Jon Wiener

GIMME SOME TRUTH

THE JOHN LENNON FBI FILES

University of California Press   Berkeley   Los Angeles   London

University of California Press
Berkeley and Los Angeles, California

University of California Press, Ltd.
London, England

© 1999 by
The Regents of the University of California

Library of Congress Cataloging-in-Publication Data

Wiener, Jon.
    Gimme some truth : the John Lennon FBI files /
Jon Wiener.
    p.   cm.
    Includes bibliographical references (p.) and
    index.
    ISBN 0-520-21646-6 (alk. paper).
    1. Lennon, John, 1940–1980—Archives.   2.
Singers—United States—Archives.   I. Title.
ML420.L38W52   1999
782.42166' 092—dc21
  [B]   99–15216
                                CIP

Manufactured in the United States of America
08 07 06 05 04 03 02 01 00 99
10 9 8 7 6 5 4 3 2 1

To Mark Rosenbaum and Dan Marmalefsky

Contents

When FBI Director J. Edgar Hoover reported to the Nixon White House in 1972 about the bureau's surveillance of John Lennon, he began by explaining that Lennon was a "former member of the Beatles singing group." Apparently Hoover wanted to show that although he was no rock fan, at least he knew who Lennon was. When a copy of this letter arrived in response to my 1981 Freedom of Information Act (FOIA) request, the entire text was withheld, as were almost 200 other pages, on the grounds that releasing it would endanger the national security. That seemed unlikely. So, with the help of the American Civil Liberties Union (ACLU) of Southern California, I filed a lawsuit under the FOIA in 1983, asking the court to order the release of the withheld pages. Fourteen years later, after the case went to the Supreme Court, the FBI finally agreed to settle almost all the outstanding issues of the case, to release all but ten of the documents, and to pay $204,000 to the ACLU for court costs and attorney fees. The most significant 100 pages of the Lennon file are reproduced in this volume.

The Lennon FBI files document an era when rock music seemed to have real political force, when youth culture, for perhaps the first time in American history, was mounting a serious challenge to the status quo in Washington, when President Nixon responded by mobilizing the FBI and the Immigration and Naturalization Service (INS) to silence the man from England who was singing "Give Peace a Chance" at his first live concert in the United States since 1966. Lennon's file dates from 1971, a year when the war in Vietnam was killing hundreds of thousands, when Nixon was facing reelection, and when the "clever Beatle" was living in New York and joining up with the antiwar movement. The Nixon administration learned that he and some radical friends were talking about organizing a national concert tour to coincide with the 1972 election campaign, a tour that would combine rock music and radical politics, during which Lennon would urge young people to register to vote, and vote against the war, which meant, of course, against Nixon.

The administration learned about Lennon's idea from an unlikely source: Senator Strom Thurmond. Early in 1972 he sent a secret memo to Attorney General John Mitchell and the White House reporting on Lennon's plans and suggesting that deportation "would be a strategy counter-measure" (see figures 1–3).

That was exactly the sort of thing John Dean, the counsel to the president, had suggested in his famous 1971 memo: "We can use the available political machinery to screw our political enemies." The word was passed to the INS, which began deportation proceedings a month later.[1] The Nixon administration's efforts to "neutralize" Lennon—their term—to silence him as a spokesman for the peace movement, are the central subject of Lennon's FBI file.

Throughout fourteen years of FOIA litigation over the files, which began in 1983, the FBI maintained that its surveillance of Lennon was not an abuse of power but rather a legitimate law enforcement activity. It's true that in 1972 Lennon associated with antiwar activists who had been convicted of conspiring to disrupt the Democratic National Convention four years earlier. It's true that he spoke out against the war at rallies and demonstrations. But the files contain no evidence that Lennon committed any criminal acts: no bombings, no terrorism, no conspiracies. His activities were precisely the kind protected by the First Amendment, which is not limited to U.S. citizens.

The story of the Lennon files is also the story of the fourteen-year legal battle to win release of the withheld pages, a story about the ways the Reagan, Bush, and Clinton administrations resisted the requirements of the FOIA. The basic issue here was not simply John Lennon. The basic issue was that government officials everywhere like secrecy. By keeping the public from learning what they have done, they hope to avoid criticism, hinder the opposition, and maintain power over citizens and their elected representatives. Classified files and official secrets lie at the heart of the modern governmental bureaucracy and permit the undemocratic use of power to go unrecognized and unchallenged by citizens.

Democracy, however, is not powerless before this practice. In the fight against govern-

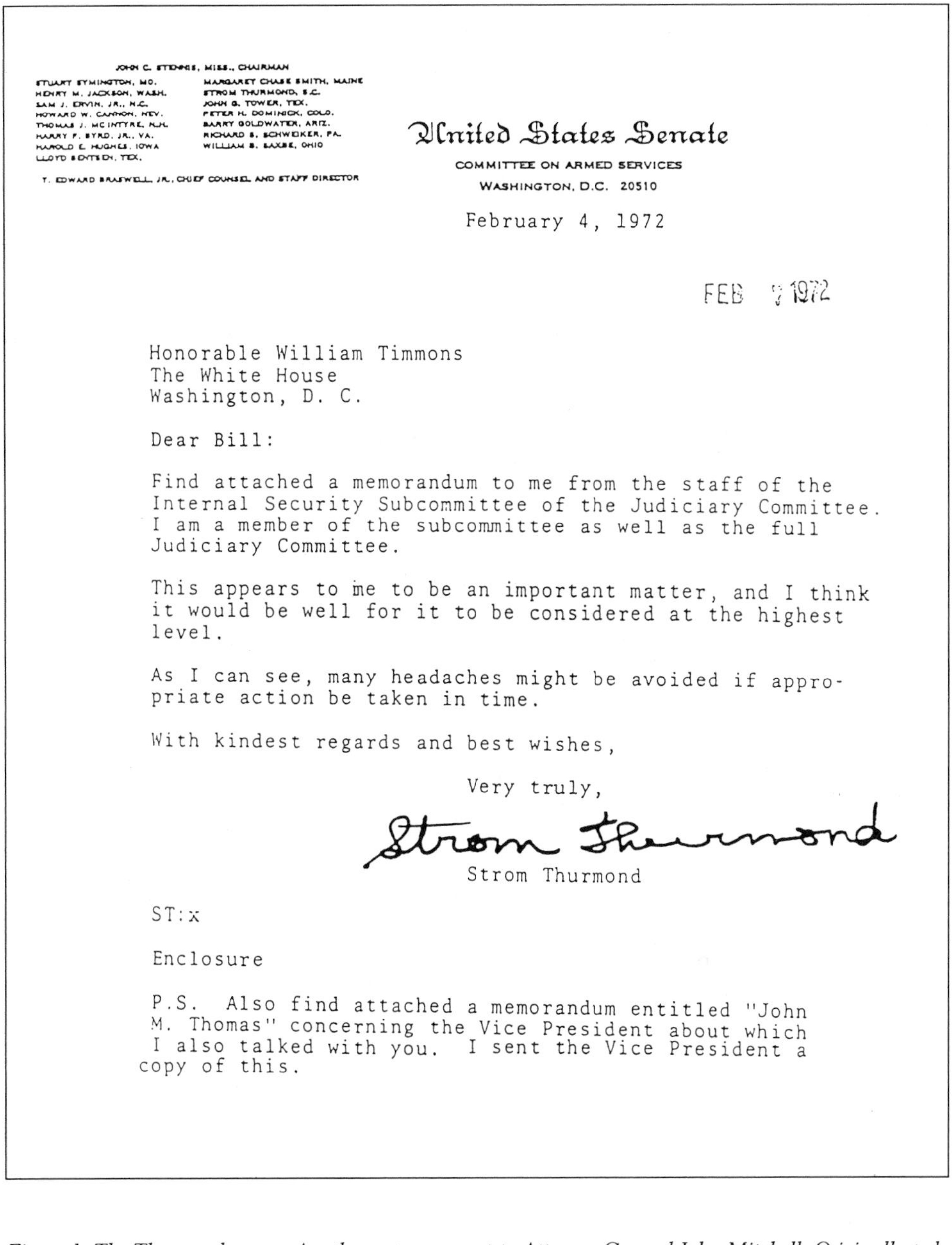

United States Senate

COMMITTEE ON ARMED SERVICES
WASHINGTON, D.C. 20510

February 4, 1972

FEB 7 1972

Honorable William Timmons
The White House
Washington, D. C.

Dear Bill:

Find attached a memorandum to me from the staff of the
Internal Security Subcommittee of the Judiciary Committee.
I am a member of the subcommittee as well as the full
Judiciary Committee.

This appears to me to be an important matter, and I think
it would be well for it to be considered at the highest
level.

As I can see, many headaches might be avoided if appropriate action be taken in time.

With kindest regards and best wishes,

Very truly,

Strom Thurmond

Strom Thurmond

ST:x

Enclosure

P.S. Also find attached a memorandum entitled "John
M. Thomas" concerning the Vice President about which
I also talked with you. I sent the Vice President a
copy of this.

*Figure 1. The Thurmond memo. Another copy was sent to Attorney General John Mitchell. Originally pub-
lished in* Rolling Stone, *July 31, 1975.*

JOHN LENNON

John Lennon, presently visiting in the United States, is a British citizen. He was a member of the former musical group known as "The Beatles." He has claimed a date of birth of September 10, 1940, and he is presently married to a Japanese citizen, one Yoko Ono.

The December 12, 1971, issue of the New York Times shows that Lennon and his wife appeared for about 10 minutes at about 3:00 a.m. on December 11, 1971, at a rally held in Ann Arbor, Michigan, to protest the continuing imprisonment of John Sinclair, a radical poet.

Radical New Left leaders Rennie Davis, Jerry Rubin, Leslie Bacon, Stu Albert, Jay Craven, and others have recently gone to the New York City area. This group has been strong advocates of the program to "dump Nixon." They have devised a plan to hold rock concerts in various primary election states for the following purposes: to obtain access to college campuses; to stimulate 18-year old registration; to press for legislation legalizing marihuana; to finance their activities; and to recruit persons to come to San Diego during the Republican National Convention in August 1972. These individuals are the same persons who were instrumental in disrupting the Democratic National Convention in Chicago in 1968.

According to a confidential source, whose information has proved reliable in the past, the activities of Davis and his group will follow the pattern of the rally mentioned above with reference to John Sinclair. David Sinclair, the brother of John, will be the road manager for these rock festivals.

Davis and his cohorts intend to use John Lennon as a drawing card to promote the success of the rock festivals and rallies. The source feels that this will pour tremendous amounts of money into the coffers of the New Left and can only inevitably lead to a clash between a controlled mob organized by this group and law enforcement officials in San Diego.

The source felt that if Lennon's visa is terminated it would be a strategy counter-measure. The source also noted the caution which must be taken with regard to the possible alienation of the so-called 18-year old vote if Lennon is expelled from the country.

Figure 2. Memo from Senate Internal Security Subcommittee staff accompanying the Thurmond memo.

March 6, 1972

Dear Strom:

In connection with your previous inquiry
concerning the former member of the Beatles,
John Lennon, I thought you would be interested
in learning that the Immigration and Naturalization Service has served notice on him that
he is to leave this country no later than
March 15. You may be assured the information
you previously furnished has been appropriately
noted.

With warm regards,

Sincerely,

William E. Timmons
Assistant to the President

Honorable Strom Thurmond
United States Senate
Washington, D. C. 20510

bcc: Mr. Harlington Wood, Department of Justice - for your information
bcc: Tom Korologos - for your information

WET:VO:jlh

Figure 3. White House reply to the Thurmond memo. William E. Timmons was Nixon's assistant for congressional relations.

ment secrecy, America has led the world. In 1966 Congress passed the FOIA, which requires that officials make public the information in their files to "any person" who requests it, unless it falls into a small number of exempted categories, including "national security." The Act was substantially expanded in 1974 in the wake of revelations of White House abuse of power during the Watergate scandal. The FOIA, in effect, created a notable challenge to the history of government secrecy; it provided a set of rules and procedures, officials and offices dedicated not to the collection and maintenance of secrets but rather to their release to the public. Journalists, scholars, and activists have used the FOIA to scrutinize the operations of government agencies and expose official misconduct and lying, including the FBI's illegal efforts to harass, intimidate, disrupt, and otherwise interfere with lawful political actions. The John Lennon FBI files provide an example.

Before considering that history, it's important to acknowledge that the FOIA in many respects has been a spectacular success, as Americans have demonstrated an impressive appetite for government information. In 1990, for example, federal agencies received 491,000 FOIA requests and spent $83 million responding to them. The Defense Department received the most, 118,000 requests, while the FBI received 11,000, and the CIA, 4,000. The FOIA further requires that agencies report the extent of their denials of such requests: the agency with the highest denial rate in 1990, strangely enough, was the Office of Ethics, which refused to release 75 percent of requested documents. In contrast, the Department of Health and Human Services denied only 2 percent of the requests it received. The staff at the FBI's Freedom of Information Section processing FOIA requests consists of eight agents and 245 support employees, 65 of whom work on national security declassification. In 1990, 421,000 previously classified pages were released; requesters filed 993 administrative appeals of decisions to withhold documents; 263 requests that had been denied were in litigation.[2]

The most fundamental justification for governmental secrecy is "national security." Thus the FOIA exempts from disclosure any material "which reasonably could be expected to cause damage to the national security."[3] What constitutes a "reasonable expectation" is obviously the issue. Because of the long-standing belief in the legitimacy of keeping secret diplomatic and military information, the claim that releasing any particular document could reasonably be expected to damage "national security" has been difficult to refute, which opens the FOIA to abuse by officials with something to hide. How federal officials have interpreted the national security exemption to the FOIA provides the most important test of government practice, and lies at the heart of the John Lennon FBI files litigation.

The original FOIA of 1966 had no provision for judicial review of "national security" information. The Act exempted material "specifically required by Executive Order to be kept secret in the interest of national defense or foreign policy." The law, however, contained no provisions authorizing courts to consider government decisions to withhold documents under the "national security" claim. In a 1973 Supreme Court ruling, Justice Potter Stewart pointed out this flaw: the FOIA provided "no means to question any Executive decision to stamp a document 'secret,' however cynical, myopic, or even corrupt that decision might have been."[4] The Court went on to note that Congress could establish procedures to permit courts to review such decisions.

This use of the "national security" exemption to conceal government misconduct came to the fore in 1974, in the wake of the Watergate revelations of White House abuses of power. At that time the issue was framed in an apolitical way as a problem of "overclassification of national security information." Congress held extensive hearings documenting the problem and accepted the Supreme Court's suggestion, passing a series of amendments that significantly strengthened the FOIA, especially in relation to "national security" claims. The 1974 amendments instructed courts to determine *de novo* whether the national security exemption was being properly applied in particular cases. Courts were authorized to conduct *in camera* reviews of documents for which the government claimed the national security exemption. Most important, courts were empowered to overrule executive officials' decisions classifying documents under the "national security" claim. For the first time, courts could order the release of improperly classified documents. President Ford vetoed the legislation, objecting specifically to the provision empowering the courts to overrule executive branch classification decisions. This provision, he declared, was an unconstitutional infringement on executive power. Congress overrode Ford's veto, and the amendments became part of the FOIA. Nine years later, the ACLU of California asked the court to overrule the Reagan administration's claims that parts of the Lennon FBI file had to be withheld to protect "national security."

Secret government files like Lennon's have a history. The Cold War provided a great impetus to government secrecy, which was justified as a necessary response to Soviet efforts to "destroy our free and democratic system" at a time when their "preferred technique is to subvert by infiltration and intimidation," as the government explained in 1950 in the policy statement "NSC 68." Cold War presidents secretly authorized the FBI to monitor radical activists, who included not just potential spies or saboteurs but "writers, lecturers, newsmen, entertainers, and others in the mass media field" who "might influence others against the national interest," as the Senate's Church Committee explained after Watergate.[5]

But the federal government began spying on Americans long before the Cold War, as Daniel Patrick Moynihan observes in his book *Secrecy*. Most of the structure of secrecy now in place, he argues, has its origin in the World War I Espionage Act, passed into law in 1917 at the urging of President Woodrow Wilson. The former Princeton history professor declared in his 1915 State of the Union message that recent immigrants had "poured the poison of disloyalty into the very arteries of our national life," and he urged Congress to "save the honor and self respect of the nation. Such creatures of passion, disloyalty, and anarchy must be crushed out." Congress responded with the Espionage Act and, in 1918, the Sedition Act, which made it a crime to "utter, print, write, or publish any disloyal, profane, scurrilous, or abusive language about the form of government of the United States." It also made it a crime to "advocate any curtailment of production in this country of any thing . . . necessary or essential to the prosecution of the war."[6]

In fact the first FBI files on people suspected of disloyalty date from before World War I. The bureau was created in 1908; it opened a file on Ezra Pound in 1911, after he published in the first issue of *The Masses*, a socialist magazine. It opened a file on Max Eastman in 1912 on the grounds that he was editor of *The Masses* and "a true believer in free love." It opened a file on Walter Lippmann the same year, noting that the recent Harvard graduate was secretary to the socialist mayor of Schenectady. Herbert Mitgang and Natalie Robins have shown that the FBI kept files on at least 150 of the country's leading writers, from Sinclair Lewis to William Faulkner to Ernest Hemingway to Norman Mailer and James Baldwin.[7] Thus the insatiable appetite of Hoover's FBI for derogatory gossip and malicious trivia, evident in the Lennon file, was nothing new. But unlike other writers and artists the FBI watched, Lennon wasn't persecuted simply because of what he thought or wrote. The Nixon administration was after him because of what he did—and what he planned to do.

The Lennon files constitute a small but significant chapter in the history of the sixties, and of the Watergate era, and also in the history of bureaucratic secrecy and government abuse of power. They confirm Richard Nixon's place in the annals of rock 'n' roll as the man who tried to deport John Lennon, and thus they support the claim that rock in the sixties had some kind of political significance. Of course some have seen Nixon's pursuit of Lennon as a simple case of paranoia, in which the president and the New Left shared the same delusion. But the record shows there was a rationale behind Nixon's campaign to silence Lennon that was not simply nutty. Lennon's plan to mobilize young voters against the war may not have affected the outcome of the 1972 election, but it had a clear and reasonable logic behind it.

The Lennon FBI files include some comic and hilarious moments. The FBI at points looks more like the Keystone Cops than the Gestapo. But the campaign to "neutralize" Lennon wasn't a joke; it was a crime.

The experiences of exaltation and anger that rock music provided in the late sixties were not in themselves political experiences. Lennon knew that. He also knew that rock could become a potent political force when it was linked to real political organizing, when, for example, it brought young people together to protest the Vietnam War. The Lennon FBI files chronicle Lennon's commitment to test the political potential of rock music. They also document the government's commitment to stop him. The investigation of Lennon was an abuse of power, a kind of rock 'n' roll Watergate.

Part One

HISTORY

1

Getting Started

Early in 1981, shortly after John Lennon's murder on December 8, 1980, I filed a Freedom of Information Act (FOIA) request for any files the FBI had kept on Lennon. The FBI released some documents in May. But of the 281 pages staff said they had reviewed, they withheld 199 (more than 70 percent) in their entirety. The documents were withheld mostly under three different FOIA exemptions: protection of the privacy of others named in a document, protection of the identities of confidential sources, and "national security."[1]

The documents that were released included one page that had Lennon's name at the top but was otherwise blacked out under the national security exemption (see p. 170); a variety of documents discussing the Nixon administration's effort in 1972 to deport Lennon, including a letter suggesting that Lennon be "arrested if at all possible on possession of narcotics charge," which would make him "immediately deportable" (see p. 289); and several pages, completely blacked out, from the Detroit FBI reporting on Lennon's appearance at the "John Sinclair Freedom Rally" in Ann Arbor in December 1971 (see pp. 110–119). Most interesting was a letter from J. Edgar Hoover to H. R. Haldeman, assistant to the president, dated April 25, 1972, that had been withheld in its entirety under the national security exemption (see p. 240). Since Haldeman was the closest official to Nixon, this document provided crucial evidence that the Lennon investigation was a political one, significant at the highest levels of the Nixon White House.

When these documents began arriving in my mailbox in the spring of 1981, American politics was beginning a shift of historic proportions toward the right. Ronald Reagan had been elected in November 1980, bringing to power the Republican right wing that had failed to elect Barry Goldwater sixteen years earlier. The "Reagan Revolution" rested on an ideological commitment to "law and order," which Lennon had challenged, and a passionate hostility to "the sixties," which Lennon personified. The fight for the Lennon files would be a battle with the Reagan administration.

When the FBI informed me it was withholding 70 percent of the Lennon files, the letter also said, "You may appeal to the Associate Attorney General." I did. My appeal argued that information about Lennon's plans to demonstrate against Nixon should not have been withheld under the "national security" exemption, a decision I called "arbitrary and capricious." I argued that the other withheld material was "not properly covered by the exemptions claimed."

Reagan's assistant attorney general for legal policy, Jonathan C. Rose, responded six weeks later: "After careful consideration of your appeal, I have decided to affirm the initial action in this case." The national security material, he wrote, was "being referred to the Department Review Committee for review," but the rest had been "properly withheld."

Six months after that, the assistant attorney general informed me that the review committee had completed its work and concluded that eight of the national security pages could be declassified. But the FBI still wasn't going to release them. While those pages were no longer being withheld on national security grounds, the bureau now claimed they fell under other exemptions: personal privacy and confidential source information. So my administrative appeal produced little of significance. The assistant attorney general's letter denying my appeal concluded, "Judicial review of my action on this appeal is available to you in the United States District Court for the judicial district in which you reside." It was time to find a lawyer.

The FOIA gives federal courts the power "to order the production of any agency records improperly withheld from the complainant." That's what I wanted the courts to do. I asked a variety of organizations and attorneys for help in bringing an FOIA lawsuit against the FBI. Victor Navasky, editor of *The Nation* magazine, suggested four criteria for picking a lawyer: find one you trust; who understands the case; who cares about it; and who will do it for no money except an award of fees at the end. Courts had awarded attorney fees in some successful FOIA appeals, recently in an appeal for documents about Vietnam Veterans against the War (VVAW), so money at the end remained a possibility.

In search of a lawyer, I talked to the Reporters Committee for Freedom of the Press, the Fund for Investigative Journalism, and the Fund for Open Information and Accountability ("FOIA, Inc."). I talked to the Media Alliance in San Francisco and the Center for Investigative Reporting in Oakland. I talked to the American Historical Association's Committee on Access to Documents. I talked to the Playboy Foundation, well known for its defense of the First Amendment. I talked to Frank Wilkinson, who had sued the FBI for his file, the largest on any individual, and who headed an organization called the National Coalition against Repressive Legislation originally established to fight HUAC. I talked to the San Francisco attorney who had been awarded fees in the VVAW case. I talked to prominent radical attorneys including Leonard Weinglass. I talked to Leon Friedman, who Victor Navasky called "the best FOIA attorney in the country."

All the attorneys told me the same thing that Leon Friedman did: "I took a couple of these, hoping to win, and got burned. I'm not in a position to do this kind of thing. You can't win on national security any more. Try the ACLU."

So I talked to Ramona Ripston and Fred Okrand of the ACLU of Southern California. Okrand, who was legal director, told me, "I don't know of anyone who'd be interested, but I'll ask around and if I come up with anyone, I'll have them call you." That was in January 1983, and it didn't sound promising. But shortly thereafter, Okrand's successor, Paul Hoffman, called to schedule a meeting at which I would present my case to him and Mark Rosenbaum, the ACLU general counsel.

At the meeting, I presented my documents and arguments, anxious that this was my last best hope. Nervously, I showed that I had followed the ACLU's model letters requesting material under the FOIA and that I had exhausted my administrative appeals. It turned out that their biggest concern was not about the case but about their potential client, the possible plaintiff: was I some kind of obsessed fan? or perhaps a burned-out hippie, living in the past? or a conspiracy buff, eager to prove Reagan had ordered Lennon's assassination? They brightened noticeably when they learned I had been granted tenure six years earlier at the University of California, Irvine; that I had published not just in *Radical America, Dissent,* and *Socialist Review* but also in the *American Historical Review* and the *Journal of Modern History,* and the distinguished British scholarly journal *Past and Present.* They saw they would be able to argue that the plaintiff was a respected historian who sought the Lennon files as part of his research on the American past. Convinced that their potential client was a mild-mannered professor and not some kind of nut, the two of them decided the ACLU of Southern California would take the case. Rosenbaum, who eventually succeeded Hoffman as ACLU legal director, served as the colead attorney throughout the next fifteen years of litigation.

In a 1998 interview, he discussed the ACLU's considerations in taking the case: "It was simple to decide. The timing was coincident with a national frustration with the administration of the FOIA, particularly in the areas of national security and informants. Agencies were coming forward with boilerplate refusals. The law's presumption in favor of disclosure had, for all intents and purposes, been dissolved, and the FBI in particular was choosing what they wanted to disclose. If any case could take us back to legislative objective favoring disclosure, this would be the one." So the ACLU's first goal was not just to get the documents, but to challenge "systemic problems in implementing the FOIA."[2]

The ACLU had a second goal: to publicize the value of the FOIA and expose the ways in which it was being subverted by the FBI. The files on Lennon provided an excellent example that could win media attention.

Mark Rosenbaum is a remarkable figure. Known as both a brilliant legal strategist and a passionate and effective courtroom advocate, he graduated from the University of Michigan in 1970 and went on to Harvard Law School. In 1973, on the verge of dropping out because the classes seemed so uninteresting, Rosenbaum went to work as a clerk in the law office of Leonard Boudin and Leonard Weinglass. At that moment, they, along with Ramsey Clark, happened to be representing Daniel Ellsberg, the government researcher who was being prosecuted by the Nixon administration for leaking the Pentagon Papers to the *New York Times*. Rosenbaum describes the experience of working on the Ellsberg defense as "the turning point of my life."

After the Ellsberg case, Rosenbaum went back to Harvard Law School and graduated in 1974. He then joined the ACLU of Southern California as a staff counsel—hired by the new executive director, Ramona Ripston. Stanley Sheinbaum, then head of the ACLU Board of Directors, personally put up the $10,000 required to pay Rosenbaum's salary for the first year. The year before taking on the Lennon FBI files case, he had gone to the Supreme Court, along with Harvard law professor Laurence Tribe, to challenge school segregation in Los Angeles.[3]

In subsequent years Rosenbaum would serve as colead counsel in the ACLU lawsuit seeking to overturn California's Proposition 187, the anti-immigrant initiative, and as the point man in the ACLU fight to maintain affirmative action programs. He also successfully defended the constitutionality of the "Motor Voter" registration act, challenged by California governor Pete Wilson before the Ninth Circuit Court of Appeals. And in 1995 he argued before the Supreme Court a case in which the Court held that residency requirements for Aid to Families with Dependent Children program recipients were unconstitutional.[4]

When the ACLU decided in 1983 to take the Lennon files case, Rosenbaum called Dan Marmalefsky, a Los Angeles attorney with the firm Hufstedler, Miller, Carlson & Beardsley (which later merged with Morrison & Foerster). Another brilliant young lawyer, Marmalefsky had graduated from the University of California, Berkeley in 1976 and from Yale Law School in 1980, where he received an award for his work in legal services. He went on to specialize in complex civil and criminal business litigation. In 1982 he had served as co-counsel for a group of Salvadorean refugees seeking political asylum, assisting with an appeal to the Ninth Circuit. He also had experience with FOIA litigation, primarily from using it for discovery in criminal cases, starting with the defense of John DeLorean in 1982, and had worked with Rosenbaum pro bono on several other ACLU cases. Marmalefsky accepted Rosenbaum's offer to work on this one, and the two served as co-lead counsel for the next fifteen years.

Marmalefsky told me that the decision to take a pro bono case was his alone and didn't require permission from anyone at his firm. "The basic question concerns time, balancing pro bono work against the amount of fee-generating work I do," he explained. "Because when I take pro bono cases, I don't do it halfway. I treat them the same as any other matters and devote the necessary time—whatever it takes."[5]

The two had just won a case before the Supreme Court in 1983, an ACLU challenge to the California Penal Code section making it a crime for a person to refuse to provide identification when asked by a police officer. The Court accepted their argument that the law violated the First Amendment and voided the statute for vagueness and overbreadth.[6]

In 1985 he and Rosenbaum would bring to the Supreme Court a case challenging the constitutionality of the enforcement of draft registration.[7] He also litigated prosecutors' duty to present exculpatory testimony before a grand jury and the right of public access to juvenile court proceedings. But Marmalefsky's practice wasn't all pro bono; in other cases he helped successfully defend Kirk Kerkorian in a $1 billion damage suit over the sale of MGM to Giancarlo Parretti in 1990, and as co-counsel, he won an $11 million verdict for an investor defrauded in commodities trading.

When Rosenbaum and Marmalefsky went to work on the case, 69 pages out of 281 in the Lennon FBI file were being withheld in their entirety under various claims, and portions of dozens of others were also withheld. The FOIA not only allows judges to order agencies to release withheld documents but also requires that if a requester brings a case before a judge, "the court shall determine the matter *de novo*, and may examine the contents of such agency records *in camera* to determine whether such records or any part thereof shall be withheld . . . and the burden is on the agency to sustain its action."[8] Equally important was the section of President Reagan's executive order on classification, which declared that "in no case shall information be classified in order to conceal violations of law . . . [or] to prevent embarrassment to a person, organization, or agency."[9]

Because the FBI cited three different exemptions under the FOIA for withholding most of the information, challenging the withholding required litigating each exemption separately, and each had a separate body of case law to be studied and invoked.

When Rosenbaum and Marmalefsky sat down to discuss strategy, they conceded that the law was clear that we would never get some of the withheld information; the names of confidential informants, for instance, were clearly protected. So we decided at the outset to notify the FBI that we were not seeking those names, the names of FBI or nonfederal law enforcement officers, or technical source symbol numbers. We were challenging the claims made for withholding only some of the information: particularly the material claimed under "national security" and the information provided by confidential sources. We were not seeking the names of the informers, but we were seeking the information they provided.

The "national security" information provided the most obvious target—how could release of twelve-year-old information about a dead rock star possibly endanger the national security?—but was also the most difficult to obtain. Mark Rosenbaum told me that the biggest problem in the case was that "courts fear divulging national security documents. They believe that courts should tread lightly in this area. They pay enormous deference to executive branch claims concerning national security."[10]

Still, Rosenbaum and Marmalefsky had at least one significant avenue of attack. The FOIA exemption covers any material "which reasonably could be expected to cause damage to the national security," but the task of determining what constitutes "damage" is assigned by the Act to the president, who issues executive orders on classification of documents. At the time my FOIA request was filed in 1981, the relevant executive order required federal agencies considering FOIA requests to consider the public interest. The benefit to the public was to be balanced against the possible harm that could result from release of documents. If the public interest outweighed the possible harm, the documents had to be released. That policy, the "public interest balancing act," had been established by President Carter.[11] Since the public benefit from release of the Lennon files would be considerable, and the possible harm to the national security was small or nonexistent, the argument for releasing those pages was a strong one.

Disaster struck almost immediately. Between the submission of the original FOIA request in 1981 and the filing of the lawsuit in 1983, President Reagan issued a new executive order on classification that eliminated the public interest balancing act. Under the new Reagan policy, the FBI was required to withhold all documents "the unauthorized disclosure of which reasonably could be expected to cause damage to the national security," period. The FBI was now permitted to withhold any information that might possibly result in damage to the national security, no matter how great the public interest that would be served by its release, and no matter how insignificant or unlikely the damage, as long as the "expectation" of damage was "reasonable." The ACLU team had lost its strongest argument for release of the national security documents in the Lennon file. Until a Democratic president could be elected, who would presumably restore the Carter-era public interest balancing act, we would face a serious obstacle to the release of that material. Nevertheless, a judge could find that the expectation of damage was not reasonable or that the files were being withheld improperly to conceal information that would embarrass the FBI—and then order their release.

Wiener v. FBI was filed by Rosenbaum and Marmalefsky on March 22, 1983, in U.S. district court in Los Angeles. The lawsuit sought three things: an injunction ordering the FBI to release the documents, a written finding stating that the FBI "acted arbitrarily or capriciously" in withholding the documents, and last but not least, an award of costs and attorney fees.[12] Rosenbaum and Marmalefsky pointed out that under the law the burden of justifying the withholding of documents rested on the FBI. But the ACLU team's strategy in the case was not to start by asking the judge to order the prompt release of the withheld documents; it was necessary to go through several preliminary procedural steps. The first was to ask the court to order the FBI to provide an index of every document at issue along with "a detailed justification covering each refusal to release agency records." Once the FBI had stated its justifications document by document, each justification could be challenged and shown to be inadequate, and on that basis the judge could then order the bureau to release the documents.

This was the established procedure: the bureau provided the plaintiffs with an affidavit known as a "Vaughn index"—the court's term for the document itemizing the government's justifications for refusing to disclose documents.[13] The purpose of the index was to provide the FOIA requester with a meaningful opportunity to contest the FBI's arguments in court. When the D.C. Circuit Court of Appeals established the Vaughn index procedure in 1973, it addressed the basic dilemma facing FOIA plaintiffs, a dilemma we faced: how to challenge a government decision to withhold a document when the contents of the document remained unknown to the challenger? The plaintiff's lack of knowledge about the contents of the withheld document "seriously distorts the traditional adversary nature of our legal system's form of dispute resolution," the circuit court explained. "Ordinarily, the facts relevant to a dispute are more or less equally available to adverse parties." An index was necessary, the court argued, to "assure that a party's right to information is not submerged beneath governmental obfuscation and mischaracterization." Preserving the adversary nature of the proceedings would turn out to be the key to the Ninth Circuit Court of Appeals ruling against the FBI nine years after the case was first filed.

Wiener v. FBI was assigned to Judge Robert M. Takasugi in Los Angeles district court. Born in Tacoma, Washington, in 1930, Takasugi at age twelve was interned in a wartime "relocation camp" for three years, along with the entire Japanese American population of the West Coast, for the duration of World War II. After the war he went to UCLA as an undergraduate in the mid-fifties, then served in the army for two years, and graduated from University of Southern California Law School in 1959. He worked in a variety of judicial positions and was appointed to the federal bench in 1976.

We thought that his wartime experience might make him more sensitive to the issue of government abuse of power—especially after Judge Takasugi called his wartime internment experience "an education to be fair" in May 1995 at a gathering sponsored by the Japanese American National Museum and the Los Angeles Jewish Federation. Along with four other Japanese American judges—including Lance Ito, who at the time was presiding over the O. J. Simpson criminal trial, Takasugi recalled indignities like sleeping on straw mattresses, sharing toilets with hundreds of other people, and using tin cans to cover knotholes in the thin walls of the wooden barracks to keep out the dust. Along with the others, he described how the experience of internment had led him toward a career in law and how it sensitized him to civil liberties issues. "It has certainly affected me 26 hours a day," Judge Takasugi told the audience. All the judges at the event warned of the dangers of anti-immigrant hysteria; Judge Takasugi "spoke caustically of the stereotypic sing-song impersonation of Judge Ito by Senator Alphonse M. D'Amato, Republican of New York, in a recent radio interview, calling it 'a disgrace.'" Judge Takasugi also told about how his father lost his home and property as a result of the wartime "relocation" program and died at age fifty-seven of a stroke, brought on, the judge said, by "feelings of helplessness" at the Tule Lake internment camp.[14]

The gathering coincided with the opening of an exhibit about the internment program, which included a reconstructed barracks moved to the museum from the Heart Mountain internment camp site in Wyoming. Reporters asked Judge Takasugi whether it resembled the place where he had lived. "Yeah, exactly," he replied, "but the floors were tar, so on a hot day we started sinking." A photographer asked him if he was willing to step inside. "I don't want to go back in, really," Judge Takasugi said. "I'll take the loyalty oath."[15]

While the Lennon files were being debated in Judge Takasugi's courtroom, a movement for "redress and reparations" for Japanese Americans interned during World War II was gaining strength in national politics. In 1988 Congress officially apologized and authorized reparation payments to victims of the internment program. It seemed as if Judge Takasugi's youthful experience of government abuse of power might make him more sensitive to the issues in the Lennon FBI files case.

THE FBI'S ARGUMENT　　The FBI was represented in the case by Peter Osinoff, an assistant U.S. attorney. He was a thirty-one-year-old New York native who had graduated magna cum laude from Yale in 1973 and then from Stanford Law School.

The FBI in due time produced its Vaughn index to the Lennon files. But instead of providing specific arguments justifying each deletion from the FBI file, the bureau submitted a master list of justifications for withholding material—a codebook. The blacked-out passages on file pages were marked with marginal notations referring to particular justifications in the codebook. Obviously the codebook justifications were generic. It turned out that the FBI submitted the same master list of justifications in all FOIA litigation. Mark Rosenbaum wrote in a letter to the FBI attorneys in September 1983 that the explanation in the codebook "is really not more than a generalized elaboration of the exemption asserted: it is mainly just wordier." Despite the vagueness and generality of the codebook, the courts had been sympathetic to the FBI's use of boilerplate justifications. Rosenbaum and Marmalefsky decided that challenging the codebook would be the first element in their strategy to win release of the Lennon FBI files.

The FBI's Vaughn index of the Lennon file was accompanied in June 1983 by the "Declaration of Robert J. Chester," supervisor of the FBI's FOIA Section, which defended the FBI's procedures for all exemptions, except national security—for that the FBI submitted a separate statement by another official. Agent Chester explained that the names of FBI agents were being withheld because targets of FBI investigations "carry grudges which last for years and [these people] seek any excuse to harass the responsible Agent." Recognizing that the target of the investigation in this case was dead and the plaintiff was a mild-mannered history professor, Chester conceded that "in the instant case, there is no apparent evidence that plaintiff constitutes a threat to law enforcement personnel." That was deeply gratifying. Nevertheless, he added, "in light of the highly publicized nature of this particular case, it is important that Agents' identities be protected even absent evidence of potential physical harm to their persons."

Chester provided an equally rich justification for withholding information provided by confidential sources: "Informant identification has become a paramount consideration to members of the criminal and subversive elements." Again, he had no evidence that the plaintiff in this case belonged to those elements. But that did not prevent him from continuing to argue: "Members of the criminal and subversive elements do not require proof beyond a reasonable doubt when they seek to ferret out the individual who has cooperated with law enforcement authorities."

The FOIA permits the FBI to withhold confidential source material only if it had been gathered as part of a legitimate law enforcement purpose; thus it was necessary for the FBI to state the law enforcement purpose of the investigation of Lennon. The Chester declaration did that: the FBI had investigated Lennon in 1972, Chester told the court, "to determine if John Lennon was in violation of Federal law," namely, "the National Security Act of 1947."

This was a strange claim, one that would turn out to be helpful for our case. The National Security Act of 1947 created the Central Intelligence Agency. Congress was concerned at the time about whether the proposed CIA would serve the president as "a Gestapo of his own if he wants it," in the words of a Republican congressman from Ohio. So the security act made it clear that the CIA would be prohibited from "investigations inside the continental limits of the United States" and would not have "police, law enforcement, or internal security functions."[16] To claim that law as one Lennon was suspected of violating was strange not only because it wasn't a criminal statute but also because eventually it would be revealed that the CIA had indeed compiled files on Lennon's domestic political activities, in violation of the very same National Security Act of 1947.

The FBI codebook for the Lennon file divided "national security" material into eleven subcategories, starting with "identity of a foreign government . . . engaged in a cooperative, confidential relationship with the United States" and ending with "intelligence information gathered by the United States about or from a foreign country, group or individual." The FBI's arguments regarding national security deletions from the Lennon files were presented in a court declaration by Special Agent Robert F. Peterson, supervisor of the National Security Affidavits Unit at FBI headquarters, who reported that he had been "designated by the Attorney General of the United States as an original Top Secret classification authority."

Information provided by a national security confidential source had to be withheld, Peterson declared, because disclosure could permit "hostile entities" to assess "areas and targets which may have been compromised." But who were the "hostile entities" in this case? Surely not the ACLU. Release of the information could also lead to exposure of the people who provided it, threatening them with "loss of life, jobs, friends, status, etc." This was the problem with the codebook approach—none of this boilerplate argument had anything to do with the Lennon file.

The most significant part of Peterson's declaration concerned the category "foreign government information," which the FBI claimed as the basis for withholding numerous documents. These had to be withheld, Peterson argued, "due to the delicate nature of international diplomacy." Release of the foreign government information in the Lennon file could lead to "political or economic instability, or to civil disorder or unrest" in the foreign country that supplied the information, he declared. It could "jeopardize the lives, liberty or property" of U.S. tourists visiting the country. It could "endanger United States Government personnel there." Then came the most remarkable claim made in fourteen years of Lennon file litigation: release of foreign government information in the Lennon file, Agent Peterson declared, could "lead to foreign . . . military retaliation against the United States."

Britain was obviously the source of the "foreign government information," but it seemed unlikely that British citizens would attack visiting American tourists or government personnel in retaliation for the release of information gathered by British authorities. British economic instability might be a problem, but it was unlikely to be exacerbated by the release of information about Lennon. Most important, we felt confident that the Thatcher government would not engage in military retaliation against the United States if our government released British information on Lennon.

What could the John Lennon FBI file contain that had been provided by the British government? The Nixon administration had begun deportation proceedings against Lennon in 1972 after learning of his antiwar and anti-Nixon activities in an election year. This is the point at which "information gathered by the United States . . . from a foreign country" enters the story. The Nixon administration claimed as the legal basis for its effort to deport Lennon his 1969 conviction on misdemeanor charges of cannabis possession in Britain. Presumably the FBI's Lennon file contained information from the British government regarding that event.

Thus in response to an FOIA request for the FBI's Lennon file, the classification officer—the man with the magic marker—blacked-out passages that originated with the British government and marked them with the code referring to "foreign relations or foreign activities of the U.S."; the reader then looked up the code in the codebook and found the official description of "damage to the national security reasonably expected to result from unauthorized disclosure"; among the boilerplate list of possible damages, the FBI included "foreign military retaliation against the U.S." To add insult to injury, Special

Agent Peterson also declared that he had made "every effort" to be "reasonable" and provide "sufficient detail" so that the court could "rationally determine" that the FBI was right.

The Lennon file also contained five documents originating with the CIA. These were part of the FBI's file on Lennon because the FBI had received them from the CIA. Confronted by an FOIA request, the FBI sent these documents back to the CIA so that the agency could decide whether to release or withhold them. The official CIA justification for withholding this material was prepared by Louis J. Dube, the information review officer for the Directorate of Operations of the CIA. In his affidavit, submitted in December 1983, he declared that he was acting on "advice of the CIA Office of General Counsel." "As a senior CIA official," he wrote, in a chain of command "running from the President of the United States to the Director of Central Intelligence . . . to me, I hold original classification authority at the TOP SECRET level." Dube declared that, in document HQ-1, a "one word CIA cryptonym" was being withheld under both the (b)(1) national security exemption as well as the (b)(3) intelligence sources and methods exemption (see p. 153).

A cryptonym, Agent Dube explained, is a code word "used to conceal the true nature or identity of some intelligence activity." The use of cryptonyms "provide[s] an additional measure of security in the event a document comes into the possession of a hostile foreign power." If the cryptonym used in the Lennon files were disclosed, "the intelligence service of a hostile foreign power" would be able to "divine the nature and purpose of the CIA activity" in question. But it was obvious to any power, hostile or not, that the purpose of the CIA activity in question had been to gather information about John Lennon's political activities. (In 1987, the cryptonym would be released; see chapter 3.)

The CIA released one of its Lennon documents in September 1984—a teletype dated February 8, 1972, reporting on Lennon's plan for a "caravan of entertainers who will follow U.S. primaries and raise funds for local radical groups along the way" (see p. 157). About half of it was blacked out under the national security exemption, but one word in the heading was released: "MHCHAOS."

Rosenbaum and Marmalefsky agreed that the word rang a bell, and since I was the historian, I was dispatched to the UCLA Research Library reference room. The news indices there were clear: "MHCHAOS" was a secret, illegal CIA program of surveillance of domestic political dissent, a violation of the CIA charter that had been revealed in 1976.

"MH" was a CIA code indicating worldwide area of operations. The CHAOS program had been launched in August 1967, under Director Richard Helms, by James Jesus Angleton, the CIA's chief of counterintelligence, and headed by Richard Ober, a counter-intelligence specialist in the Directorate of Plans, Harvard '43. Ober's tasks had already included developing CIA strategy to respond to the revelation by *Ramparts* magazine in February 1967 that the CIA had been secretly funding the National Student Association for fifteen years. Under the CHAOS operation, the investigation of *Ramparts* was expanded to cover the entire underground press and given "highest priority." To keep the illegal activity from being leaked by CIA employees, the operation was housed in the basement of CIA headquarters in Langley, Virginia, in specially shielded vaults that blocked electronic eavesdropping.

The CIA sent Operation CHAOS domestic intelligence reports on political dissent first to President Johnson and later to Nixon, as well as to Henry Kissinger and John Dean, counsel to the president. Under Nixon, the CHAOS program was expanded to sixty agents, who, according to Angus MacKenzie, "became the Nixon administration's primary source of intelligence about the antiwar leadership."[17]

CIA Operation CHAOS was revealed in 1976 by Representative Bella Abzug's House Subcommittee on Government Information and Individual Rights. The CIA director at the time was George Bush, who conceded in congressional testimony that "the operation in practice resulted in some improper accumulation of material on legitimate domestic activities." He defended the agency, declaring that "only a very small fraction of reporting on the activities of American citizens in the US was done by the CIA." Abzug proposed that individuals who had been targets of Operation CHAOS be notified by the CIA and given a chance to review their dossiers. Bush replied that notification was unworkable and proposed instead that the CIA "destroy . . . all the information which was improperly collected under the so-called CHAOS program." Because of congressional insistence, Bush agreed that the FOIA would make Operation CHAOS files available under the Act.[18] Thus the appearance of the CHAOS memo here (see p. 157).

Just eight months after the ACLU suit was filed, the government changed attorneys. Peter Osinoff, who had represented the FBI, left the U.S. Attorney's Office for private practice, and the Justice Department reassigned the case in November 1983 to Stephen D. Petersen, a forty-year-old graduate of the University of Iowa and Iowa Law School. Dan

Marmalefsky promptly wrote Petersen, expressing "concerns with the delays in the FBI response to this lawsuit," protesting that two months had passed since he had requested a more specific Vaughn index. Fourteen years later Rosenbaum and Marmalefsky would still be arguing many of the same issues.

The FBI accounting of file pages in their Vaughn index included two unexpected and previously unknown sets of materials: Lennon files from the FBI field office in Washington, D.C. (as opposed to headquarters) and in Houston. When filing FOIA requests, it is vital for requesters to contact not only FBI headquarters in Washington, D.C. but also FBI field offices in cities where investigations were conducted. The field office files contain the raw material from investigations, while headquarters files contain mostly summaries. I had requested Lennon files from field offices in New York, Detroit, and Los Angeles but not from Houston or Washington, D.C.; nevertheless the FBI provided copies of those documents.

A careful examination of the released pages in Lennon's New York file indicated that a Lennon file had also been opened in Miami, yet no Miami file had been produced along with those from Houston and Washington, D.C. So in 1983 I filed a new FOIA request for Lennon files in the Miami field office, providing the Miami file number for Lennon that appeared on New York FBI memos. In May 1983 I received a reply: "A search of the index to the central records system of the Miami Office reveals no information identifiable with your request." As for the file whose number I requested, it "was destroyed in connection with the routine file destruction program during September of 1977."

The Miami file could have been an important one; it may have contained evidence of the government's efforts to set up Lennon for a drug bust. A memo from the New York FBI dated July 1972, released in the first batch of pages, suggested that "Miami should note that LENNON is reportedly a 'heavy user of narcotics'. . . . This information should be emphasized to local Law Enforcement Agencies covering MIREP, with regards to subject being arrested if at all possible on possession of narcotics charges" (see p. 289). ("MIREP" was FBI newspeak for the 1972 Miami Republican National Convention.) The Miami Lennon file that the FBI said it had destroyed might have contained further information about that element of the FBI's harassment of Lennon.

The ACLU team raised the issue of the Miami file with FBI attorneys. Petersen replied in November 1983 that the statement provided by the Miami FBI "was a statutorily sufficient response." He added, "I hope this information is responsive to your letter."

The *Miami Herald* picked up the story and quoted local FBI spokesman Joe Del Campo confirming that "there once was a Lennon file in Miami, but there is no way to know what was in it." He explained that "the local office has a carefully regulated file destruction program, in which outdated closed files are destroyed at specified intervals."[19] Yet none of the other offices with Lennon files had destroyed theirs.

THE ACLU'S ARGUMENT In an effort to provide the courts with a sense of the historical significance of the Lennon files, and of the broader context in which they had been created, the ACLU team submitted a document in October 1987 modestly titled "The Declaration of Jonathan M. Wiener." In it the plaintiff argued that FBI files released under FOIA requests had become a major research tool for historians of the 1960s; that Lennon was widely regarded as a significant historical figure; that the lawsuit was seeking only information of genuine historical significance; and that the Lennon FBI files contained evidence of Nixon administration abuses of power.

The declaration sketched out some recent history: for Nixon and Hoover, another historian had written, "The world was a battlefield filled with active or potential enemies." Lennon became identified as one of those enemies because he publicly opposed Nixon's reelection. In Nixon's mind, "he was a victim forced forever to defend himself against unrelenting and unscrupulous enemies." Hoover supported Nixon's beliefs: he told Nixon at a private meeting in October 1971, "More than anything else, I want to see you reelected in 1972."[20]

Hoover's rhetoric about antiwar activists like Lennon "was even more violent than Nixon's," according to his biographer. Hoover characterized the antiwar activist of the sixties as " 'new . . . different . . . a paradox because he is difficult to judge by the normal standards of civilized life. . . . His main reason for being is to destroy, blindly and indiscriminately, to tear down and provoke chaos. . . . They conceive of themselves as the catalyst of destruction—bringing to death a society they so bitterly hate.' "[21] This attitude helped shape the FBI's conduct in its investigations of Lennon.

The declaration reminded the court that the bureau acknowledged it had engaged in illegal and unconstitutional activities in investigating antiwar activists during the sixties.

The man who headed the FBI's Intelligence Division during the sixties, who was deeply involved in the FBI's investigations of the antiwar movement, William Sullivan, testified before a congressional committee in 1975: "Never once did I hear anybody, including myself, raise the question: 'Is this course of action which we have agreed upon lawful, is it legal, is it ethical or moral.' We never gave any thought to this line of reasoning, because we were just naturally pragmatic."[22]

The declaration quoted John Ehrlichman, who served as J. Edgar Hoover's contact with the Nixon White House and received Hoover's reports. "The Bureau dealt excessively in rumor, gossip and conjecture," he wrote in his memoir of this period. "Sometimes a report was based on 'a confidential source'—the Bureau euphemism for wiretapping or bugging. Even then the information was often hearsay." The FBI had repeatedly refused to release documents from the Lennon file it described as based on "confidential sources." But the FOIA does not permit the bureau to withhold information gathered by improper law enforcement techniques. The 1976 report of the Senate Select Committee on Intelligence, chaired by Frank Church, concluded that the FBI during this period engaged in a "pattern of reckless disregard of activities that threatened our constitution."[23]

The declaration argued that the Nixon campaign against Lennon was related to the Watergate abuses of power. Lennon was not the only one of Nixon's "enemies" to feel the power of the White House early in 1972. Gordon Liddy and E. Howard Hunt proposed in January that the Committee to Re-Elect the President spend $1 million on covert operations, including mugging demonstrators at the Republican National Convention and abducting the leaders to Mexico. Jerry Rubin and Abbie Hoffman were selected for abduction; Lennon was not. When the plan was presented to Attorney General Mitchell, he said it was "not quite what I had in mind" and cost too much.[24] Liddy came back with a plan to break into Democratic National Committee headquarters in Washington to plant bugs and photograph documents. Mitchell liked that better. The operation was carried out on June 17 at the Watergate offices of the Democratic National Committee; Washington police caught the perpetrators in the act. A cover-up directed by H. R. Haldeman and John Ehrlichman successfully kept the press from developing the story until after Nixon's reelection.

The declaration concluded that the Nixon administration's persecution of Lennon was one small part of a massive, illegal effort to ensure Nixon's reelection, one example of an abuse of power that eventually led Congress to move toward Nixon's impeachment, and that Lennon's FBI file contained the best and in some cases the only documentation of some Nixon-era abuses of presidential power. Release of these documents therefore would contribute to establishing a complete record of those historically significant events.

Judge Takasugi held a hearing February 6, 1984, in which both sides presented their arguments. In the courtroom, Rosenbaum and Marmalefsky looked splendid in their dark blue suits, although it was not hard to tell the ACLU team from the FBI attorneys: Rosenbaum and Marmalefsky were the ones with beards. Rosenbaum was also wearing cowboy boots.

The ACLU team had four specific objections to the FBI's codebook approach. First, Marmalefsky rose to challenge the bureau regarding confidential source material: the FOIA distinguished between information provided under a guarantee of confidentiality that was explicit and one that was not. If an FBI source had received an explicit promise that his or her identity would not be revealed, the information in question was absolutely protected from release under the FOIA. That was not the case for information provided by sources who had only an implied promise of confidentiality. Marmalefsky argued that the FBI had failed to distinguish between guarantees that were explicit and those that were only implied. That issue was called "expressed versus implied confidentiality." Second, the FBI had failed to explain how the information provided by confidential sources was gathered as part of a legitimate law enforcement investigation. What was missing was the "rational nexus."

Then Rosenbaum addressed the issue of national security information. The FBI's claims regarding the damage that would be caused by the release of foreign government information were too broad, he argued — they had a "lack of specificity." Finally, he told the court that the withholding of numerous entire pages was unacceptable; the courts required the segregation of all nonexempt portions of particular pages and the release of the rest of each page. This issue was called "segregability."

The ACLU team cited some important precedents in support of its argument. The closest parallel FOIA case had been brought in 1976 by a Berkeley graduate student, David Dunaway, who was writing a Ph.D. dissertation on Pete Seeger. That suit concerned the FBI file on the Weavers and other folk music groups and organizations. In 1981 Judge Peckham of the Northern District of California wrote that "we cannot blindly accept" the vague generalities in the codebook. The documents in that case "concern the comings and goings of U.S. citizens 20 to 30 years ago. . . . [V]irtually all of the information is of the most mundane character, information which has no apparent relationship to the security of this nation today, if it ever had." He ordered the documents to be released in their entirety.[25]

Another key case was that of Frank Wilkinson, executive director of the National Coalition against Repressive Legislation, founded to organize opposition to the McCarthy hearings and to the House Committee on Un-American Activities. In that case, Wilkinson argued that in the early 1960s the FBI targeted his organization as part of the illegal COINTELPRO operation, that the FBI investigation was intended "not to uncover potential criminal activity, but instead to monitor and disrupt plaintiff's lawful activities through the use of various illegal techniques such as warrantless electronic surveillance, 'black bag jobs,' and *agents provacateur* [sic]." In that case 12,000 documents were at issue. Judge Tashima of the Central District of California ruled that the FBI coding system consisted of vague generalities that "do not enable this Court meaningfully to assess the validity of the agency's claims."[26] Because the government had not met its burden, he ordered the FBI to release the documents. By citing these cases, Rosenbaum and Marmalefsky were providing Judge Takasugi with precedents he could rely on if he were to rule that the FBI's Vaughn index was inadequate.

The government attorneys replied that the FBI had done what was legally required and that if the judge wanted they would submit the original uncensored FBI file pages for *in camera* review by the judge. In response to the ACLU team's arguments that confidential source information could not be withheld if the government lacked a legitimate law enforcement purpose in the investigation, FBI attorney Petersen replied that the prevailing law in three federal circuits held that FBI records "are *inherently* records compiled for 'law enforcement purposes.'" That was a chilling argument. The standard in the Ninth Circuit, where the case was being tried, required a "rational nexus" between the documents and a legitimate law enforcement purpose.

The government had already responded briefly to the "Declaration of Jonathan M. Wiener": "While interesting reading," the FBI told the court in its reply, the declaration was "mostly composed of hearsay, improper opinion, and irrelevant matter." It urged the court to ignore it.

Petersen reminded Judge Takasugi that the FBI brief had provided an explanation of

"The Origination of the FBI Investigation Concerning John Lennon." He cited the 1968 Civil Obedience Act and the Anti-Riot Act, which made it a felony to travel interstate with the intent to encourage, incite, or participate in a riot. Congress had passed this law in response to the demonstrations at the Democratic National Convention in 1968, in the hope of preventing a recurrence in 1972. Lennon had been associating in 1971–72 with Jerry Rubin and Rennie Davis, who had been convicted of similar crimes in Chicago in 1968 and who had formed a group "apparently dedicated to creating disruptions," Petersen told the judge, at the 1972 Republican convention. Therefore, Petersen continued, the FBI's investigation of Lennon had a legitimate law enforcement purpose, and the withholding of confidential source information was required under the FOIA. That had a certain logic; however, the government had earlier given a different basis for the investigation of Lennon, the National Security Act of 1947. Rosenbaum and Marmalefsky would highlight this contradiction in subsequent litigation.

On the "national security" material, Petersen argued that Judge Takasugi should defer to executive branch decisions. Judges were unqualified to overrule decisions made by career officials whose responsibility was national security classification. Thus, he argued, the assignment of a "national security" classification to any FBI document was "absolute." The judicial review process provided for in the FOIA, he argued, was "limited to a determination that the procedures set forth by the applicable Executive Order have been followed and that the classification decision was made in good faith"; in other words, Petersen told Takasugi, "the court may not review or second-guess the substantive decision to classify." He cited the D.C. Circuit making precisely that argument.

The brief Petersen had submitted pointed out that another court went beyond the "reasonable basis" standard for withholding documents. "In view of the knowledge, experience and positions held by the three affiants regarding military secrets, military planning and national security," a D.C. Circuit judge declared, "their affidavits were to be treated by the courts with 'utmost deference.'"[27] The implication was clear: if "utmost deference" were to become the prevailing standard, the judicial review provisions of the FOIA would become virtually useless, and the withheld Lennon files would never be released.

Judge Takasugi responded five weeks later, in March 1984, to the ACLU motion to compel a new and more adequate Vaughn index. He agreed that the FBI's index to the Lennon documents lacked the required specificity. But instead of ordering the bureau to provide the plaintiff with a new and detailed Vaughn index, he ordered the FBI to submit more specific affidavits to him *in camera*—affidavits Rosenbaum and Marmalefsky would not be allowed to see. The FBI promptly filed two *in camera* affidavits by Agents Peterson and Chester, which presumably made new arguments, and gave the judge a copy of the uncensored Lennon FBI file. Apparently they were confident he would conclude that the files indeed did contain national security information.

The ACLU team objected to the FBI's submission of documents to the judge *in camera*, pointing out that the Vaughn decision that governed this kind of case criticized *in camera* inspection of documents because "it is necessarily conducted without benefit of criticism and illumination by a party with the actual interest in forcing disclosure." In August 1984, Rosenbaum and Marmalefsky filed a motion asking the judge either to release the *in camera* affidavits or order the FBI to prepare a more adequate Vaughn index. Without such rulings, "the litigation will essentially have lost its adversary character," the ACLU team concluded.

MEDIA WATCH: 1983–84   The first steps in the ACLU's project of publicizing the value of the FOIA and its subversion by the FBI came when the lawsuit was first announced and my book *Come Together: John Lennon in His Time* was published, drawing on files that had been released. The publisher, Random House, organized a ten-city author tour in 1983, which featured the story of the withheld files and the historian who had sued the FBI to win their release. As the ACLU had hoped, the story was covered by Dan Rather, *ABC 20/20*, the *CBS Morning News, People* magazine, and most of the country's newspapers. CNN's Dave Rinn was energetic enough to ask Haldeman and Nixon for comment; both refused.[28]

The *Today* show producers didn't want to have me on alone. They invited the White House to send a spokesman to respond to my account of the Reagan administration's fight to prevent release of the Lennon files. Senator Orrin Hatch, one of the smartest and most articulate spokesmen of the Right, was chosen to provide the administration response. For anyone who thought the Reagan White House didn't care about the Lennon files, the selection of Senator Hatch must have been illuminating. (He canceled at the last minute.)

The ACLU was delighted to get the story on TV, but often the context undermined the seriousness of the issues. In Chicago on a live morning TV show, the other guests were Soupy Sales, Miss USA—a J. C. Penney promotion—and a drug-sniffing dog that was sent out into the studio audience. Another live morning TV show, in Detroit, had a smaller budget for their dog segment: "Coming up, John Lennon and the FBI—but first, Name That Breed!" A picture of a dog went up on the screen, and viewers were invited to phone the station and "name that breed. We'll be back with the correct answer—and the John Lennon FBI files—right after this message." Cut to commercial.

Some treated the story seriously but got it wrong: instead of "FBI refuses to release files on Lennon," dozens of newspapers ran stories in June 1984 headed "Senator Thurmond Tried to Deport Lennon," attributing that information to documents released in *Wiener v. FBI*. But that story had been told almost a decade earlier, in 1975, by Chet Flippo in *Rolling Stone*.[29]

And occasionally the story provided a platform for diatribes against "the sixties." Ronald Radosh, a former sixties leftist who had joined the right, reviewed *Come Together* in the *Washington Post*, where he wrote that the book shared J. Edgar Hoover's delusions about Lennon's political significance.[30] The *Princeton Alumni Weekly* ran a report on the Princeton graduate, class of '66, who had sued the FBI for the Lennon files, which prompted Bill Black Jr., class of '67, to write a letter to the editor declaring that another Princeton alumnus of the same era had "bombed a computer center at the University of Wisconsin in 1970, killing a graduate student and wounding four other persons. I do not understand how Wiener could have forgotten so prominent a member of his small group, who graduated to terrorism and murder." That claim was completely untrue and indeed libelous, as editor Charles Creesy '65 was informed. The next issue bore an abject apology from Black, who conceded that his statement was "without basis and completely in error. I regret this error and any harm it may have caused." That ran next to a box from the editors headed "An Apology and Retraction."[31]

From District Court to the Supreme Court

JUDGE TAKASUGI'S 1988 RULING: THE FBI WINS ROUND ONE The FBI case regarding information provided by confidential informants became considerably stronger in 1986, when the Republican-dominated Congress adopted something called "the Reform Act" to strengthen the protections of confidentiality for informers and confidential sources under the FOIA. The FBI promptly informed Judge Takasugi that Congress made its intentions clear in debate on the floor of the Senate, when Republican Senator Orrin Hatch of Utah provided examples of the risks in releasing confidential source information: "If a record says that the informant, Joe Jones, drove away in a green sedan," and the FOIA requester "knows that he only has one friend with a green sedan," the identity of the source has been revealed. Or "the criminal may know that one of his friends always calls a party a 'bash' or a soft drink a 'pop.' If one of those words appear in a requested record, he has identified the informant."[1] As a result, the FBI told the court, the 1986 amendment to the FOIA "permits deletion of apparently innocuous information, such as reports of public events."

The FBI went further: while the purpose of withholding information provided by confidential informants was to protect the identity of the sources, the information they furnished could still be withheld, the FBI declared, citing a recent decision, "even if the identity of the sources have been revealed."[2] And "even if the identity of the source is known and the person is dead," the confidential source information would still be withheld.[3] Therefore, the FBI said, there were no circumstances under which it would release any of the information provided by confidential sources.

Before the FBI sent its final briefs to Judge Takasugi, the bureau in 1987 abandoned its "national security" claim for ninety-six pages or passages, but that did not mean the information on those pages would be released. Thirty-seven passages previously withheld as national security material were now withheld as law enforcement confidential source information. Nineteen more passages were now withheld as law enforcement "source symbol numbers or letters." Seventeen were now withheld as relating to "internal FBI personnel rules and practices." Only twenty-six pages remained for which the FBI asserted the national security exemption. The bureau felt it was unable to defend its claims for a whopping 80 percent of the original material it had called "national security" information; but clearly it didn't want to release those pages.

Judge Takasugi never ruled on the ACLU team's motion for a more adequate Vaughn index. Instead, after waiting more than two years, he invited the FBI to file a motion for summary judgment, a ruling without a trial, which he granted on February 29, 1988. The district court's ruling adopted exactly the language proposed by the FBI—a listing of the nine affidavits submitted by the government, followed by a declaration that "the above-listed affidavits and declarations carry the government's burden of proof to show that FOIA exemptions were properly applied in this case." Although the FBI had submitted the uncensored Lennon files to Takasugi, he did not say that he had read them; he did not say that his decision was based on his own examination of the withheld material. Five years of litigation had produced only a terse affirmation that the FBI had fulfilled its statutory obligations.

Thus five years of litigation had accomplished virtually nothing. *Wiener v. FBI* was beginning to seem like *Jarndyce v. Jarndyce*, the case in Dickens's 1853 novel *Bleak House*, where the court "so exhausts the finances, patience, courage, hope, so overthrows the brain and breaks the heart, that there is not an honorable man among its practitioners who would not give—who does not often give—the warning, 'Suffer any wrong that can be done you, rather than come here!' "[4]

When Mark Rosenbaum called me with the bad news, he said, "The first thing I want to say is I'm sorry. The second thing is that we're going to appeal." Rosenbaum later told me that Takasugi's 1988 ruling was "a major blow. He was a judge who, by virtue of his track record, we thought would not be bowled over by empty government assertions of privilege. His decision reinforced just how bad the state of the law was."[5]

Takasugi's decision "reflected the custom of the time," Rosenbaum continued, "which was that if the government affidavits passed the 'straight face test,' they would be accepted.

That meant the grounds cited by the government in withholding the documents were found to be legitimate on the surface, even if they were not clearly related to information on individual pages at issue."

Although the FBI won the case at the district court level, it had periodically released documents that had been previously withheld. Just four months after the case was filed, the FBI released some of the Haldeman letter, which had been completely blacked out originally (see p. 240). The letter began at the beginning, identifying Lennon as a "former member of the Beatles singing group," and summarized the state of the case for deporting Lennon. Hoover reported that Lennon "has been offered a teaching position at New York University for the summer of 1972," hardly a criminal matter (see p. 231). He also informed the White House that Lennon claimed to have been appointed to "the President's Council on Drug Abuse." In fact the FBI had confused the National Commission on Marijuana and Drug Abuse, to which Lennon had not been appointed and never claimed to have been, with the American Bar Association Committee on Drug Abuse, to which he indeed had been appointed. Nothing in the letter to Haldeman identified any violations of the law that would justify an FBI investigation.

The FBI continued to maintain that release of the remaining blacked-out portions of Hoover's letter would endanger the national security, arguing that the withheld sections contained foreign government information. The FBI stated in its codebook that the damage to the national security "reasonably expected to result from disclosure" of these lines included "foreign military retaliation."

Despite Judge Takasugi's decision, Rosenbaum and Marmalefsky were not about to give up. They promptly appealed to the Ninth Circuit Court of Appeals in 1989. "We had no hesitation over appealing," Rosenbaum told me in 1998. "The ACLU's commitment had always been open-ended. We litigate virtually all our cases without any time boundaries. We still believed in the case. The problem wasn't Judge Takasugi, it was the state of appellate law. And our larger strategy required moving the case forward. If you were timid about this case, you might as well fold up the FOIA tent."[6]

Dan Marmalefsky, who was doing the case pro bono, said he too "never had any doubt about appealing. When we did not get what we felt was an adequate Vaughn affidavit, it was clear that we would have to appeal. And we were confident that we stood a good chance on appeal."[7]

The three judges on the panel that heard the ACLU team's appeal, appointed by lot, all turned out to be Democratic appointees, unusual at a time when the Ninth Circuit had become almost two-thirds Republican. James Browning, who would write the published decision, had been a Kennedy appointee to the federal bench. Born in Great Falls, Montana, he was seventy-one at the time the appeal was filed. He had gone to college at Montana State in Missoula during the Depression and had graduated from the University of Montana Law School in 1941. In the forties he had been a government antitrust lawyer and worked as executive assistant to the U.S. attorney general in 1952–53. The year before he was assigned the appeal on *Wiener v. FBI*, he completed twelve years as chief judge of the Ninth Circuit Court of Appeals.

Warren Ferguson, the second member of the appeals panel, had been born in Eureka, Nevada, and was sixty-nine years old when the case was filed. He had graduated from the University of Nevada in 1942 and then from USC Law School in 1949. During the fifties he had been city attorney for Buena Park, Placentia, La Puente, Baldwin Park, Santa Fe Springs, Walnut, and Rosemead, California, and then had begun a judicial career. He was a Lyndon Johnson appointee to the federal bench and at the time of the appeal was senior judge on the Ninth Circuit in Santa Ana. He was also a faculty member of the USC Medical School, where he taught psychiatry and the law. In *Who's Who* he described himself as "Democrat. Roman Catholic."

The third judge on the appeals panel was Mary M. Schroeder, a Carter appointee. She had been born in Boulder, Colorado, and was forty-nine at the time the appeal was filed. She had graduated from Swarthmore College in 1962 and from the University of Chicago Law School in 1965. She had worked as a Department of Justice trial attorney during the sixties and became a judge in Arizona in 1975. Her office was in Phoenix. Rosenbaum had argued a draft registration case before Judge Schroeder, and she had voted in favor of his argument. When the membership of the panel was announced, Rosenbaum said he thought we had a shot now, but it would still be an uphill fight.

Representing the FBI before the Ninth Circuit was Miriam MacIntyre Nisbet. She was forty-two at the time and had been an undergraduate and law school student at the University of North Carolina, Chapel Hill. (She later left the Justice Department to work on the staff of the general counsel of the National Archives and Records Administration, where she remained in 1998.)

The climax of the case came at noon on December 5, 1989, when both sides met in courtroom two of the U.S. Court of Appeals in Pasadena.[8] Mark Rosenbaum spoke first: "Your honors, this appeal tests whether there exists, in the context of a request for decades-old documents about John Lennon, any bounds to the national security exemption to the Freedom of Information Act. It tests whether the government, by invoking the national security exemption, may automatically shield from disclosure documents upon arguments so broad, and so categorical in nature, that the mere act of classification confers on the government virtual carte blanche authority to restrict access." He emphasized that the law required the court to perform a *de novo* review of the case, not simply accept the government's assurances. He conceded that, under the president's executive order on classification, the release of classified foreign government information is "presumed" to cause damage to the national security; nevertheless, he argued, "the government must show that the presumption is properly applied in this particular case." And he pointed out that, under the law, classification cannot be used to conceal "violations of the law or politically embarrassing situations."

Rosenbaum asked the judges to look at a couple of documents: first, the letter to H. R. Haldeman from J. Edgar Hoover, from which several lines had been withheld as foreign government information (see p. 240). The withheld information, he said, probably involved Lennon's 1968 conviction in England for cannabis possession and perhaps his political activities there. He then read from the FBI codebook stating that release of this information would "lead to diplomatic, political or economic retaliation." "It is our position, your honors," he declared, "that under *no* set of facts could *any* of those matters result from the document we're talking about."

The second document was one that had originally been withheld on national security/foreign government information grounds but, after that classification was lifted, had been withheld as (b)(7) confidential source information. Forty national security documents had been similarly declassified, and 85 percent of them were still being withheld under exemption (b)(7). "How was it," Rosenbaum asked, "that an FBI agent swore under oath that he had followed all the rules of classification and come up with national security, and now instead they involve a domestic investigation. How did that happen? How did that agent get it wrong? That gives us some indication as to the character and the nature of the national security exemption claim." If the government claim regarding national security was upheld, he concluded, "the exemption is absolute and the rights of citizens to foreign information is gone altogether."

Dan Marmalefsky then challenged the FBI's claim that it had a legitimate law enforcement purpose in investigating Lennon. He reviewed the change in the FBI's claim regarding the law under which Lennon was being investigated and declared "there is no plausible connection between Lennon and the National Security Act, and there's no plausible connection with the Civil Obedience Act."

The government claimed that they were investigating Lennon because of his involvement with the Election Year Strategy Information Center (EYSIC), the organization led by Jerry Rubin and Rennie Davis committed to defeating Nixon in the 1972 presidential election. According to the FBI, EYSIC disbanded on March 1, 1972, but twenty-seven of the thirty-four documents in the Lennon headquarters file postdate that event. "So this has nothing to do with a continuing investigation of a relationship between John Lennon and EYSIC," Marmalefsky argued. In fact the documents in the file "don't concern themselves with enforcement of the Anti-Riot Act, they concern themselves with statements being made at INS hearings . . . and 'how can we get John Lennon out of the country before the Republican convention?'" Marmalefsky quoted from a memo from Acting Director L. Patrick Gray, declaring that the FBI wasn't really the pertinent agency to be involved with the INS effort to deport Lennon. Marmalefsky said, "I suggest that this has nothing to do with a legitimate concern that Lennon is involved in a potential violation of the anti-riot act."

Marmalefsky also raised the issue of "segregability"—whether any part of a withheld document could be released, as required under a Ninth Circuit Church of Scientology case. Sixty-nine pages had been withheld in their entirety, but the Ninth Circuit had previously ruled that a government agency "cannot justify withholding an entire document simply by showing that it contains some exempt material."[9] "I presume that John Lennon's name appears somewhere in those documents," Marmalefsky said, "because we requested John Lennon's files and we got those deleted documents. But there is no finding that says that John Lennon is mentioned on this page and there's no finding that tells us why information about John Lennon is not reasonably segregable."

Then Miriam Nisbet rose to argue the government's case. Judge Ferguson interrupted her almost immediately with a question centering on one deleted document, called "exhibit

OO." Nisbet said, "Your Honor, exhibit OO pertains to an entirely separate extortion file that the appellant did not wish to get," which was true. In its Vaughn index, the FBI was required to list all its Lennon documents, including the file on a 1977 investigation of an attempt to extort money from Lennon. Because it had nothing to do with the Nixon administration effort to silence him as an antiwar spokesman, we had not requested that file. But it was described briefly in the FBI's court papers, along with the reason why it was not being released. The Vaughn index stated that the perpetrator "has never been identified or prosecuted. If the details of this investigation, such as the contents of letters, a description of the subject's voice, and the physical description of a suspect, were released, media publicity would undoubtedly follow. . . . The result effect on him is obviously unknown but can be speculated upon. Perhaps this refreshing of his memory would cause him to resume this type of threatening activity against the Lennon family."

"I understand," Judge Ferguson said. "Now exhibit OO is the only exhibit in the file in which there is a personalized reason why the exhibit is not being released. All of the other exhibits refer to a coded index, and that coded index states with assurance that national security is going to be violated etcetera, etcetera, etcetera." The codebook arguments, he pointed out, identify the damages that would result from release of the pages at issue with certainty, but in the one file in which they did not use a codebook, "you use the words 'we speculate' or 'perhaps.' Now can you justify the difference?"

"Your Honor, I'm sorry," Nisbet said, "I'm not sure I'm understanding the significance."

"Oh sure you can."

"Because this explanation is, I believe, for one thing this file was not at issue in this lawsuit. That is, I believe, . . . "

Ferguson interrupted: "It was a matter of the record. I'm not indicating whether or not it's an issue. All I'm indicating to you is the fact that when you are required to specifically state a reason, particularized reason, why we are withholding a document, you use the words 'speculate upon' and 'perhaps,' but in every instance in which you use a coded index, you are absolutely certain. Now can you see a little difference in that?"

Nisbet struggled to answer: "The statute only requires that the information be such that its disclosure reasonably could be expected to disclose—or to cause—particular harm."

"I understand all that," Judge Ferguson replied impatiently. "I understand all that."

"Am I not responding to your question? I'm very sorry."

"Your response is very effective," Judge Ferguson told the FBI attorney, "because you're not responding." That was a devastating thing for an appeals court judge to tell a Justice Department litigator.

"I sure am trying," Nisbet replied. "I really am. I'm not trying to avoid it at all. I'm not sure I understand exactly."

Judge Ferguson tried again. Nisbet gave a long answer, concluding that "substantial deference should be given to the agency's determination. I recognize that the appellant may not feel that these harms might occur, but that is not the test. The test is whether or not the agency has made the correct determination, and that is something that the district court was able to verify, and you will be able to verify as well. You have access to the documents here. You can look at the *in camera* declarations. You can look at the information withheld, and I am confident that you will be able to see the harm as well."

Judge Ferguson challenged her on that argument: "What if we decide that the administration of the Act is such that we should not review *in camera*? The government should disclose its case, in an affidavit open to the public, [for] the need for nondisclosure." That's exactly what the ACLU team had been arguing. Asking the judge to decide the case *in camera*, Ferguson declared, "violates the Act"—a striking affirmation of the ACLU position. "To require all courts to examine *in camera*, both the district court and the court of appeals, regarding these documents, defeats the purpose of the Act." That was a strong statement.

Finally Nisbet was allowed to return to her presentation. She argued that the Lennon investigation had taken less than a year, short by FBI standards, and that "there were in fact very few documents that we even created after the summer of 1972, and in fact what happened is the FBI concluded, as a result of the investigation, that it need not further investigate Mr. Lennon."

Here Nisbet was interrupted by Judge Schroeder: "Which way does that cut in terms of disclosure? How can you make those points and then argue that these dire consequences may reasonably occur if this is disclosed?"

"Well, Your Honor, the investigation ultimately concluded that there was no violation of any sort of crimes certainly. Nonetheless, in order for it to conduct its investigation, the FBI did have to gather information. That's how it determines whether or not to go forward, to conduct further investigation, or in this instance, to close its file."

Since her time was almost finished, Nisbet tried to sum up: "I would simply like to conclude, unless there are additional questions, in our firm belief, again, the district court had an entirely adequate factual basis for its decision. I urge this court, if it wishes, to look at the *in camera* materials. It too can confirm what [the] district court saw." But there was nothing in Takasugi's decision indicating that he had looked at the uncensored files. "What the district court saw," according to the text of the decision, was the declarations of the FBI officials.

But the judges didn't challenge her on that point, and she continued: "There's no wrong-doing being hidden here. The claims for exemption are very narrow, they're very discrete, they're entirely within what the Freedom of Information Act envisioned. The Act, the purpose of the Act, of course, is to open up government files. But the exemptions are there because Congress recognized that there were legitimate government reasons why information, in some cases, had to be withheld, and that's all that's being withheld here."

Now Judge Browning interrupted: "Do we need the assistance of some kind of an index that would relate the objections, the denial of which are under appeal, to particular documents and particular pages?"

"No, Your Honor, I don't think that you do."

"Do you think we might need that," Judge Browning repeated, "assuming that we're going to examine the documents?"

"Your Honor, I do not," Nisbet said. She saw where this was headed—to a victory for the ACLU team's argument that the FBI's Vaughn index was inadequate. "Let me explain why. The documents really are not voluminous. They're not very lengthy. I have certainly looked through them. I believe that you can look through them without spending a great deal of time. The reason for the exemptions, particularly in context, are quite straightforward. Certainly if you feel the need of something like that, I'm sure we could provide something." The "something" she had in mind was another *in camera* affidavit, but Judge Ferguson had already argued against *in camera* proceedings.

Dan Marmalefsky commented later that "basically the government's argument had been 'trust us.' It's not much of an argument, but it is supported by law and precedent."[10] Indeed the Justice Department's reply brief before the Ninth Circuit had pointed out that the Supreme Court had held in 1983 that even "speculative or ambiguous prediction of harm" resulting from the release of foreign government information was "sufficiently reasonable and plausible" to justify withholding the information.[11]

Nisbet had completed her presentation. Now Mark Rosenbaum asked for the opportunity to respond. "You may have two minutes," Judge Browning told him, "though as you know, you've used your time."

First, Rosenbaum argued that "the business of the government is not to put a sheaf of documents in front of a judge and say, 'See what you think, see if you can find some basis for an exemption here.' . . . All of the cases say that the government has to make its case. It's not for the judge to sit and speculate and try to find a basis for it. . . . In fact, the record on this case shows the constantly shifting position of the government: on one hand the statute that they're utilizing is the National Security Act, the next time it's the Anti-Riot Act. One time it's the (b)(1) exemption, next time it's a (b)(7) exemption."

Second, Rosenbaum argued, "the government misstates the standard with respect to classification." In describing damage that could result from the release of national security documents, what was required was "not some agent's fathoming of every possible horror that could take place, but with specificity. . . . The case law says that there is substantial deference in the area of exemption 1 [(b)(1)], but that doesn't mean that the courts are supposed to roll over."

Rosenbaum made one final point: "Knowing what we know about those documents, the government shouldn't be saying it's OK that there were 280 pages. There ought to have been no pages." He was arguing that the FBI lacked a legitimate law enforcement purpose in investigating Lennon. "I don't know whether or not what's behind those deletions is politically embarrassing to the government. There's already plenty of that in what we've seen. And I don't know whether it's mundane. I don't know whether any of that information would ever find its way into Professor Wiener's new book on John Lennon. But that isn't the point. The point is that the public has a right to know under that Act, and the government can't hide behind categorical conclusory claims."

He ended by criticizing Judge Takasugi's ruling, calling it "a sign-off on a simple statement that the government met its burden. We have no clues whatsoever as what the reasoning was that upheld the government's case." With that, the session ended.

YEAR EIGHT: THE NINTH CIRCUIT DECISION   While the Ninth Circuit deliberated, President Bush organized an alliance to attack Iraq after Saddam Hussein invaded Kuwait, and the BBC banned Lennon's song "Imagine" for the duration of the Gulf War.

Sean Ono Lennon recorded a new version of "Give Peace a Chance," featuring Lenny Kravitz, M. C. Hammer, Peter Gabriel, Bonnie Raitt, L. L. Cool J., Randy Newman, and Tom Petty; during the first days of the war, MTV played the new "Give Peace a Chance" video hourly.[12] Lennon's political message seemed as relevant at the beginning of 1991 as it had twenty years earlier.

The three judges issued a strong decision on July 12, 1991, sharply criticizing the FBI. The Ninth Circuit decision was significant because it held not just that the FBI had failed to process the Lennon files correctly but that the bureau's codebook approach was itself unacceptable henceforth throughout the Ninth Circuit, the western U.S. The codebook approach, the Ninth Circuit declared, provided the requester with "little or no opportunity to argue for release of particular documents," because "the index provided no information about particular documents." The court endorsed Rosenbaum and Marmalefsky's argument that an adequate Vaughn index must "not merely inform the requester of the agency's conclusion that a particular document is exempt from disclosure . . . , but afford the requester an opportunity to intelligently advocate release of the withheld documents." The FBI cannot give "broad explanations of alternative harms that might result from the release of withheld information," the judges declared. Instead, the FBI must tie its "general concern about disclosure" with "the facts of this case" by describing specifically the damage that would result from each particular disclosure.

On the national security exemption, the Ninth Circuit ruled unanimously that the FBI's boilerplate claims were not adequate, because the codebook procedure lacked specificity; the FBI had failed to provide a description of the injury to national security arising from the disclosure of each document. (The panel commented on the FBI's claim that releasing the foreign government information in the Lennon file could lead to "foreign military retaliation." The judges called that claim "farfetched.")[13]

The principle at stake, the appeals court held, was the preservation of the adversary process, which had been subverted by the FBI's boilerplate codebook. The plaintiff had been unable to "intelligently advocate release of the . . . documents," and the district court was unable to "intelligently judge the contest." In order for a judge to be able to rule fairly, he or she had to hear the best arguments of both sides.[14]

Significantly, the Ninth Circuit accepted the ACLU team's argument that *in camera* examination of documents by the judge was not sufficient for him to determine whether they should be released. The fact that Judge Takasugi had made such a determination was no substitute for a genuine adversary proceeding. The court of appeals declared that resort to *in camera* review was "appropriate only after the government has submitted as detailed public affidavits and testimony as possible."[15] The judge had an obligation to hear full, informed argument from those seeking the files. The FBI's obligation was to maximize their opponents' ability to argue for disclosure.

The three-judge panel also agreed with Rosenbaum and Marmalefsky that the FBI had "failed to explain with sufficient specificity the 'law enforcement purposes' underlying its investigation of John Lennon." The FBI, the court continued, had not demonstrated a "rational nexus" between the bureau's legitimate responsibilities in law enforcement and the withheld documents, because it had failed to describe "the kinds of criminal activity of which John Lennon was allegedly suspected."[16]

The appellate court also ruled that the government had not adequately justified its claims of withholding information to protect confidential informants. "The most obvious flaw," the court stated, was the FBI's "failure to state whether the purported grant of confidentiality was express or implied." It agreed with the FBI that an express grant of confidentiality was "virtually unassailable" and required the withholding of information. But it agreed with the ACLU that the same was not true if the promise of confidentiality was only implicit. In such cases, withholding information required explaining "the circumstances surrounding the receipt of information which led the FBI to conclude the informant would not have given the information without an implicit assurance of confidentiality." The principle the court sought to uphold was that the requester of an FBI file should have enough information to "argue [that] no inference of confidentiality was justified."[17] Finally the appeals court criticized Judge Takasugi for failing to provide adequate written explanations of his findings of fact and conclusions of law regarding each document in dispute.

As for the strongest precedent claimed by the government, the 1989 ruling by the Fifth Circuit that the CIA's decision to withhold information could not be "second guessed" by a court in an FOIA suit "in the absence of evidence of bad faith,"[18] the Ninth Circuit judges declared, with admirable directness, that they "declined to follow" it. The judges acknowledged that the CIA's judgment was "entitled to great deference," but argued that "the Agency still bears the burden of proving the withholding is justified."[19]

Although the Ninth Circuit found the FBI had failed to make an adequate case for withholding the documents, the panel did not rule that therefore the pages had to be released. They could have ordered the release of documents on the grounds that the government had failed to meet its burden. But instead the appeals court sent the case back to District Court Judge Takasugi with instructions to start over—for the FBI to prepare an adequate Vaughn index, which would give Rosenbaum and Marmalefsky an opportunity to argue about each document. That was a striking victory, with great significance as a precedent for other cases, and a vindication of the ACLU team's arguments; but it was not the victory we had hoped for.

The Ninth Circuit went so far as to take two documents the FBI had withheld from the public, but had provided for the court; the judges described these documents to provide an example of the kind of detailed description the bureau had an obligation to provide. First they took an "airtel" from J. Edgar Hoover to the FBI in New York, dated April 10, 1972, in which Hoover conveyed information about Lennon provided by an informer in Alexandria, Virginia (see p. 219). Large sections were completely blacked out. The appeals court declared that, instead of providing abbreviations in the margins that referred to boilerplate passages in the FBI codebook, the FBI's Vaughn index "could have stated that HQ-8 recites information provided by a third party to an FBI informant detailing the third party's knowledge of several activists and protest activities planned at the 1972 Republican National Convention, discussing the possibility that John Lennon would organize a series of concerts to raise money to finance the activity, and describing rivalries and jealousies within activist organizations."[20]

Their second example was an informant report that had been withheld in its entirety—we subsequently learned it was the one that included the parrot story (see chapter 4, p. 87). "The FBI could have stated that [it] describes a series of meetings between a third person and various activists, discusses contests over the leadership of activist groups and complaints that activist leaders receive more publicity than the groups themselves, and reports tangential information about activist leaders, such as their habits of personal hygiene and the peculiar behavior of their pets."[21] Apparently the parrot story had made an impression on the judges.

The implication here was clear: the court's examples of suitable descriptions of withheld documents suggested there was no legitimate legal basis for withholding them. Once the FBI declared it was withholding information about the "personal hygiene" of various activist leaders and "the peculiar behavior of their pets," it would not be hard for Rosenbaum and Marmalefsky to argue that those documents had no legitimate law enforcement purpose and ought to be released. Still, the court refused to order the release of either document, holding fast to its principle that only an adversary proceeding should resolve the case, not *in camera* inspection carried out by judges.

The Ninth Circuit decision in *Wiener v. FBI* appears to be one of the most important published decisions enforcing a plaintiff's rights against government agencies in FOIA cases. The court's holding and reasoning are frequently cited, often with lengthy quotations from the decision.[22]

THE FBI INFORMER WHO CHANGED SIDES   While the appeal was on the way to the Ninth Circuit, I received a phone call from a woman who had read a news article about the Lennon FOIA lawsuit; she told me, "At long last maybe I should come clear: in 1972 I was undercover for the FBI." Her name was Julie Maynard, she lived in Madison, and she said she had been "Miami office manager for Jerry and Abbie—I ran the YIP [Youth International Party] office. I was in on the ground floor of the planning for a rock concert to disrupt the Republican convention in Miami—to tie it up with a Woodstock-like event." She said she'd like to help with our lawsuit.

To have a former FBI informer join our side would be a stunning development. But skepticism is always required when dealing with statements from undercover agents and informers, since their livelihoods depend on persuading their superiors that the information they provide is unique and significant. This information from Maynard about Lennon was available in news accounts and in my book on Lennon, so maybe that was where she got it.

She continued: "We contacted rock groups; they wanted insurance. Jerry went to John, and John wrote a check for $40,000. Our legal people said put it in the bank. I Xeroxed the check and made copies for the FBI. That's why they were interested in Lennon." It was true that Lennon's financial contribution to the group the FBI called "the Allamuchy tribe" played a big role in his FBI file. But Maynard's account put her at the center of the Lennon investigation, which seemed unlikely.

"I was not a sworn agent," she said. "There was a hippie sworn agent I worked for—Cril Payne. He wrote the book *Deep Cover*." Indeed *Deep Cover* includes a first-person account of the FBI undercover operation at the Miami conventions, but again this was a published account that would have been available to Maynard.[23] "I was sworn May 2, 1972," Maynard continued, "the day after Hoover died." The FBI was "agitated about the rock concert plan—Bob Mardian from the Justice Department was down there—he was getting pressure from Haldeman, who was getting pressure from Nixon." Mardian was assistant attorney general at the time and eventually would be convicted in the Watergate trial, along with Mitchell, Haldeman, and Ehrlichman, for conspiracy, obstruction of justice, and perjury.[24] His name had never come up in this context before.

Regarding the plans for a rock concert in Miami, "We couldn't get it together," she told me. "We couldn't get groups to come. Maybe the money went back to John. We worked on Lily Tomlin to do a phone freak conference, but she didn't do it. She did call on the phone a lot. She always wanted to talk to Abbie. I wasn't in touch with them directly, but other people would say 'I talked to John last night'—Patty Oldenburg, Claes's wife, was part of the collective. She may have been in touch with him. Suzy Creamcheese was there and went on to be a receptionist for Apple in New York. She was in touch with him. I knew John wasn't going to come—that was a given. But we thought we could get some money out of him. We thought it would be too dangerous for him—we'd been through Chicago in 1968, where we were paranoid and thought they might kill us all."

I was not convinced that Maynard was as important as she wanted me to think she was. I asked about the time frame for her story, pointing out that, originally, the Republican convention had been planned for San Diego but had been moved to Miami after the Dita Beard scandal exposed corporate payoffs to put the convention in San Diego.

"I was instrumental in getting the convention moved to Miami," she answered. "The reasons why it was moved weren't all made public." This seemed dubious and made her sound more unreliable.

She wanted to talk about the "national security" claim the government was making in withholding Lennon documents. "I can key into that," she said, "because I later became a CIA operative and went on to become a double agent for the Chinese—Deng was in charge of intelligence in China at the time. I was working for the CIA but I allowed the Chinese to recruit me. The CIA wanted me to do that—it hadn't been done. It would embarrass the CIA if this info got out. The claim of 'national security' in your case doesn't refer to Lennon, it refers to me." That seemed extremely unlikely.

She went on to say that "the Madison police chief blew my cover" in 1976 "to establish that he was a liberal fellow," and since then she had not worked for the FBI. I concluded that she was probably a paid informer and possibly involved with the Chinese, but I was not at all certain she was a reliable or significant source on the Lennon files.

In a January 1990 follow-up letter, Maynard wrote "I am very happy to be of any service to you" and, to document the fact that she had worked as a paid FBI informant, provided the ACLU with a 1979 FBI affidavit "summarizing the contents of the records and documents concerning Julie Maynard's role as an FBI informant." She said she had sued the city of Madison in 1979 for income she lost as a result of having had her cover blown, and the affidavit was part of that lawsuit.

The FBI affidavit reported that the Milwaukee FBI office had a "main file" on her consisting of 267 pages of administrative data and "documents pertaining to the quality and quantity of the information Plaintiff provided," and seven volumes, consisting of 2,136 pages, of "reports" she provided "during her tenure as an informant regarding organizations, members of organizations, and their activities." That was impressive. The FBI declared that Maynard initially received payment from the FBI on June 5, 1972, in connection with services performed in Miami; that she received additional payment on September 5, 1972, because she "provided reports" on the "Youth International Party" (the Yippies). The FBI declared that it had paid her $960 for "services" in 1972 and considerably more in the next three years, when she provided reports on the Revolutionary Union, the Revolutionary Student Brigade, and the U.S.-China Peoples Friendship Association. Clearly Julie Maynard had been a paid FBI confidential informant reporting on the Yippies in Miami in 1972—but how closely she had been involved in the bureau's surveillance of Lennon was still not certain.

How could she help our case? The FBI was withholding from us confidential informant reports she had written on the grounds that they were obligated to conceal her identity. But she no longer wanted her identity concealed. Rosenbaum and Marmalefsky saw an opportunity here and helped her draft a formal statement in a notarized declaration dated January 9, 1990: "I, Julie Maynard, hereby authorize the FBI to release to Jon Wiener and his lawyers all references to me included in any files or 'see Reference' files pertaining to John Lennon, as well as any information provided by me in those files. This includes all references to the check John Lennon wrote in 1972 for $40,000 in connection with a proposed rock concert to be held in Miami that summer."

They submitted Maynard's affidavit to the court and declared that "she is cooperating with Professor Wiener in this litigation." Since she had provided the FBI with written consent for its disclosure of the information she provided about Lennon, the ACLU team argued, "there exists no legitimate basis for the FBI to withhold this information."

Julie Maynard, Rosenbaum later noted, "undermined the last line of their defense—if the informants who they were asserting had to be protected were coming forward and expressing a willingness to testify on our side—and to provide evidence as to the insubstantiality of the government's case, that meant their legal arguments fell apart. Practically speaking they had to be very fearful of the possibility of a trial in which this key player from their side would undercut their arguments."[25]

Dan Marmalefsky recalled not being as enthusiastic: the Julie Maynard declaration was "helpful" but "not a triumph. It didn't mean winning or losing, unless she was the source for everything, which she wasn't."[26]

The FBI responded that the request for Maynard's reports was "irrelevant, beyond the scope of discovery, and not reasonably calculated to lead to the discovery of admissible evidence." Moreover, the FBI declared it would "neither confirm, deny nor explain the role of this individual or any third party in the Lennon investigation." Frustrated on the Julie Maynard front, the ACLU team hoped to find a future opportunity to seek release of her confidential informant reports.

MEDIA WATCH: 1991   The media gave the Ninth Circuit decision extensive coverage, accomplishing the ACLU's goal of publicizing the value of the FOIA and its subversion by the FBI. Often, however, what should have been a legal story was presented as show biz news. *CBS This Morning* did a segment featuring the plaintiff in the story: "Coming up, the John Lennon FBI files, but first . . ." First came Emmy-Award winning host Harry Smith, in studio with an older couple; he told them, "I know this isn't easy for you, and we are very grateful to you for coming here today to talk about the CBS *Movie of the Week*, premiering tonight, featuring the murder of your son. I understand you had something to do with making this movie?"

The father replied, "Yes, we had creative participation in the script."

On KFI talk radio in Los Angeles, an interview with the plaintiff in the Lennon FBI files story followed a segment called "Dial a Date" where women came down to the studio and described themselves on the air. Announcer Tom Leikes then said, "Who out there wants a date with Kitty? Guys, call 543-1KFI. Daryl in Costa Mesa, you're on KFI, say hi to Kitty."

"Hi Kitty, I'm thirty-four, I'm a native Californian, and I work in a motorcycle shop."

"Well, what do you do there? Are you the manager?"

"No, I'm a mechanic."

Kitty said, "Dump him, Tom."

Tom: "Daryl, you're a loser!" A loud buzzer sounded, and a tape loop of a heavy voice came on: "Loser! Loser!"

Tom: "Next we have Bill from Santa Monica, a first-time caller. Bill, say hi to Kitty."

Bill: "Hi Kitty, I'm thirty-four, I'm in great shape, I'm a sincere guy looking for a fun time."

"What do you do?"

"I'm an FBI agent."

(squeals of laughter from Kitty)

Tom: "Bill, you're quite a kidder."

"No, I really am an FBI agent."

Kitty: "Oh. Well, what do you like to do for fun?"

"I like a lot of things—like going to museums."

"Tom, dump him."

"Bill, you're a loser!" Loud buzzer, etc. "And don't forget, in just ten minutes, the *Joe Crummey Show,* this afternoon talking about John Lennon and the FBI—be sure to stay tuned. Now, a word from Maybelline."

YEAR NINE: TO THE SUPREME COURT   The FBI appealed the Ninth Circuit decision to the Supreme Court.[27] The appeal was submitted in April 1992 by Bush administration solicitor general—and future Clinton impeachment independent counsel—Kenneth W. Starr, a longtime Republican who had been appointed to a federal appeals judgeship by Ronald Reagan.

The government brief objected strenuously to the requirement that the FBI explain the reasons for withholding each document, instead of providing generic explanations. That ruling "imposes a staggering burden on the government," the petition declared. To prepare specific descriptions of the documents at issue "threatens an immediate and devastating drain" on the FBI's limited resources. It would "require virtually unlimited manpower and ingenuity." In the Ninth Circuit alone, they pointed out, fifty FOIA suits were pending, some of which involved "tens of thousands of pages of disputed documents." Other courts of appeal, they pointed out, had not imposed such a requirement. On the question of confidentiality, the FBI petition to the Supreme Court again argued that other courts of appeal had come to the opposite conclusion.

The Kenneth Starr petition expressed particular anger over the sample descriptions of two documents the Ninth Circuit had provided as examples of what an adequate Vaughn index ought to contain. The appeals panel had described what we subsequently learned was "the parrot story" as one containing information about activists and "the peculiar behavior of their pets." The FBI's petition protested that "the court did not consider whether its own descriptions . . . actually disclosed information exempt from disclosure." It declared that the Ninth Circuit had, in the solicitor general's opinion, in fact revealed protected information. Because of the "enormous burden" of preparing detailed descriptions and the "significant risk" of unintentionally revealing exempt information, Kenneth Starr's brief asked the Supreme Court to hear the FBI's appeal.

Rosenbaum and Marmalefsky's opposition brief began by describing for the Supreme Court the most egregious examples of "a pattern of abuse of executive agency power to suppress political dissent." It started with the confidential informant report that recorded the lyrics to "John Sinclair," which had been classified as "confidential" for ten years (see p. 115). The ACLU team went on to describe a newspaper clipping in the FBI file in which the writer reviewed the John Sinclair concert and reported that the song "John Sinclair" was "lacking Lennon's usual standards"; a newsletter report that Lennon was publicly supporting McGovern; several memos discussing Lennon's appointment to a teaching position at New York University; and another in which the FBI expressed concern about "adverse publicity" (see pp. 121, 231, 277, 293). The ACLU team also highlighted for the Supreme Court the CIA "CHAOS" memo on Lennon, regarding the program of domestic political surveillance that violated the agency's charter (see p. 153).

Rosenbaum and Marmalefsky's brief reiterated that Congress, in drafting the FOIA, had placed the burden on the FBI to establish that a given document was exempt from disclosure. They repeated the argument that *in camera* review was not an adequate substitute for the adversary process. The ACLU team argued that, because the appeals court had refused to rule on the merits of the case or order a release of documents, limiting itself to requiring a more detailed explanation of the grounds for withholding documents, it would be premature for the Supreme Court to review the decision.

The procedures of the Supreme Court gave the FBI the final word, and in a second brief replying to the ACLU team's arguments, the bureau reiterated the crushing burden compliance would create. Kenneth Starr cited an FOIA case against the IRS that involved 53,000 pages, in which the IRS "devoted 2200 hours of attorney time and 500 staff-support hours to produce a 5436-page Vaughn index."

On June 22, 1992, the Supreme Court denied the FBI's petition for a review of the case. The Court made no comment. Of the nine justices, all of the Reagan and Bush appointees voted in support of the ACLU position, including William Rehnquist, Antonin Scalia, and Clarence Thomas. Only one justice voted to hear the case: lone Kennedy holdover Byron "Whizzer" White. For the FBI and Solicitor General Kenneth Starr to find no support among the conservative law-and-order Republican appointees must have been humiliating.[28]

"Normally the Supreme Court would have granted cert [certiorari, or review of the lower court ruling] in a case like this," Mark Rosenbaum later explained to me. "I thought there was a better than 50 percent chance that the Court would grant the petition. In the past when the government went to the court arguing that a lower court had gone too far, they usually granted a hearing. The Justice Department made it clear to the Court that they regarded this as a very serious matter." Why then did he think the Supreme Court turned it down? Because the Ninth Circuit had not ordered any release of documents—just the preparation of a new and detailed and specific Vaughn index, to strengthen the adversary process. "Maybe the fact that the Ninth Circuit decision had focused on process made them less interested in taking the case," he said.[29]

The FBI then prepared a new Vaughn index, in compliance with the Ninth Circuit ruling. Despite their protests to the Supreme Court that preparing a new index would impose a "staggering burden on the government," requiring "virtually unlimited manpower and ingenuity," the FBI was able to produce a new index by September 11, 1992, less than three months after the Supreme Court ruling. Devoting one page to each document, it made for a stack two inches high; it was accompanied by three declarations, two from FBI officials and one from the CIA. The description followed the examples provided in the Ninth Circuit decision to which the FBI had objected so strenuously.

Along with its new Vaughn index, the FBI in September 1992 released some previously withheld, and mostly mind-numbing, information. One sentence that had been withheld for eleven years as national security/foreign government information was in a cablegram from J. Edgar Hoover to the head of the FBI in London: "Request permission from sources to disseminate information obtained to U.S. State Department and US INS" (see p. 163). This was one of the passages the FBI had previously claimed that, if released, would lead to foreign military retaliation. Presumably the information in question had something to do with Lennon's arrest for cannabis possession in London in 1968.

Some CIA national security information that had been withheld for eleven years was also released: for example, a sentence from HQ-5, an "airtel" from FBI headquarters to field offices: "essential captioned organization be further identified expeditiously and logical investigation initiated" (see p. 167).

Despite these revelations, the continuing refusal of the FBI to release documents was striking. The government declassified secrets about H-bomb design in September 1992 but still kept dozens of pages in the Lennon files confidential.[30]

A third FBI attorney now replaced Stephen Petersen, who left the U.S. Attorney's Office to become a Los Angeles Superior Court judge in Van Nuys. Sanjay Bhambhani was thirty years old in 1992, when he took over the case. He had been an undergraduate at Washington University in St. Louis and got his law degree from Rutgers University; Dan Marmalefsky said he was "the easiest to work with" of all the attorneys who represented the FBI.[31] For Bhambhani, it was just another case, even if it was the one that brought phone calls from international media. I thought he was particularly intense and argumentative: when we met in a courthouse elevator before one hearing, he said angrily, "Why don't you just drop the case?"

3

Deposing the FBI and CIA

Rosenbaum and Marmalefsky launched an aggressive new strategy in September 1992. If it could be shown that the FBI's files on Lennon were not "compiled for law enforcement purposes" but rather for the purpose of suppressing dissent, if it could be shown that the FBI's stated purpose in investigating Lennon was "pretextual," the government would have to release all the information withheld under exemption (b)(7) of the FOIA, the law enforcement investigation exemption. To gather evidence that the FBI's claim was a pretext for political surveillance and harassment, the ACLU team filed a motion for "discovery," seeking information from the FBI about the purposes of its investigation of Lennon. They asked the court to permit them to question "third parties familiar with the Lennon investigation" and the FBI officials who prepared the government affidavits justifying withholding documents.

Rosenbaum and Marmalefsky argued that the documents the FBI had already released showed the FBI's real purpose was not to investigate crime but rather "to neutralize dissent" and "to impair the effectiveness of opponents to the re-election of President Nixon." As evidence their brief cited the effort to deport Lennon prior to the Republican National Convention, the FBI noting his support for George McGovern, and, in general, the bureau's recording "in excruciating detail . . . matters regarding his lawful political views, professional career and private life."

They emphasized the significance of three agents supervising the Lennon investigation: E. S. Miller, R. L. Shackelford, and R. L. Spence, whose names or initials appear on dozens of documents. E. S. Miller served as head of the Domestic Intelligence Division beginning in 1971. He was regarded as a key, trusted loyalist to Director J. Edgar Hoover. Miller was convicted in 1980, along with Mark Felt, of conspiring to violate individuals' civil rights by authorizing break-ins and searches of the homes of five people suspected of having ties to fugitives who belonged to the Weather Underground. The prosecutor said that he had "tons of examples of [illegal] entries that continued from 1966 to 1972." Miller and Felt were at that point the only FBI agents ever to have been convicted of crimes committed while on duty. Shackelford was an unindicted co-conspirator in the same case.[1]

Miller and Felt received "full and unconditional" pardons from President Reagan before they were sentenced. The following day former President Richard Nixon sent champagne to the two men. "I think he's a fabulous guy," Miller told the press afterwards.[2] Rosenbaum and Marmalefsky pointed to the involvement of Miller and Shackelford as evidence that the FBI may have committed unlawful acts in the Lennon investigation.

The Thurmond memo and the CIA "CHAOS" memo also were cited as evidence that the FBI investigation of Lennon lacked a legitimate law enforcement purpose but instead was "pretextual." The court, they argued, should let the ACLU proceed to gather evidence to "confirm the pretextual nature of the FBI claim of law enforcement purpose, as well as to demonstrate that other, unauthorized purposes drove the investigation."

The FBI strenuously opposed the ACLU team's discovery motion and argued that no discovery was appropriate in any FOIA litigation. They also argued that their investigation of Lennon was a legitimate one, motivated by a concern that the 1972 Republican National Convention would be disrupted by a group led by the same people who had been convicted of disrupting the 1968 Democratic National Convention. And the FBI attacked the evidence of "pretext" presented by Rosenbaum and Marmalefsky. "Wiener's claim of pretext," the FBI brief declared, "is nothing more than a strident and impermissible effort to second-guess the wisdom of the FBI's investigation." The court again was urged to reject the "Declaration of Jonathan M. Wiener," which had linked the Thurmond memo to other historical evidence to try to show a pattern of FBI misconduct; the FBI described that declaration as "a potpourri of conjecture, supposition, innuendo and surmise."[3] Rosenbaum and Marmalefsky pointed out that none of the released documents in the Lennon file mentioned the laws the FBI claimed it suspected Lennon of violating — the Civil Obedience Act of 1968 and the Anti-Riot Act.[4] Indeed those statutes were not mentioned in the first four and a half years of the litigation. The FBI replied that the absence of references in the released file pages "in no way proves that the FBI fabricated its concerns about disruptive demonstrations at the RNC."

The ACLU team argued that participating in protests or contributing money to support antiwar organizing was constitutionally protected activity. The FBI replied that "Wiener merely draws a different conclusion from the FBI" about Lennon's plans.

After Rosenbaum and Marmalefsky demonstrated that numerous courts had permitted discovery in FOIA cases, Judge Takasugi in October 1992 denied the FBI's motion to block discovery. Two months later Rosenbaum went to Washington to take depositions from FBI and CIA officials.

Rosenbaum's depositions of three top FBI and CIA officials provide a rare glimpse into the inner workings of the FOIA, the world where top secret classification authorities make the decisions about which passages get blacked out in documents requested under the Act. The three officials in question had prepared the government's affidavits justifying the withholding of documents, and Rosenbaum's objective was to get each to admit under oath that they had no idea, and had never made any effort to find out, whether the original investigation had a legitimate law enforcement purpose. If the FBI could not show that it had such a purpose, then the material withheld under the confidential informant exemption would have to be released.

THE STRICKER DEPOSITION: VOICE OF THE CIA   Katherine M. Stricker, information review officer for the Directorate of Operations of the CIA, answered questions at the ACLU Washington office in December 1992, under oath. At the time of the deposition, Stricker had worked for the CIA for thirty years. She said she had prepared "dozens" of Vaughn indices describing classified documents sought in FOIA litigation. Ms. Stricker was accompanied at her deposition by three government attorneys: Sanjay Bhambhani of the Justice Department's Civil Division, Federal Programs Branch, who had been representing the FBI in the case; Elizabeth Pugh, assistant branch director of the Justice Department's Civil Division; and Fred Crawford, attorney in the Office of General Counsel of the CIA.

Asked whether any portion of document HQ-5 (see p. 167) that had been withheld under the confidential source exemption could be released, Stricker told Rosenbaum, "There is no phrase or sentence within that paragraph that could be released without reflecting upon the identity of the source." Rosenbaum asked if she knew how many other people knew the information in the withheld paragraph. She said she didn't know. What if ten million other people knew the withheld information—would she still withhold it on the grounds that releasing it would cause damage to the national security? "That is correct," she answered.

Asked about Operation CHAOS, she conceded that "the entire operation was considered to be outside the CIA charter." She said its purpose was "to collect information on dissent groups in the United States to determine if there were any foreign connections with these organizations." When Rosenbaum asked whether she knew anything about the relationship of Operation CHAOS to John Lennon, she said, "No. I do not."

Rosenbaum asked, "Do you have any information . . . that Mr. Lennon had any connections with a foreign government or a foreign nation with respect to his political activities?"

"I have no information," she answered.

Rosenbaum asked whether her reference to "certain activities of John Lennon" referred to political activities. Bhambhani objected to the question and advised her not to answer on the grounds that the answer "would disclose the very information that is classified and withheld." Rosenbaum then asked about a "CIA intelligence source" she had referred to in her declaration, and Stricker replied, "It is a human being." Rosenbaum asked whether "that human being is still alive," because dead people cannot be damaged by the release of information. Stricker answered, "When I checked about a year ago that human being was alive."

She said she trained CIA personnel in the proper application of the (b)(1) national security exemption, but when Rosenbaum asked, "Have you read any judicial decisions regarding the (b)(1) exemption?" she could not name any that she had read and could not recall anything in any such decisions. That was a devastating admission.

"Do you know anything about the investigation per se of John Lennon?"

"No," she answered.

"Did you make any effort to inquire regarding that investigation?"

"No," she answered.

"Did you make any effort to determine whether agents engaged in the reporting of information violated any laws?"

"No," she answered.

THE DAVIDSON DEPOSITION: NATIONAL SECURITY, AGAIN   Richard D. Davidson was a supervisor in the Document Classification Unit at FBI headquarters, responsible for preparing the government's affidavit justifying withholding of (b)(1) national security material. He came to the deposition at the ACLU's Washington office accompanied by four attorneys, one of whom, Sanjay Bhambhani, opened the session by declaring, "It is our position that the Vaughn declaration is sufficient for the purposes of summary judgment. Therefore, this proceeding is wholly unnecessary." Rosenbaum replied, "As you know, you have made many of these same objections to the judge. They were rejected."

Then Davidson was sworn. He explained that he had been an FBI agent for "twenty-one-plus years," but that he had worked as a supervisor in document classification for slightly more than a year. His responsibilities included "teaching the people in the unit how to classify." The FBI had no written criteria explaining how to apply the (b)(1) exemption, he said; in his class he did not discuss court decisions regarding the exemption. That seemed negligent. He had not looked at all the Lennon file documents, just those classified (b)(1). Asked whether he had concerned himself with "the nature of the criminal investigation" of Lennon, he answered, "No, I did not."

"Can you define 'damage to the national security of the United States'?" Rosenbaum asked, referring to a phrase in Davidson's declaration. Davidson went to look up the definition in his affidavit, but Rosenbaum stopped him and asked if he could define the term without looking it up.

He replied, "The damage to the national security in this case would be a chilling effect." He seemed to be referring to a chilling effect on exchanges with foreign government intelligence agencies.

Rosenbaum asked him to define "serious damage," another term in his affidavit.

"'Serious damage' is damage above and beyond confidential," Davidson replied.

"And what is 'confidential'?"

"That would be just damage." These were not "definitions" in the usual sense of the term. Rosenbaum asked how Davidson defined "national security."

"Anything involving the information that is gathered by the United States in regards to the government doing business that the knowledge of which would be detrimental to the workings of the government if it were given out." If he really meant it, that was a frightening answer.

Davidson said he did not know what the relationship between the FBI and the INS was with respect to Lennon.

He said he was not aware of any improprieties committed by Shackelford, Miller, or Felt. He did concede that if FBI agents had acted outside the scope of the law, that "would be a reason to declassify" the documents they produced.

He said he did not know what H. R. Haldeman had to do with the Lennon investigation, even though the Haldeman letter was one where he had asserted a "national security" exemption.

Davidson did report one major new fact about the Haldeman letter. Three lines had been withheld, described as "intelligence information provided by a foreign government." "The foreign government was recently contacted about releasing this information," Davidson wrote in his declaration. "The foreign government continues to insist that the information remain confidential and not released to the public." We were not allowed to know even the name of the foreign government.

Rosenbaum then turned to the "foreign government information" that was being withheld. Davidson said only one foreign government had provided information that was being withheld. "Which one is that?" Rosenbaum asked innocently.

"I can't give you that," Davidson replied. Rosenbaum asked exactly how Davidson determined that the foreign government wished the information to remain confidential. He explained that on August 13, 1992, he telephoned the foreign government for "one to three minutes," asking them to "come in and review the documents." One representative of the foreign government "came in and talked with me, reviewed the documents." Then he took the documents back to his government. "In writing it came back" that they wanted "these matters to remain classified."

Rosenbaum asked what Davidson meant in his affidavit when he used the term "express" guarantee of confidentiality.

"I mean by 'express' it is inferred that they want their information protected." Another terrible answer: of course "inferred" is the opposite of "expressed."

Rosenbaum asked if Davidson knew whether the information in the Lennon file "was compiled pursuant to a criminal investigation."

"No," Davidson said, "I don't know."

Rosenbaum pointed to Davidson's written statements that information still being withheld was provided to the FBI with the explicit understanding that it would be kept confidential. He asked whether there was a written statement to that effect. Davidson said no. Rosenbaum asked whether there was an oral statement. "I can't answer that. I wasn't involved in that at that time."

"And you haven't done any research to find out?"

"No, sir."

Rosenbaum asked about the meaning of the caption on one page of the Lennon file, headed "Security Matter-New Left." "New Left was a title of a group," Davidson replied.

"That was the name of a group?" Rosenbaum said, barely able to disguise his astonishment.

"It covered a wide range of individuals that were involved in the purported or violent overthrow of the government," Davidson explained.

"Do you know that for sure?" Rosenbaum asked, even more amazed.

"That is my opinion of it."

THE BOLTHOUSE DEPOSITION: FBI CONFIDENTIAL SOURCES FBI Special Agent Karlton Bolthouse had prepared the FBI declaration justifying withholding of material from the Lennon files under FOIA exemptions (b)(3), intelligence sources and methods, and (b)(7), personal privacy and law enforcement confidential source information. The transcript of the Bolthouse deposition is 238 pages long, a hefty volume. The questions started at 8:40 in the morning and ended just before 5:00 P.M. Bolthouse came with four attorneys—Sanjay M. Bhambhani, Elizabeth Pugh, James M. Kovakas of the Justice Department's Freedom of Information unit, and James G. Fidler, the FBI legal counsel.

Bolthouse said he had been with the FBI for eight years, that he had been a supervisor in the Freedom of Information office for a year. Prior to that, for three years, his "sole responsibility was investigations concerning foreign counterintelligence and national security." Asked whether he had read the Ninth Circuit decision in *Wiener v. FBI*, he answered that he had read it "several times." He said that drafting his forty-three-page declaration on the Lennon file took him two months, during which he worked on it 50 percent of his time.

Asked whether he knew if FBI agents Shackelford or Miller had "any involvement in the Lennon matter," he answered that he did not know, even though their names were on dozens of documents Bolthouse had supposedly reviewed. Asked whether he knew if Shackelford, Miller, or Felt had ever been found to have violated any FBI guidelines, rules, or laws, he answered that he didn't know. Asked whether he had looked at the files to detect whether agents may have violated laws or regulations, he answered no.

Asked whether he knew if Strom Thurmond had any interest in John Lennon during the period covered by the files, he said he didn't know. Asked whether he knew what "MHCHAOS" meant, he said he didn't. Asked whether he knew if members of the Election Year Strategy Information Center, the group Lennon had been supporting, participated in demonstrations at the Republican National Convention in 1972, he said he didn't know and had made no inquiry to find out. Asked if he knew whether John Lennon participated in demonstrations at the Republican National Convention, Bolthouse answered that he didn't know—even though the files he had reviewed clearly reported that Lennon did not.

"Do the documents have anything in them," Rosenbaum asked, "where John Lennon is purportedly advocating criminal conduct?"

FBI attorney Bhambhani interrupted: "I am going to instruct him not to answer."

Bolthouse answered anyway: "His financial support." He seemed to be referring to Lennon's financial support for the organization planning demonstrations at the Republican National Convention, not exactly the same as "advocating criminal conduct."

"Do you know, sir, whether or not there were files related to John Lennon that were in the Miami headquarters of the FBI?" Rosenbaum was referring to the file the FBI had said was destroyed "as part of a routine file destruction procedure."

Bolthouse answered, "I believe so. Yes."

"Do you know what happened to those files?" Rosenbaum asked.

"I think to my recollection they were independently processed by the Miami office and released," Bolthouse replied. That was news to us.

Rosenbaum pointed out that Bolthouse in his declaration used the phrase "the public's right to know." Rosenbaum asked, "Can you define that phrase as you use it there?"

"Not accurately," Bolthouse replied. "No."

Rosenbaum moved on to ask about withholding names of third parties in the files. They have a privacy right not to have their names released, but Bolthouse agreed that "privacy interests would normally be extinguished by death." Rosenbaum asked whether he made any effort to determine if the third parties whose names were withheld were alive or dead. Bolthouse answered no.

"So, some of them you don't really have a clue as to whether or not they are alive or dead; is that right?"

"None are known to be dead to me," Bolthouse replied.

Rosenbaum then turned to the issue of confidentiality. An explicit guarantee of confidentiality protected the identity of a source absolutely and could not be overruled. But an "implied" guarantee of confidentiality did not have that degree of protection. Rosenbaum asked Bolthouse whether he could remember "any" express promise of confidentiality documented in the Lennon files.

"No," Bolthouse replied.

Rosenbaum asked whether, before going to work on the Lennon file, Bolthouse had had any knowledge of the groups mentioned there. Regarding "Election Year Strategy Information Center," Bolthouse said, "I remember the group . . . from 1970, '71, '72, '73, that general period of time." If this was true, it was remarkable—the FBI first noted its existence in 1972, and no press indices from 1972 or earlier list it. Bolthouse would have been twenty-one years old in 1972.

"So, were you a member of the Election Year Strategy Information Committee?" Rosenbaum asked.

"No, sir."

"Were you on the other side of the Election Year Strategy Information Committee?"

"No, sir."

Rosenbaum in 1998 recalled his feeling at the end of the day of depositions: "I was stunned at how shallow their review of the docs had been. I thought their case had been destroyed. They didn't have any plausible justifications. They didn't even know what these documents were about—the names, places, and events. They were relying on the claim that they were the government and didn't intend to disclose. It was like everything we had been saying turned out to be true in spades."[5]

Marmalefsky got a call from Rosenbaum after depositions were finished. "He told me the stories of what they had said," Marmalefsky recalled. "They were incredible. We would now be able to demonstrate to the judge that all the evidence they were submitting was from people who knew nothing about the documents. I thought the depositions were great. But I wasn't sure how much we would profit from them."[6]

SUBPOENAS FOR SHACKELFORD AND MILLER   After deposing the three current FBI and CIA officials and determining that they had no knowledge about the original FBI investigation of Lennon, Rosenbaum and Marmalefsky took the next step: in January 1993 they served subpoenas to take depositions from the two key FBI agents who had directed the investigation of Lennon: Robert L. Shackelford and Edward S. Miller, both retired. Seeking to interview under oath retired FBI agents about work they had done twenty years earlier was a bold tactic. It had a clear rationale: since the issue whether the FBI had a legitimate law enforcement purpose in investigating Lennon couldn't be determined through questioning current FBI officials, it would be necessary to interview the agents who actually conducted the investigation.

The FBI was outraged and used all its resources to prevent the depositions, which from the bureau's point of view would create an ominous precedent. Shackelford, the FBI stated, retired from the FBI in 1978 and had worked from 1968 to 1973 as section chief of the Domestic Intelligence Division at FBI headquarters. In response to the subpoena, he filed a declaration stating that he possessed no documentary information about the Lennon investigation and lacked "any recollection of what the investigation was about, why the investigation was initiated or the manner in which it was conducted." Miller had retired from the FBI in 1974 and had worked from November 1971 to October 1973 as assistant director in charge of the Domestic Intelligence Division. He too filed a declaration in response to the subpoena saying the same thing as Shackelford.

Because Judge Takasugi had permitted discovery, authorizing the depositions of FBI and CIA officials, the FBI now fought the subpoenas in a different court, the federal district court in the District of Columbia. There they filed a flurry of objections: deposing former FBI agents was beyond the scope of discovery permitted in FOIA litigation; it was irrelevant to exemption (b)(7); it wasn't permitted because the information was protected; if it was permitted, it would frustrate the underlying purpose of the FOIA.

The FBI's argument indicated they understood clearly where Rosenbaum and Marmalefsky were headed. "Contrary to plaintiff's assertions," the FBI brief stated, "the case is not about 'the FBI's surveillance of John Lennon.' Nor is it about whether, in hindsight, the FBI's investigation of John Lennon should or should not have been undertaken." The ACLU, according to the FBI, was basing its arguments on "rank speculation, rumor and innuendo," in an attempting to "transform this run-of-the-mill FOIA action into a full-blown inquisition of the FBI's conduct." As for the information submitted by the ACLU team regarding Miller's conviction for illegal acts in an FBI investigation, the FBI told the court that those reports were "based on . . . 'media accounts' . . . of a questionable nature." This was an incredible statement: Miller's conviction had been headline news everywhere—to be sure, in "media accounts." The FBI brief did make one reasonable point: "plaintiff relies on nothing more than inference and innuendo" to suggest a link between the crimes for which Miller had been convicted and "the Lennon investigation."

Without acknowledging that the section chief of the FBI Domestic Intelligence Division had been convicted of illegal acts in conducting an investigation, the FBI argued that, even if he had authorized illegal methods in the surveillance of Lennon, "the methods used in an investigation are irrelevant to the 'law enforcement purpose' requirement" of FOIA exemption (b)(7). The purpose was legitimate even if the methods were not; that was a bold claim.

In opposition to the FBI's arguments that Shackelford and Miller should not be required to answer questions under oath, Marmalefsky submitted his own declaration pointing out that there was no better source on the conduct of the FBI investigation of Lennon than the agents who supervised it. How better could the plaintiff's attorneys show that the FBI records had not been "compiled for law enforcement purposes"? Marmalefsky based his argument on the depositions Rosenbaum had taken from the FBI officials. Each had acknowledged that he had no contact whatsoever with anyone who participated in the original investigation. Marmalefsky noted parenthetically that the FBI did not object to depositions of FBI agents who had no knowledge of the details of the case; their only objection was to the ACLU's deposing those FBI agents who actually could respond to questions. Of the 34 documents in the headquarters file on Lennon, he pointed out, "Shackelford's name is reflected on the first 22 and most of the remainder." Notable among them was a memo from Shackelford to Miller requesting approval for a proposed memo to the White House concerning surveillance of Lennon.

The purpose of deposing Shackelford and Miller, Marmalefsky declared, was to demonstrate that "Lennon was the victim of FBI abuses" and thus to argue that Lennon FBI file pages should not be withheld "to conceal violations of law . . . or prevent embarrassment to a person, organization, or agency," as the Ninth Circuit had declared in its decision, quoting the FOIA. In the depositions, the ACLU team intended to show that Lennon was subject to surveillance "as part of an effort to monitor political opponents of the Nixon administration, rather than because he was the subject of a legitimate law enforcement investigation."

In response to the declarations of Shackelford and Miller that they had no "present" knowledge of the Lennon investigation, Marmalefsky commented that "it should not be difficult to refresh their memories." If a witness could avoid a subpoena by citing lack of memory, Marmalefsky pointed out, the federal courts would grind to a halt. And if the two continued under oath to insist they had no recollection of the events in question, "it will mean that the depositions will be short."

Nevertheless, in February 1993, Judge John H. Pratt of the D.C. Circuit granted the FBI's motion to quash the two subpoenas. Taking statements under oath from retired FBI agents, Pratt declared, "concerning the purpose and conduct of the investigation of John Lennon over 20 years ago, is beyond the scope of allowable discovery in a Freedom of Information action." The FBI was delighted and declared that Judge Pratt had "repudiated implicitly, if not explicitly, Wiener's so-called 'evidence' as well as his legal arguments."

YEAR TEN: DISCOVERY OF "UNLAWFUL ACTIVITIES"   Blocked from questioning the FBI agents who supervised the original Lennon investigation, Rosenbaum and Marmalefsky went back to Judge Takasugi in April and asked for a more limited kind of discovery: an order that the FBI be required to answer a series of "narrowly crafted" questions about the law enforcement purpose of the Lennon investigation. In October 1993, despite strenuous FBI objections, Judge Takasugi ordered discovery reopened. Rosenbaum and Marmalefsky submitted their list of "interrogatories" directed toward proving the following in a trial: that "unlawful activities" were utilized in the investigation of John Lennon and related investigations; that Shackelford, Miller, and others involved in the Lennon investigation participated in or authorized unlawful activities in related cases; that people opposed to the reelection of Nixon were subjected to FBI investigations because of their political views; that the FBI investigated opponents of Nixon at the request of members of the White House staff and members of Congress; that Lennon was a target of Operation CHAOS; that no current FBI employee had personal knowledge of the 1972 investigation, and no current employee had attempted to learn why Lennon was the subject of an investigation in 1972. The ACLU team argued that they were entitled to discover all this as evidence of the FBI's "impermissible motive" and "unlawful activities."

The FBI responded with predictable outrage, declaring the interrogatories "nothing short of a full-scale fishing expedition." The plaintiff was "using the discovery process" to obtain information that we were not entitled to receive under the FOIA. Again the FBI declared that it was "pure speculation and conjecture on Wiener's part" to argue that Lennon was the target of illegitimate harassment and intimidation. And again the FBI declared that responding to the ACLU team's interrogatories "would place an impossible burden upon federal agencies."

To document the impossibility of bearing the burden of responding to further discovery, the FBI submitted the "Declaration of Robert A. Moran," a supervisor in the FBI's FOIA Section. Between 1986 and 1993 the FBI had received an annual average of 15,165 FOIA requests, and the backlog was growing: in 1985 the backlog was 4,736 requests; by 1994 it had grown to 11,828. The bureau was also dealing with 206 FOIA lawsuits. In 1993 the FBI devoted 33,006 hours to FOIA litigation. One case—*Rosenfeld v. Dept. of Justice*, dealing with FBI surveillance of the Berkeley Free Speech Movement—required the work of thirteen full-time experienced paralegal specialists for an entire year.

Robert A. Moran blamed part of the backlog problem on the Ninth Circuit decision in *Wiener v. FBI*, which required the FBI to "abandon its coded format of Vaughn declarations, which had been widely accepted by courts throughout the United States." Compliance with the Ninth Circuit decision "has placed an additional burden" on the FBI. Along with the problems created by the decision in *Wiener v. FBI*, the bureau's FOIA Section was required by the Kennedy Assassination Records Collection Act, passed by Congress in 1992, to review one million pages of FBI material on the assassination for release to the public.

Moran objected in particular to the proposed interrogatory seeking the names of FBI personnel who had participated in the investigation of Lennon. "The retirement, transfer and death of many of these Special Agents would further compound the difficulty of this search," Moran wrote. He concluded that responding to the ACLU team's interrogatories would "greatly burden the FBI's resources and further delay the processing of other FOIA requests."

But the central argument of the FBI was that the law did not require the FBI to answer the kinds of questions the ACLU was asking. The bureau's lawyers were able to cite a frightening variety and number of court rulings giving the FBI extensive and unchecked power. The Ninth Circuit, they pointed out, had held that the FBI was entitled to "special deference" from the courts in determining whether the "law enforcement purpose" exemption to the FOIA had been properly applied. They cited a Second Circuit decision in 1984 that warned about "the vagaries of judicial hindsight as to the merits or wisdom of an investigation. Such judgments involve rank speculation." Indeed, the Ninth Circuit had ruled that information need not be released under the FOIA "even in FBI investigations of questionable legality."[7]

In a particularly frightening 1994 ruling in the D.C. Circuit, the court considered an FOIA case brought by Donald Williams, who in the late sixties and early seventies had belonged to a group called the Afro Set, which had been targeted by the FBI as part of its illegal COINTELPRO campaign. Williams argued the FBI's investigation of him was illegal and he sought discovery to buttress his claims. The D.C. Circuit acknowledged that COINTELPRO had been condemned, but it nevertheless argued against "corrective hindsight" that "distorts the real issue." It declared that "in view of the mind set of the late 1960s and early 1970s, the FBI's concern about such groups was rational. Events such as the tumultuous riots in 1968, the assassinations of both Martin Luther King and Senator Robert F. Kennedy . . . set the country, and certainly the FBI, on edge." In that historical context, "the FBI's broad mandate to protect the internal security of the country" meant that surveillance of the Afro Set was "justified." That court concluded that the FBI's rationale for an investigation was "not the proper subject of FOIA discovery requests."[8]

But Rosenbaum and Marmalefsky had a response: in that case, they pointed out, Donald Williams did not dispute the FBI's suspicion that the Afro Set's involvement in criminal activity "had some basis in fact." In the Lennon case, there was never any admission that Lennon was involved in criminal activity.

In summarizing its objections to the proposed ACLU questions, the FBI argued once again that there was a "rational nexus" connecting their investigation of Lennon with criminal law, namely, "Lennon's reported involvement with a group planning to disrupt a national political convention." Had Lennon participated in such demonstrations, he could have been prosecuted under the anti-riot provisions of the Civil Obedience Act of 1968; when the FBI learned that he had not participated, they closed their investigation.

But the FBI response didn't stop there. Even if the FBI's investigation of Lennon had "other purposes" than legitimate law enforcement, according to the government brief, in order to show pretext FOIA plaintiffs had to demonstrate that the investigation "lacked *any* law enforcement purpose."[9] Thus even if Rosenbaum and Marmalefsky could show in court that during this era the FBI had a pattern of investigating people because of their political views, that would not establish the "pretext" required to justify the release of documents withheld under the law enforcement exemption. This argument represented a significant step away from the FBI's previous position, that the bureau did not engage in illegitimate or unlawful activities.

The ACLU team responded by citing some key cases in which courts had allowed the kind of discovery they were seeking. Without such a procedure, Rosenbaum and Marmalefsky argued, the only way to establish FBI misconduct in FOIA cases would be if "the FBI were to announce its improprieties on paper." And since FBI abuse of power during the Hoover years had been widely documented by scholars and journalists, "we are hardly operating on a blank slate." Most important to the ACLU team was the *Pratt* case, the 1982 decision of the D.C. Circuit that established that FBI records are not automatically deemed to have been "compiled for law enforcement purposes."[10] Their legitimacy has to be established by showing the "rationality" of the connection the FBI claims between the investigation and a possible violation of law. The court did say the burden of showing the FBI had an illegitimate pretext rested on the plaintiff, not on the bureau, but it allowed plaintiffs to submit "direct evidence of impermissible motive." That direct evidence, the ACLU team argued, "could only come from the FBI. It is that same direct evidence of impermissible motive that Wiener seeks here."

A recent decision in an FOIA case involving FBI surveillance of the Free Speech Movement provided the ACLU team with the best case supporting their position. In *Rosenfeld v. Dept. of Justice*, a federal court in northern California found in 1991 that the FBI had failed to establish that it had a legitimate law enforcement purpose. The FBI had investigated the infiltration of the Berkeley Free Speech Movement by "subversive organizations." Although the investigation was begun "in good faith and with a plausible basis," the court found, the bureau's continuing investigation lacked the "rationality" required by the courts. The subsequent "routine monitoring, surveillance and information-gathering" did not have "a permissible law enforcement purpose"; the plaintiff had "provided persuasive evidence" that by 1965 "another, nonqualifying purpose came to drive the FBI" investigation, and thus the FBI file could not be withheld under exemption (b)(7).[11]

As for the FBI's claim that as long as it had one legitimate law enforcement purpose, information could be withheld under the FOIA, Rosenbaum and Marmalefsky had a withering reply. "Pretext," they pointed out, was defined as "a purpose alleged in order to cloak the real intention." Since the FBI always stated a legitimate rationale for an investigation, "a pretext, by nature, is always legitimate. The FBI will hardly tender an illegal motive as a cover." Numerous cases established that plaintiffs were entitled to introduce evidence that the FBI had a reason other than the one stated for an investigation.

Moreover, Rosenbaum and Marmalefsky argued, the FBI had to show a legitimate law enforcement purpose for each document they were withholding. "It is difficult to see how FBI collection of criticism of the government's effort to deport Lennon, or of Lennon's support for George McGovern, or plans to perform at a peace concert can be supported by a legitimate law enforcement purpose." And they argued that "a music reviewer's opinion of Yoko Ono's singing can hardly qualify as information properly gathered in a bona fide criminal investigation of possible violation of the Anti-Riot Act."

Further evidence that the FBI lacked a legitimate law enforcement purpose was provided to the court in a declaration by Stewart Albert, an antiwar activist whose name appears in the Lennon file several times, almost from the beginning (see p. 122). Contacted by the ACLU, he agreed to file a declaration in May 1993. In his declaration, Albert explained to the court the events to which the FBI pages referred: along with Jerry Rubin and Rennie Davis, he met with Lennon late in 1971 to discuss "ways of expressing our opposition to the Vietnam War and the presidency of Richard Nixon." Lennon at this meeting "stated very firm guidelines" for any protest events in which he would participate: they would have to be "(1) legal; (2) within the framework of pacifism; and (3) at an ideological level, . . . [supportive of] the rights of dissidents in Communist countries—there were to be no double standards." "At no time in this or any other meeting on this matter," Albert stated, "was there ever any discussion or advocacy of illegal activities."

The FBI dismissed the Albert declaration as "a wholly dubious attempt to second-guess the FBI's decision to investigate with 'evidence' gathered over two-decades after-the-fact." Moreover, "the Stewart declaration," as the FBI brief erroneously called it, "unwittingly confirms the legitimacy of the FBI's concerns." Albert had recalled that Lennon stated he did not want another violent confrontation like the one that occurred at the 1968 convention in Chicago. "While Lennon's intentions may now be perfectly clear to Wiener," the FBI declared, "Mr. Albert's post-hoc assertions . . . do not negate the FBI's then-existing concerns about disruptive demonstrations at RNC."

But Lennon wasn't the only antiwar radical who didn't want a violent confrontation in Miami. Jerry Rubin and Abbie Hoffman publicly sought negotiation and compromise. The Miami political establishment responded positively. "Anxious to avoid a replay of Chicago," it "opened its doors" to Jerry and Abbie and "treated them like visiting dignitaries." The mayor and the chief of police invited Rubin and Hoffman to speak to the police force and city council, and the Yippies were granted permits to camp in Flamingo Park, parade on Collins Avenue, and "perform guerrilla theater almost anywhere." Both sides were trying to avoid a repeat of Chicago '68.[12]

The mysterious CIA cryptonym withheld for the previous twelve years was released in January 1993: it was "CACTUS." It appeared in the sentence "Please transmit reply via CACTUS channel" (see p. 153). It had been withheld by the CIA through ten years of litigation under the national security exemption; the CIA had claimed that releasing it would permit "the intelligence service of a hostile foreign power" to "divine the nature and purpose of the CIA activity with respect to which the cryptonym is employed."

The CIA explained its change of mind in a sworn statement from Lee E. Carle, the information review officer of the Directorate of Operations, and the successor to Louis J. Dube, whose earlier affidavit had justified withholding the cryptonym. "Cactus," Carle declared, "had recently been released in another litigation," so he was releasing it in this litigation as well. He reaffirmed all the other claims regarding withheld CIA information and quoted the Supreme Court's 1985 ruling that the CIA director should receive "great deference" from judges in FOIA cases, "given the magnitude of the national security interest and potential risks at stake" in protecting all intelligence sources. "It is the responsibility of the Director of Central Intelligence, not that of the judiciary, to weigh the variety of complex and subtle factors in determining whether disclosure of information may lead to an unacceptable risk of compromising the Agency's intelligence-gathering process," the Supreme Court had recently declared.[13]

CIA officer Carle added that these words "apply with full force" to the information withheld from the Lennon file. "Mr. Weiner [sic] may assert that the CIA had no right or need to collection information on Mr. Lennon," Carle told the court. "However, his personal views are irrelevant to the issue of whether the CIA can protect its sources." Moreover, "Mr. Lennon was a foreigner who engaged in activities opposing U.S. policy. Clearly, the CIA had the duty and right to monitor such activities, despite Mr. Weiner's belief that this is improper or illegitimate." But "opposing U.S. policy" was not a crime, it was an activity protected by the First Amendment, whose scope extends beyond citizens.

Ten years of litigation has resulted in the release of the word "cactus." But what did "cactus" mean to the CIA? To find out, I called the CIA in October 1987 and asked Peter Earnest, the agency's chief of media relations.

"I don't know what it means," he told me. "I've never heard of it."

How could I find out what it meant?

"The best way to find out is to go to the CIA information coordinator with a written FOIA request asking for any information previously released on 'cactus channel.' In a second request, ask for any information that is releasable. Be as specific as possible. Include a copy of the document you received."

If something like this is declassified, I asked, is there any public notice of it?

"Director Gates mandated as part of his new openness policy that an index of released documents be made available to the public. That has not yet been accomplished. Ultimately that would be the quickest way in the future."

But getting a response to an FOIA request can take years. Is there any faster route?

Here Peter Earnest had a surprising suggestion: "There are some folks around like Scott Armstrong," he said. (Armstrong was founder of the National Security Archive, an independent organization that collects CIA documents and monitors CIA compliance with the FOIA.) "He might know, or have an index if it has been released officially. You might call him. I'm just trying to be helpful here." The CIA spokesman was suggesting I call Scott Armstrong, one of their nemeses, to find out information the spokesman himself did not know about his own agency.

When I called Armstrong and told him what the CIA spokesman had said, he laughed. When I asked if he knew what "CACTUS channel" meant, he said, "I haven't a clue."

I also filed my new FOIA requests with the CIA for "any and all documents previously released concerning the CIA 'cactus channel.'" With astounding speed, the CIA replied less than a month later with copies of three pages on the topic. The pages were part of the same secret memo, stamped "enciphered," from CIA Director Richard Helms to J. Edgar Hoover, dated April 1970. "The cryptonym cactus has been assigned as a teletype indicator covering teletype communications between this agency and your bureau dealing with the new left, black militants and related matters," the CIA director informed Hoover. "Use of this indicator will facilitate prompt and effective action on such communications by this agency." The second page was completely blacked out, and the third repeated the statement on the first.

MEDIA WATCH: 1992   The ACLU made more progress in publicizing the value of the FOIA and its subversion by the FBI when *New York Times* reporter David Margolick, who would later cover the O. J. Simpson trial for the paper, wrote a column in 1991 headed "Assessing John Lennon, with a Little Help from His Foes." "Imagine that in the early 1970's," the story began, "the FBI began tailing John Lennon." He referred to the case that had taken a "magical mystery tour through the courts," a journey he described as "a long and winding road." And he described the "big black blotches" on the released documents as "the work of some anonymous deskbound Rothko in the Federal apparat."[14] Margolick's essay was the most thorough and comprehensive account of the legal issues in the case that had appeared in nine years—and also the best written.

The *Los Angeles Times* published an editorial making precisely the points the ACLU had hoped for. Under the headline "Bureaucracy Watch: Suspect Beatle," the editorial declared, "John Lennon engaged in such subversive activities as urging people to imagine what it would be like to have world peace. The FBI was watching on the sidelines, keeping secret files on his activities." The editorial concluded that the Lennon file litigation "has focused attention on how spurious claims of national security exemptions can be in freedom-of-information cases."[15] That was exactly the point we had hoped to get to the public.

June 1992 marked the twentieth reunion of the class of 1972 at Denmark High in Green Bay, Wisconsin. Back in 1972 they had voted to make their class song "Imagine." But the principal rejected their choice, claiming the song was "anti-religious and anti-American with communist overtones." The students sent a delegation to the principal's office to protest, with no success. "That incident is one we'll always remember," Chris Wood later wrote.

And they did. In 1992 the class made "Imagine" the official theme of their twentieth reunion. The reunion booklet cover read "Denmark High School/Class of 1972/Twenty Year Reunion/'Imagine'." At the climax of the evening, the band played the song that had been banned from their graduation twenty years earlier, and class members sang the lines that had expressed the utopian dreams of the sixties.[16]

4

The Clinton Administration Takes Action

CLINTON'S "OPENNESS INITIATIVE"   In October 1993, President Clinton issued a ringing endorsement of the FOIA. He announced an "openness initiative" under which all federal agencies were required to "renew their commitment to the Freedom of Information Act . . . and to its sound administration." All agencies were required to "take a fresh look at their administration of the Act, to reduce backlogs of FOIA requests," and to conform to a new standard in litigation. Up to that point, almost a year into Clinton's first term, the Reagan administration guidelines still governed Clinton Justice Department FOIA litigation.

Under the new litigation guidelines promulgated the same day by Attorney General Janet Reno, the Department of Justice was required to conduct a comprehensive review of all FOIA cases in litigation at that point, including *Wiener v. FBI*, to determine whether they met the new and higher standard required to justify withholding information: "foreseeable harm." Under this new policy, "the department will no longer defend an agency's withholding of information merely because there is a 'substantial legal basis' for doing so," Reno declared in revoking the Reagan policy. "Rather, in determining whether or not to defend a nondisclosure decision, we will apply a presumption of disclosure." The government would no longer go to court to prevent the release of information that "might technically or arguably fall within an exemption," unless a specific "foreseeable harm" would result from its disclosure. And she "strongly encouraged" agencies to make "discretionary disclosures" of previously withheld information.[1]

Less than a month later, FBI attorney Bhambhani suggested that the FBI was interested in settling my case. He proposed on November 1 that the FBI would release the information on Lennon provided by confidential informants, but not the national security information, if the ACLU team dropped the other issues in the case, including discovery. The possibility of settlement had arisen following Clinton's "openness initiative" and because he was expected to issue a new, more liberal executive order on classification soon.

Before considering the possibility of settlement, the ACLU team wanted to see the results of the FBI's litigation review of the Lennon files case under the new "foreseeable harm" standard. That review resulted in the release a month later of substantial previously withheld material. In releasing the new pages, the FBI emphasized that this was a "discretionary release . . . based exclusively on the new policy" of the Clinton administration that "should in no way be construed as an admission, tacit or otherwise, that the government's litigating position was not 'substantially justified.'" The Justice Department letter accompanying the newly released pages declared that, in withholding them for the previous twelve years, the law had been "properly applied" and that "the policy upon which the release is being made does not give FOIA litigants any additional rights."

The new release covered 150 pages, almost all previously withheld under exemption (b)(7)(D)(2), information provided by a confidential source "under an expressed or implied assurance of confidentiality." Apparently the FBI concluded it lacked the necessary documentation to establish that the informers had received a guarantee of confidentiality that was explicit.

The principal piece of new information was a report that Lennon contributed $75,000 to EYSIC, the Election Year Strategy Information Center. Much of the rest of the new material reported that Lennon was *not* participating in plans to disrupt the Republican National Convention—thus undermining the entire pretext for the FBI investigation of his activities. An FBI confidential informant report dated February 23, 1972, reported that "[NAME WITHHELD] has had numerous conversations with John Lennon and his wife about becoming active in the New Left movement in the United States, and that Lennon and his wife seem uninterested. [NAME WITHHELD] can't seem to convince them they should become more active" (see p. 179).

Another newly released document, dated March 31, 1972, described Lennon's plans to hold a concert in Ann Arbor "in the near future" (see p. 220). Instructions followed to "discreetly ascertain" if such a concert was indeed scheduled. This memo showed how confused and inefficient the FBI could be. The Ann Arbor concert had been held three months earlier and had been documented in the file at that time.

Other newly released documents described perfectly legal activities: a proposal of Lennon's back in 1970 to set up a network of radio stations to broadcast five-minute "peace" programs; a report that "there may be a Peace Concert next month in the Boston Garden"; a report that "New Hampshire PCPJ [People's Coalition for Peace and Justice] hopes to have the peace conference sometime during the New Hampshire Presidential Primary and John Lennon . . . is hoped to attend" (see pp. 127, 149). Another document reported that the "International Society for Krishna Consciousness was backed by George Harrison and John Lennon, not further identified. It appears that these individuals are members of the Beatles singing group who reside in England." That was what the FBI had gone to the Supreme Court to prevent the public from seeing. The release raised grave questions about the actions and integrity of the FBI—not only in investigating Lennon but also in fighting release of the files.

The Justice Department's hope in implementing Clinton's openness initiative had been to bring a significant amount of FOIA litigation to an end—either by yielding disclosure of all withheld records or by yielding disclosure of so much additional information that FOIA plaintiffs would decide not to contest the decision to withhold the remaining information. But with the Lennon case, the ACLU team was determined to continue the litigation. They had won on the issue of express versus implied guarantees of confidentiality, but two other issues remained: national security documents and confidential informant material compiled for a legitimate law enforcement purpose.

While the Clinton administration moved slowly toward revising the Cold War system of government secrecy, Congress moved ahead. In March 1994, with Democrats in control of both the House and Senate, the chairmen of the Senate and House intelligence committees introduced legislation that would greatly reduce both the number of classified documents and the time they remained secret. Senator Dennis DeConcini, Arizona Democrat, pointed out in introducing the legislation that the government was classifying seven million documents a year, which amounted to one every second of the working week. He noted that some World War I records were still being withheld on the grounds that releasing them would endanger national security. "This is simply nonsensical," he declared, "and it must change."[2]

The two bills provided for automatic declassification of secret documents after ten years and top secret documents after fifteen. They allowed exemptions for "extremely sensitive information like the names of foreign agents working for the US."

A similar proposal was put forward at the same time in a report by a joint Pentagon-CIA commission, consisting of ten senior military intelligence officials working with a nineteen-member staff. They agreed that "the classification system, largely unchanged since the Eisenhower Administration, has grown out of control." For Pentagon officials and the CIA to make such a statement was truly a major transformation in official attitudes toward secrecy. That report described a system in which classified documents were "stored in locked containers inside locked strong rooms within secure buildings in fenced facilities patrolled by armed guards." Apparently this was where they kept the Lennon files. The commission termed that system "overkill even at the height of the cold war." The Pentagon-CIA report also criticized the enormous cost of secrecy, which it estimated at $14 billion. They recommended that "a great deal of information" be automatically released ten years after classification and the rest after twenty-five.[3]

In response to Clinton's openness initiative, the National Security Council drafted a new policy on classification that was described by the *New York Times* in March 1994. The draft policy, which Clinton at that point was expected to sign, established automatic declassification after twenty-five years. Historians were quoted welcoming the proposed changes, while the CIA's general counsel expressed concern about the twenty-five-year rule.[4] Since the Lennon files ended in December 1972, a twenty-five-year rule would have automatically declassified them at the end of 1997—at that point three years away—if Clinton signed the draft executive order.

YEAR TWELVE: CLINTON'S 1995 EXECUTIVE ORDER ON CLASSIFICATION Clinton finally issued a new executive order on classification in April 1995, more than two years after taking office. The order required automatic declassification of all information more than twenty-five years old that had been classified, unless the information fell into one of nine categories of exemptions. Documents exempt from release included those revealing the identity of a confidential source, the most frequent justification for withholding documents in the Lennon files, and foreign government information that would "seriously and demonstrably undermine ongoing diplomatic activities of the US," another category the FBI was claiming for the Lennon files.

In Clinton's statement announcing the new policy, he declared that "we will no longer tolerate the excesses of the current system" and that "the order will lift the veil on millions of existing documents." He promised it would "make available to the American people and posterity most documents of permanent historical value that were maintained in secrecy until now."

The Clinton executive order also declared that information could not be classified merely to "prevent embarrassment to a person, organization, or agency" or to "conceal violations of law, inefficiency, or administrative error," which arguably applied to the Lennon files. Clinton also declared that "we will resolve doubtful calls about classification in favor of keeping the information unclassified."[5]

Most important for the Lennon files litigation was the issue of the "public interest balancing act." Under the Reagan executive order on classification, the public interest in release of particular documents could never outweigh even the tiniest possibility of damage to the national security. Historians and journalists had long argued for the restoration of the Carter policy, which required that the public interest in disclosure be balanced against the possible harm that might result. Since the Lennon files were of great public interest, while their release would bring very little if any damage to the national security, restoring the public interest balancing act would bring the release of information withheld under the national security exemption.

Clinton declared that the new executive order "will authorize agency heads to balance the public interest in disclosure against the national security interest in making declassification decisions." But "authorize" is not the same as "require." The text of the executive order did not mandate that the public interest be considered. Instead of requiring such a balancing act, as the Carter policy had, Clinton made it "an exercise of discretion." "In some exceptional cases," the executive order declared, "the need to protect information may be outweighed by the public interest in disclosure of the information, and in these cases the information should be declassified." So far, so good. But the next sentence gave the senior official of the classifying agency the power to "determine, as an exercise of discretion, whether the public interest in disclosure outweighs the damage to national security that might reasonably be expected from disclosure."[6]

Even more damaging to freedom of information, the executive order declared that "this provision does not . . . create any substantive or procedural rights subject to judicial review." Thus if the head of the FBI wanted to consider the public interest in release of a particular document, the executive order permitted him to do so, but it didn't require him to do so, and it didn't give the public any right to appeal to the courts a decision not to do so. Under the new Clinton order, the public interest balancing act was optional and not subject to judicial review. The event we had been waiting for since Reagan abolished the Carter policy twelve years earlier did not happen.

Clinton was condemned for this failure by many voices. The *Los Angeles Times* editorial on the Clinton policy on classification was headlined "Still Too Many Secrets." It criticized the president for exempting from declassification information that would "damage relations" with a foreign government and for failing to "compel classifiers to balance the public's need to know and that state's interest in secrecy by subjecting such judgments to judicial review."[7] An Associated Press story quoted the director of the Center for National Security Studies describing the order as "a major disappointment."[8]

The *New York Times* coverage reported that "the new policy was less open than the one the National Security Council proposed a year ago." The *Times*, citing "administration officials," explained that "the version reflected White House efforts to accommodate complaints of officials at the CIA, the Pentagon, the National Security Agency and elsewhere." The officials were quoted as saying the effect of the new policy would depend "on how vigorously the CIA and others strive to protect their secrets." White House spokesman Mike McCurry "conceded that the overhaul might not satisfy some of the historians who have been pressing for swifter and more complete access to government documents," but McCurry defended the limitations on declassification as "striking an appropriate balance."[9]

While Clinton failed to make the public interest balancing act mandatory, he did open the possibility that the FBI could decide to release previously withheld information. No court could order them to do so, but still Rosenbaum and Marmalefsky had a slight chance of negotiating further release by the FBI "as a matter of discretion."

DECISIONS ON "UNLAWFUL ACTIVITIES" In February 1995 the ACLU team began lining up expert witnesses in preparation for a trial, which we anticipated could begin in June. Those who agreed to testify included Herbert Mitgang, former cultural correspondent of the *New York Times*, member of its editorial board, and author of *Dangerous Dossiers: Exposing the Secret War against America's Greatest Authors*, a highly respected

1988 book on FBI files on thirty-five American writers; Natalie Robins, author of *Alien Ink: The FBI's War on Freedom of Expression*, a widely reviewed 1992 book based on 150 FBI files released under the FOIA; Curt Gentry, author of *J. Edgar Hoover: The Man and the Secrets*, the acclaimed 1991 critical biography; Stanley Kutler, professor of law and American history at the University of Wisconsin and author of *The Wars of Watergate*, the foremost history of the period; Max Holland, an expert on national security issues and frequent contributor to *The Nation*; and Professor Athan Theoharis of Marquette University, widely recognized as the leading scholar on FBI domestic surveillance and on the FBI files, author of half a dozen books on the topic. All were prepared to offer expert testimony regarding the FBI's patterns and practices of surveillance of politically active artists during the Nixon era.

The ACLU team filed a motion in February 1995 to compel the FBI to answer its interrogatories—in particular, whether the FBI had engaged in unlawful activities in the Lennon investigation—and to provide information concerning the FBI's motivation in investigating Lennon. The FBI filed another blistering reply. Judge Takasugi assigned the issue of the interrogatories to Magistrate Judge Brian Q. Robbins—magistrates ordinarily hear discovery matters and read interrogatories, and their decisions are subject to review by the district judge. Magistrate Robbins held a hearing on discovery in April, when several hours were spent in oral argument.

The next day Robbins issued a tentative ruling, granting and denying the motion in part and permitting further supplemental briefing. Both sides promptly submitted voluminous supplemental briefs. The biggest help for the ACLU team came in June 1995, when the Ninth Circuit issued its decision on *Rosenfeld v. Dept. of Justice*, the FOIA case concerning FBI records on the Berkeley Free Speech Movement that had been appealed. The Ninth Circuit concluded that that FBI investigation had been pretextual and ordered the release of documents—an excellent precedent for the Lennon case.

Dan Marmalefsky had his own confidential sources, from which he learned that the FBI used asterisks in its files to indicate when information was obtained in an illegal search. Marmalefsky was told about the asterisks in the course of preparing for the depositions of Miller and Shackelford, by someone familiar with the prosecution of Miller and Felt. One of the interrogatories asked the FBI to "identify each document in the Lennon files that contains a source symbol number . . . that contains an asterisk," and to "explain why there is an asterisk."

To support the significance and validity of that interrogatory, the ACLU team enlisted the help of Athan Theoharis, the Marquette University historian and expert on the FBI. He provided a sworn declaration stating that, during the period when the Lennon files were created in 1971 and 1972, the FBI inserted an asterisk adjacent to a symbol number whenever the source involved an illegal investigative technique, that is, when "the source of the information was not a person but an illegal investigative technique." Rosenbaum and Marmalefsky emphasized Theoharis's expertise: he was at the time a consultant to the National Archives' FBI Records Appraisal Project and had worked with the Senate Select Committee on Intelligence—the Church Committee. He had authored or edited eleven books on the FBI and related topics. Rosenbaum and Marmalefsky argued in their brief that the presence of an asterisk would contradict the FBI's claim that the investigation of Lennon was "lawful" and provide evidence that the decision to withhold the information was improper. They noted that the FBI did not refute Theoharis's declaration.

In July 1995, Judge Robbins finally issued tentative written orders denying discovery concerning related investigations but approving a few of the ACLU interrogatories, including one stating that "defendant shall answer . . . whether illegal activities were used in connection with the investigation of Mr. John Lennon." That was the big one. Judge Robbins also ordered a response to the interrogatory asking the FBI to identify the names and duties of agents involved in the management and supervision of the Lennon investigation. In December, Judge Takasugi issued the formal order requiring the FBI to respond to the interrogatories Judge Robbins had affirmed; the way was now clear for a trial.

MEDIA WATCH: 1995   The ACLU, in its continuing effort to publicize the subversion of the FOIA by the FBI, held a press conference to announce Takasugi's order to the FBI, which made international news—much of it reported erroneously. But some got it right: the *Sacramento Bee*, under the headline "I Am the G-Man," reported correctly that "a federal judge has ordered the FBI to tell why it kept John Lennon under surveillance." A wire service reporter got confused, however, and newspapers across the U.S. ran headlines reading, "Nixon Tried to Deport John Lennon." In fact that wasn't anything new— it was a well-established historical fact, which had been in the headlines in 1972—but it wasn't what had been won in Judge Takasugi's courtroom. Typically, news of the court decision regarding Lennon ran in "celebrity" columns: for example, the *Boston Herald* ran it next to reports that Michael Jackson was "15 minutes away from death" when paramedics arrived at a rehearsal and that O. J. Simpson "turned up for the deposition of his former girlfriend, Paula Barbieri."[10]

The *Washington Post* was even more confused: they reported that the court ordered "the release of the FBI's dossier on John Lennon," consisting of 250 pages of documents. That erroneous statement appeared in the *Post's* "Style" section, following a report that the Knopf guidebook "The Holy Land" omitted the name of Israel from several maps, which Knopf president Sonny Mehta called "an astonishing editorial error."[11] Judge Takasugi's order was never mentioned in the *Post* story. The American media for the most part had once again turned a hard news legal story into an entertainment report. And once again the news they did report was not new.

YEAR THIRTEEN: THE FBI'S SETTLEMENT OFFER   Less than two months after the FBI was ordered to answer whether it had engaged in illegal activities in investigating Lennon, in February 1996, before a trial could begin, government attorneys formally offered to settle the case.

For the ACLU team, any settlement would have to include a virtually complete release of the documents still at issue, as well as compensation for attorney fees and court costs incurred in thirteen years of litigation. For the FBI, settling the case would accomplish three things: it would absolve the bureau of the need to respond to the court's orders concerning discovery of information about whether the FBI had a legitimate law enforcement purpose in investigating Lennon; it would avoid a published court opinion on the scope of discovery under the law enforcement exemption section of the FOIA, one that might be favorable to future plaintiffs challenging the legitimacy of the FBI's declared law enforcement purposes in other cases; and, of course, it would avoid not only the continued expense of litigation but also the possibility of a judgment against the FBI in a trial.

The new Clinton executive order on classification had made the public interest balancing act "a matter of discretion," which meant that the FBI had the power to release all the remaining material in the Lennon file as part of the settlement. The FBI offered, "as a matter of its discretion," to release the eighty pages of material claimed under the confidential informant exemption. That meant the FBI was no longer going to defend its claim that it had a legitimate law enforcement purpose in investigating Lennon. The FBI preferred to release the withheld information rather than face discovery about the legitimacy of its purpose and practices, followed by a trial and judgment.

In March 1996, Department of Justice trial attorney Bhambhani informed the ACLU team that "it is unlikely that any information currently withheld under Exemption 1, will be declassified and released as a matter of discretion." This meant that litigation over the national security pages would continue after any settlement of the other issues in the case.

A settlement agreement was finally signed in September 1997, under which the FBI released eighty pages of previously withheld confidential informant reports and paid $204,000 for attorney fees and court costs (amounting to $2,000 per page for the documents in this volume). The ACLU estimated its true costs, however, at more than $400,000, and the government was likely to have spent at least as much. The actual cost to the taxpayers for the documents in this volume, therefore, was closer to $6,000 per page, making this book one of the more valuable, or at least more expensive, ever published.

In exchange for the eighty new pages and the $204,000 for attorney fees, the ACLU team dismissed its claims regarding confidential source information. There was no settlement on the national security documents; the agreement identified ten documents withheld on national security grounds as "remaining at issue in this litigation." The agreement established a schedule for submitting motions for summary judgment on these documents.

The settlement agreement declared that the release of documents "shall not be construed either by the parties or the Court as an admission, tacit or otherwise, that such information was 'improperly withheld.' . . . Nor shall such release be construed as an admission, tacit or otherwise, that the FBI was not justified in withholding such information." Of course that was what the settlement meant.

Under the settlement, the FBI insisted that Rosenbaum and Marmalefsky withdraw "any and all outstanding discovery requests" regarding the Lennon file. Obviously, eliminating these had been one of the government's principal motives in settling, to avoid responding to the questions concerning the legitimacy of the Lennon investigation. The ACLU team had to promise "not to file any motion seeking to reopen discovery or to propound any further discovery in this action." The FBI also insisted that Rosenbaum and Marmalefsky agree "not to take the position that the Government's revised Vaughn index does not provide enough or sufficient information for plaintiff to intelligently advocate the release of the documents."[12]

Rosenbaum recalled that "we had no hesitation about the settlement. It still gave us the opportunity to litigate the serious remaining issues around national security. And we got the documents. But there was a lingering feeling that, gosh, it would have been great fun to have put on the stand the FBI agents who were involved in these investigations and re-visit that history. But that would have been years down the road. It would have kept the documents from us, and it had many uncertainties. We had too many other cases to work on."[13]

The FBI sent the taxpayers' $204,000 by wire transfer; Dan Marmalefsky and Morrison and Foerster donated their share to the ACLU of Southern California. The eighty new pages were delivered in October by FedEx.

Eighty pages of reports on Lennon from undercover agents seemed like a gold mine; but the work of informers must be treated with caution and skepticism. Police informers are the least reliable of all sources of information about popular movements, historian Richard Cobb argued in his book on police surveillance during the French Revolution. The informer's situation has changed little in two hundred years: to justify his continued employment, "he has to convey the inestimable and unique value of his information," Cobb wrote; "to be successful, he needs to prove that he has access to secrets that would otherwise be unknown to the authorities." In order to make a living at being a police informer, "he needs to provide a great deal of information, whatever its worth." So informers turn in reports, which typically contain "a great deal of padding—with a view to volume—and a great deal of special pleading—with a view to illustrating the trouble that the informer has taken and the cunning demonstrated" in deceiving the objects of scrutiny.[14]

Informers typically have connections to only a few people the officials are interested in. In such cases, the typical informer turns in reports "repetitively denouncing the same people, the same categories, in the hope that they will last him out for as many months or as many years as possible." The smart informer never provides all the information he has about all of his subjects; to do so would make him valueless in the future. "To make a clear sweep of a 'faction' at one go," Cobb points out, "would be a form of professional suicide."[15]

This dribbling out of information over an extended period often coincides with the interests of police officials, whose own careers depend on the existence of continuing threats to security. Thus for both the informer and his supervisors, "a 'plot' must be made to last as long as possible." Then increased budgets can be justified and continued employment made necessary. The result is that informers and their supervisors have strong motivation to "construct an elaborate 'plot' where there is an open and probably harmless association," to "make Machiavellian conspirators" of ordinary people critical of the status quo, to "scent daggers—or pretend to scent daggers—where there are kitchen knives and spoons." For the informer, when people come together, when they meet, it can't be merely for an insignificant social occasion; "these are merely covers for activities far less innocent." Especially in a society where there is a sharp divide between government authorities and their critics, "any coming together of any locals, for any purpose, may be potentially seditious."[16]

Many of these elements that Cobb found in the reports of police informers in Paris in the 1790s can also be found in the confidential informant reports released in the 1997 Lennon file settlement. Padding with irrelevant information, exaggerating the subversive significance of meetings that were perfectly legal, implying that serious violations of law were imminent, hinting that things were coming together in sinister ways, repeatedly naming a few people the government considered troublemakers, thereby keeping the case going when it had no legitimate rationale—all these practices can be found in virtually every confidential informant report in the Lennon file.

The eighty pages released in the 1997 settlement revealed very little that was new about Lennon, but they unveiled a great deal about the FBI and its informers. The most striking feature of the previously withheld information was how trivial it was. "The parrot story" provided the best example. A report written by an informer in April 1972 described a trip to New York by antiwar activists from Madison to meet with movement leaders. The second page described "a girl there name Linda" who had a parrot that "interjects 'Right on' whenever the conversation gets rousing" (see p. 251). The FBI had classified this information as "confidential" and refused to release it for twenty-five years, going all the way to the Supreme Court in an effort to prevent the public from learning about the parrot.

Another document that the FBI had been concealing put the bureau in a particularly bad light; after trying to get local police to arrest Lennon on narcotics charges, and thus ensure his deportation, "(name withheld) of the New York Police Department advised that his department has been unable to make a narcotics case on the Lennons" (see p. 265). This document had been kept secret for sixteen years. According to another newly released 1972 document, "British authorities stated that Lennon's narcotics conviction in England is not likely to be overturned" (see p. 254). Why that had been kept secret since 1981 was a mystery.

Many of the confidential informant reports described meetings of antiwar groups and the comings and goings of antiwar activists. The documents showed the obsessive and irrelevant detail with which the FBI monitored the antiwar movement. Informers reported that "Mike Drobenare is using his parent's car again," and that "George Vicers was in the office today" (see p. 125). There are reports of disagreements within the antiwar movement: associates told Jerry Rubin that the fact that he and Abbie Hoffman were "superstars . . . does not impress us at all" (see p. 253). At the Ann Arbor rally for John Sinclair, Bobby Seale "made the following public statement: "You FBI m_____ f_____, we know you're here." The FBI kept this statement secret for twenty-five years, even though 15,000 people in the audience heard him.

Given the logic of self-interest of informers, the most remarkable single sentence in all the confidential informant reports is the one where the FBI's paid informer wrote that Lennon said he would participate in demonstrations at the Republican National Convention only "if they are peaceful" (see p. 252). This comes close to what Cobb called "professional suicide" for any informant—if there is no crime in the offing, then the informant can be dismissed. It underscores the significance of the informer's report and provides additional evidence that it was in fact true. The report also seriously undermined the claim the FBI had been making for the previous fourteen years that their investigation of Lennon had not been an illegitimate abuse of power, but rather a legitimate law enforcement investigation based on the FBI's knowledge, provided by confidential informants, that Lennon intended to participate in violent, disruptive demonstrations at the Republican National Convention. The document in which Lennon said he would participate in demonstrations only "if they are peaceful" had been kept secret by the FBI since the initial FOIA request sixteen years earlier. It was a document for which the FBI went to the Supreme Court seeking to prevent its release. That was what they didn't want the public to see: the evidence from their own files that contradicted their claims.

ORIGINS OF THE PARROT STORY   When the story of the parrot trained to say "right on!" appeared in the news in 1997, two people called to say the same document had been published twenty years earlier in an underground newspaper in Madison called *Take Over* and that its author was Julie Maynard, the former FBI informer who had joined our side of the FOIA case. Research in the Wisconsin State Historical Society in Madison, beloved by historians as a gold mine of archival material about radical groups and movements, confirmed that the callers were right. *Take Over* had published several confidential informant reports written by Julie Maynard, including the one the FBI had just released under the FOIA. But *Take Over* had published the report in 1976, twenty-one years earlier.

The facts behind the parrot story go back even farther, to 1967, when the Madison Police Department had a special undercover unit, the "Affinity Squad," that infiltrated and spied on the radical community there. When local activist Paul Soglin was elected mayor in the mid-seventies, the city of Madison established its own freedom of information policy, and various local activists filed requests for information about themselves contained in what was known as the "Affinity Files."

What happened next was exactly the sort of thing the FBI fears from releasing confidential informant reports. In December 1975, the city released to one requester, John Mattes, heavily censored pages from the Affinity Files that described a 1972 trip to New York he had taken with two others to attend a meeting planning Yippie protests during the 1972 election season. Although the author's name on the document was blacked out, Mattes knew that one of the other two on the trip had to have written it and concluded that it was Julie Maynard. In typical Madison fashion, Mattes was at this point an elected city alderman. He brought the information to *Take Over*.

Take Over then published a series of articles outing Maynard as a police informer, running pictures of her at demonstrations, quoting from the confidential "Affinity File" reports she had written that had been released by the Madison police, and describing the editors' confrontation with her. In subsequent issues they published a grotesque cartoon portraying her as an immensely fat nude cover girl for "Oink, the magazine for postpubescent perverts."[17]

Maynard then sued the city for depriving her of her livelihood as an FBI informant. Up to that point, her work for the FBI remained unknown to the public; it was only her work for the Madison Police Department that had been publicized. Maynard told the *Madison Capital Times* that she had given up a "fairly good career in library science" to become an FBI informant. "And the reason I made that leap, which was a kind of astounding leap for a middle-class girl, was that I was assured that my privacy and my identity would always be protected." Initially, she sought damages of $200,000.[18]

The case went to trial in Madison in 1979, with Maynard asking the city for $37,000 in lost wages from the FBI and an unspecified amount for emotional distress. The trial produced four days of dramatic testimony recalling the heyday of radical activism in Madison. Maynard testified about harassment she suffered as a result of the *Take Over* articles. Her supervisor in the Madison Police Department, detective George Croal, also testified; he had been in charge of Affinity Squad infiltration of radical groups. Former FBI agent George Baxtrum testified that Maynard's "performance" for the "resident agency and to her country" was one of "excellence and integrity." He also testified that he had burglarized the Socialist Worker's Party headquarters in New York numerous times. Another witness was former Madison police inspector Herman Thomas, who had been field commander for the local police for several of the big antiwar demonstrations and who had left the force after it was disclosed that he took some of the Affinity Files home with him rather than allow them to fall into the hands of the newly elected activist mayor Paul Soglin.[19]

Amazingly, Maynard won the case. The jury in a liberal community in the wake of Watergate concluded that the police chief had been negligent in releasing files that revealed her identity and awarded her $21,800 for lost wages. They rejected her claim for emotional distress. The city carried only $5,000 in insurance, so the taxpayers had to pay Maynard the remaining $16,000. The jury foreman, a car company executive, told reporters afterwards that the six men on the jury wanted to "beat the shit out of the *Take Over* people in the courtroom."[20]

The trial had made for some strange bedfellows: *Take Over* wrote subsequently that "the police chief's only ally in the courtroom was the city's scandalous underground newspaper." They complained that the defense, provided not by city attorneys but by the attorney for the city's insurance company, failed to ask Maynard "if she had used dope, committed any illegal acts or advocated violence while an informant."[21]

Maynard also sued *Take Over* for libel and defamation, not for reporting that she was an undercover police informant but for writing that her brother "began taking sexual liberties" with her and for the grotesque nude drawing, both of which "greatly injured . . . her good name and reputation," her attorney said, and exposed her to "public comment and ridicule." *Take Over* published a retraction and an apology in 1979 and ceased publication shortly thereafter. Its editors deposited twenty-four boxes of archival material at the Wisconsin Historical Society, including their copies of the Affinity Files.

But in 1979, and for the next eighteen years, no one connected Maynard to the Lennon files, because the FBI had steadfastly refused to release any informant reports. She had provided a copy of Lennon's check to Rennie Davis and company that gave the FBI its rationale for investigating Lennon; she had also written the report that Lennon said he would attend demonstrations at the Republican National Convention only "if they are peaceful." The FBI confidential informant report with that information, released in the 1997 settlement of the case, had indeed been published twenty-one years earlier in an underground paper. When I attempted to contact Julie Maynard after the 1997 settlement, I discovered she had died two months earlier in Madison. She was only fifty-four. But at last we had conclusive evidence confirming her central role in the FBI surveillance of Lennon and a rare glimpse of an FBI informer at work.[22]

5

After the Settlement

MEDIA WATCH: 1997 Media coverage of the settlement of the Lennon FBI files case was extensive. Most newspapers and TV reports led with the parrot story. The *New York Times* ran the story across the front page of their arts section, but with the unfortunate headline "F.B.I. Files on Lennon Reveal Little Beyond Some Weird Details." Reporter Dinitia Smith told about the parrot trained to say "right on." The FBI, asked to comment, said the FOIA required the bureau to release "raw information from its files that was collected during an earlier era in our history when different concerns drove the FBI, the U.S. government, the news media and public sentiment. Under today's laws and investigative guidelines, this type of investigation would not have been initiated by the FBI."[1] This was the first time the FBI had publicly suggested that they lacked a legitimate law enforcement purpose in their surveillance of Lennon during that "earlier era."

Several editorial writers picked up the story, making precisely the points the ACLU had hoped for: The *Tampa Tribune* ran an editorial headlined "Keep Politics out of the IRS and FBI," in which they called the original surveillance of Lennon an example of "political abuses of police powers," and cited the parrot trained to say "right on." The editorial concluded "Wiener states the obvious: 'The FBI is supposed to catch criminals, not stop people from criticizing the president.'"[2] The *Denver Post* editorial on the case, playing off the parrot story, was titled "Bird-Brained Surveillance." "The case illustrates the disturbing extent to which federal agencies keep secrets from the American people," the editorial declared. The surveillance of Lennon was "deeply disquieting because the agency was investigating lawful free speech." The paper concluded that "Wiener's quest showed there's a need for agencies—including the FBI—to honor existing laws, such as the Free-dom of Information Act."³ The *Baltimore Sun* published a strong column by Dan Ro-dricks declaring that for the FBI to fight the release of the Lennon files on the grounds of national security was "absolutely moronic. . . . And it cost taxpayers hundreds of thou-sands of dollars."⁴

Yoko Ono commented on the case for the first time in fourteen years in the *Minneapolis Star-Tribune*. Reporter Jon Bream interviewed her about plans for son Sean's first solo al-bum; asked about the FBI files, she said, "I was there. I knew all that, John was not being Communist or being violent or anything like that. It was obvious to all of us. It was kind of surprising, I think. We were being bugged, so we knew they were after us. I think it's nice that they're releasing it now. It's due to the fact that the then-government and the now-government are totally different."⁵

The *Tom Snyder Show* ran an interview with the plaintiff in the Lennon FBI files case, which followed one featuring the president of CBS Television, Les Moonves. "My boss," Snyder pointed out. Viewers were invited to call toll-free with questions about the CBS prime time schedule. "Phil in Cincinnati, welcome to the Tom Snyder show, you're on the air live with Les Moonves."

"Tom, I love your show, and I wanted to say to Mr. Moonves, scheduling 'Brooklyn South' up against Monday Night Football was a gutsy decision—what makes you think you can win in that time slot?" After three segments with Moonves, Snyder said, "Com-ing up next: the FBI surveillance on John Lennon a few years back, and more of you on the toll free line—after this short break."

The story worked its way down the media food chain from Dan Rather and the BBC to Tom Snyder and the CBC and then to the Fox News Channel and MSNBC, finally ending up on *The Moose Miller Show* on WCCO radio in Minneapolis, a live morning drive-time show. "Coming up next, we'll be live on the phone with the professor who sued the FBI for their files on John Lennon. But first: Your Soybean Minute! Brought to you by the Minnesota Soybean Council. White mold is spreading across Minnesota soybean fields. . . . For a free brochure on managing soybean white mold, write to the Minnesota Soybean Council. And boy, I'll tell ya—soybeans had real good export numbers this week."

Two months after the settlement, Bill Clinton spoke at a private fund-raising luncheon at the Dakota, where Lennon had lived and Yoko Ono still resided. Tickets for the event cost $5,000 a person. Among those attending were Lauren Bacall, Leonardo DiCaprio, Uma Thurman, Kevin Spacey, and Christie Brinkley. After a lunch of chili and vegetable tarts, the crowd gathered in the living room of the hosts' $4 million apartment to hear the president speak. It was the day after the seventeenth anniversary of Lennon's murder outside the Dakota, and Clinton was in his lip-biting mode: "I'm a very schmaltzy person and I get all choked up when I come here," he said. "I keep imagining whether I'm standing in a place where John Lennon was, and all that." According to the *New York Times*, his listeners "shuffled uncomfortably in the dim light of the drizzly afternoon."[6]

"FOREIGN GOVERNMENT INFORMATION": THE MI5 FILE   A remarkable phone call came in response to the news of the FBI settling the case. Peter Sheridan, the Los Angeles correspondent for the London tabloid *Mail on Sunday*, called to say he knew the foreign government "national security" information the FBI was continuing to withhold. We had assumed they were records about Lennon's 1968 arrest in London for possession of cannabis, which had been the pretext for the Nixon administration campaign to deport him in 1972. But, Sheridan said, the *Mail on Sunday* had recently published an article by Richard Norton Taylor suggesting that the withheld information almost certainly originated with Britain's MI5, the government intelligence service. David Shayler, a "rogue" MI5 agent, had revealed in the August 24 issue of the *Mail on Sunday* that starting in 1968 Lennon was under close surveillance by the MI5 because of his financial support for the Workers' Revolutionary Party. Shayler apparently said the FBI approached MI5 for information, but MI5 withheld it to avoid compromising its sources inside the Workers' Revolutionary Party. According to the *Mail on Sunday*, the MI5 file on Lennon also included a copy of the lyrics to "Working Class Hero" in Lennon's own handwriting.[7]

The British government's reaction to the revelation about MI5 having had Lennon and others under surveillance in the sixties was not friendly: the MI5 ripped Shayler's house apart and arrested his girlfriend, and he went into hiding.[8] The *Mail on Sunday* was served with a draconian injunction preventing the paper from publishing further revelations from Shayler about MI5, on the grounds of "national security."[9] Although the *Mail on Sunday* is a tabloid, no one challenged the accuracy of their MI5 story, which created a scandal of sorts in British politics—not because of the MI5 Lennon file, but because of MI5 files on two members of Tony Blair's cabinet.

Shayler's revelations in the *Mail on Sunday* raised the hope that the final ten documents the FBI was withholding on the claim that they contained "foreign government information" might now be released. Indeed, in December 1997, the Blair government proposed Britain's first freedom of information law, requiring that government agencies release official documents to the public. The proposal represented a historic transformation in a country where the Official Secrets Act had prohibited any unauthorized release of information by government officials. The new law would "give every individual a statutory right to know about the information and records which the government holds," according to David Clark, minister of public service.[10] In the meantime, however, MI5 set out to destroy the files whose existence had been revealed in the *Mail on Sunday*. In January 1998 the *Mail on Sunday* reported that MI5 "pledged to pulp tens of thousands of secret files hoarded during the Cold War." The spy agency intended to "shred up to half of the 250,000 files it holds at its headquarters," including many on those who "were once considered a threat to national security." Destruction of the files was demanded by those who feared they contained scurrilous information about prominent figures in Britain today.[11]

But even if the MI5 destroys its Lennon file before Parliament enacts a British freedom of information law, the FBI could still release its documents containing MI5 information. Martin Kettle, who covered the MI5/Lennon story as the Washington correspondent for *The Guardian*,[12] said in an interview that a lot has changed in the British government since 1992, when the FBI informed Rosenbaum and Marmalefsky that the unnamed foreign government that provided the classified information had still insisted on confidentiality. In Britain today, he said, there is a new openness and interest in freedom of information; he suggested that the Tony Blair Labour government might agree to approve the release by the FBI of the withheld information, if the FBI were to ask.[13] We hoped they would and that the Blair government would agree to the FBI's release of documents.

The FBI did ask, and the answer was no. In March 1998 the FBI filed for summary judgment on the remaining ten documents, asking Judge Takasugi to rule that the bureau's withholding of those pages on national security grounds was legal and legitimate. The FBI submitted a new Vaughn index, eighty-seven pages long, describing the ten documents and providing detailed reasons for withholding them under the "foreign government information" exemption of the FOIA.

The "Declaration of Sherry L. Davis," chief of the Litigation Unit of the FBI's Freedom of Information Section, reported that "the foreign government which provided the information at issue in this case was contacted on Sept. 30, 1997"; it replied on November 17, requesting that the information "continue to be protected and not released to the public." The foreign government, still unnamed, declared that "release of this information will cause serious and demonstrable harm to its sources, which remain sensitive." She concluded that this fulfilled the FOIA requirement prohibiting the release of information that would "seriously and demonstrably impair relations between the US and a foreign government." The withheld information in the Lennon FBI files, Davis concluded, has not been "desensitized by the passage of time." The foreign relations issues, she said, remained "delicate and sensitive." She included some boilerplate language about how release of the information "reasonably could be expected to strain relations between the US and foreign governments and lead to diplomatic, political or economic retaliations."

What about releasing the information provided by the foreign government without identifying the name of the government that provided it? That would be wrong, Davis declared: "The danger remains that if the information were to be made public, the originating government would likely recognize the information as material it supplied in confidence. Thereafter, it would be reluctant to entrust the handling of its information to the discretion of the United States." Thirty-six pages in the ten documents thus contained information the FBI claimed it was required to withhold. Given the foreign government's request, it seemed unlikely that Judge Takasugi or any other court would order the release of this information.

What motivated the FBI to settle? Mark Rosenbaum gave several reasons. "First was the content of the documents themselves. The silly stuff in the pages they released helped our case: the song lyrics, the parrot story, the bed-ins. The embarrassment factor was a problem for them. They had taken a beating in the press on this case."[14]

Second, "Judge Takasugi had granted our request to take depositions of the key agents involved in the original monitoring and surveillance. We had the prospect of taking more, of going up the ladder. That meant FBI agents would have to respond to aggressive questioning about the legitimacy of the original investigation of Lennon. They feared that this would set a precedent for other cases in which they had made similar claims and not had those claims probed."

Third, Rosenbaum argued, "time worked in our favor." The new Clinton executive order, while it wasn't ideal, helped. "It became increasingly difficult for the FBI to sustain
the claims it had made in the early eighties, whatever the merits they had had when they
were first made."

Fourth, Rosenbaum said, "the depositions we took were great. We dug out contradic-
tions in their case. We showed how purely perfunctory their review of the documents had
been. We showed that the agents who we deposed had no knowledge of the case background or history. They had no independent basis for saying there would be any injury
to any of the agents or sources. A wall had been built around the original agents and the
original surveillance. That surfaced how thin the justifications the FBI provided in court
were."

Dan Marmalefsky recalled that in the status conference with Judge Takasugi after taking the depositions about whether the ACLU team would get any more discovery, "he
was impressed and disturbed to learn what the FBI had *not* done in preparing its affidavits
justifying withholding documents. Thus the depositions were very helpful not only in getting the information from those sources but in getting further favorable rulings on the discovery motions we subsequently filed. It was terrific to be able to cite back the nonsensical testimony from these witnesses who were telling the court about all the horrible things
that were supposedly going to happen if this material got released, but they didn't really
know anything about it. They were arguing the investigation had been legitimate when
they had made no effort to contact anyone who had anything to do with the investigation."[15]

The government strategy in fighting discovery, Rosenbaum held, had been to try to move
the case away from Judge Takasugi to the D.C. Circuit Court. "The high point for them,"
Rosenbaum recalled, "was getting discovery regarding Shackelford and Miller [the two
key FBI agents involved in the original surveillance of Lennon] quashed by the D.C. judge.
But when we were able to move the question of discovery back to Judge Takasugi's courtroom, that was very worrisome to them—they were not going to be able to control just
how far this case would go."

"From an intellectual standpoint, that would have made for an interesting exercise,"
Marmalefsky said. "If we had continued to litigate, there clearly were conflicts between
other decisions and our position. One of the things they had to be concerned about was
not just the district court judge. Remember that the three-judge panel in the Ninth Circuit explicitly retained jurisdiction over all appeals."

Rosenbaum added, "That was a decision that had been openly skeptical of the government's case. The FBI had to worry about that. Judge Schroeder was shocked at the selection of documents we presented."

Another factor that motivated the FBI to settle, Rosenbaum argued, was that "they had gotten themselves in trouble at the beginning when they shifted the basis of their argument that the Lennon investigation had a legitimate law enforcement purpose. Originally they had said Lennon had been investigated under one law [the National Security Act of 1947], then they changed to another [the Civil Obedience and Anti-Riot Acts]."

Additionally, the FBI was motivated to settle because "we had been aggressive in presenting affirmative evidence supporting our side," Rosenbaum argued: the declarations of Stewart Albert and Julie Maynard. "We showed we had an affirmative counter-case to present. We were prepared to litigate that era. Most FOIA cases involve just the judge ruling on their arguments. The fact that we had one of their informants prepared to testify on our side was particularly significant. They knew we were not afraid of a trial."

If the case did go to trial, Marmalefsky explained, "they were going to have to answer the question: did the government break the law in connection with the investigation? They were going to have to answer that under the threat of perjury. The government didn't want to go through that."

Finally, they were willing to settle, in Marmalefsky's view, because "they realized that the documents in fact were not all that significant to them. As they told the press, they were documents 'from another era,' way in the past. No matter how bad the documents looked, they were from 1971–72 and were not necessarily going to reflect poorly on the FBI of the 1990s. There was no strong principled reason for them to resist giving us the stuff. And they faced risks if they went forward—the possibility of a published court opinion on discovery citable elsewhere in the country that would be unfavorable to them. Whereas this settlement is not."

Why then didn't they settle on the last ten documents? Marmalefsky explained: "They aren't concerned about the danger of releasing these particular documents. They are truly fearful of precedent. And they believe the law favors them on foreign government information. John Lennon doesn't matter; the issue is that the information comes from another government's intelligence agency."

Why didn't the FBI stick with its argument that they did have a legitimate law enforcement purpose? They could have repeated that they were investigating plans for disruptive demonstrations at the 1972 conventions, organized by the same people who had been found guilty of crimes in the 1968 convention demonstrations. Dan Marmalefsky answered, "They still can't have whatever kind of surveillance they want. There has to be a legitimate connection between what Lennon was doing and what constitutes criminal activity."

But the courts might have accepted the FBI's argument, Mark Rosenbaum added. "A court could easily have said, 'There were excesses, but not sufficient evidence of pretext to make this an illegitimate investigation. In hindsight maybe it looks excessive, but at the time it was legitimate in an excess of caution.'"

Marmalefsky agreed: "We wanted to litigate the propriety of the 1972 investigation. But most courts wouldn't want to second-guess past government actions. Their biggest concern is not FOIA cases, it's criminal cases involving habeas corpus." He added that "there is strong case law on their side regarding what constitutes a legitimate law enforcement purpose—half of the appeals courts say *any* investigation by the FBI is legitimate. Fortunately the Ninth Circuit hasn't said that. It hasn't said anything on the subject. Elsewhere in the country, we would have lost."

"These were reasonable questions we were asking," Mark Rosenbaum said in summary. "What was driving our case was the documents themselves. If they had kept them all secret, we'd have had a much harder time. And we were fortunate to have a courageous federal judge saying, 'I want to find out about this.' The best thing we had going," he concluded, "was the facts of the case."

Conclusion: The Culture of Secrecy

"The concept of the 'official secret' is the specific invention of bureaucracy," Max Weber wrote, "and nothing is so fanatically defended by the bureaucracy."[1] The Lennon files case provides a small but vivid example of this larger problem, the culture of secrecy that undermines democracy. Fighting the FBI's national security and confidential informant claims was hard work, but it could have been worse; at least the Lennon files weren't threatened with destruction or carted away in the middle of the night. That's what happened to files Scott Armstrong had requested under the FOIA, the e-mail messages of the Reagan administration (the "PROFS" system), after he learned that Reagan intended to destroy all eight years of the records the day he left office.[2] Here the stakes were much higher than in the Lennon case, because the PROFS tapes contained documentation on the entire Reagan presidency, including the crucial evidence of official misconduct in the Iran-Contra scandal.

Armstrong's lawsuit prevented their destruction, but the same issue arose when the Bush administration prepared to leave office. Bush asked the U.S. Court of Appeals for the District of Columbia to allow the destruction of records while they were appealing the restraining order Armstrong had won. The court refused. Then, at midnight on the eve of Clinton's inauguration, the Archivist of the United States, Don Wilson, signed a secret agreement granting Bush exclusive legal control over the e-mail tapes of his administration. "Working all night," Armstrong writes, "a National Archives team used rented trucks to cart away from White House offices 4,852 tapes and 135 hard disk drives in cardboard boxes before the incoming Clinton appointees arrived." The archivist, the *Washington*

Post later discovered, was already negotiating secretly to become executive director of the George Bush Center at Texas A&M University.[3]

The Clinton administration resisted release of the Lennon files for five years, but it could have been worse. After Bush gained control of the White House e-mail as his private property, the American Historical Association filed suit, but the Clinton administration went to court to defend the agreement Bush had signed with his archivist.[4] Clinton went even further and accomplished what Reagan and Bush had failed to do: he created a legal basis for destroying his own White House records. Clinton's argument was that the records of the National Security Council (NSC) were not subject to the FOIA, because the NSC was not a government agency. Neither Reagan nor Bush had thought of this one. The fact that the NSC had been treated as a government agency since its founding was irrelevant, Clinton argued; it was simply a group of personal advisers to the president, and thus its records were exempt from disclosure under the FOIA. The judge in the case, Charles Richey, called Clinton's argument "arbitrary and capricious" and "contrary to history, past practice, and the law," and declared the NSC an agency. The Clinton administration appealed, and in August 1996 the U.S. Court of Appeals for the District of Columbia reversed that ruling by a vote of two to one. The Supreme Court refused to hear Armstrong's appeal. That means Clinton and future presidents have the freedom to destroy with impunity whatever NSC documents they want. The Clinton administration had won the most sweeping expansion of secrecy in the past twenty-five years.[5] The fight against secrecy thus involves not just a battle against government claims regarding "national security" and "confidentiality" but also a more elemental battle against removal or destruction of records.

Even when new legislation gave historians greater power to obtain particular documents than that provided by the FOIA, it still wasn't easy to prevail over the FBI and CIA, as the Kennedy assassination records demonstrate. After Oliver Stone's film *JFK* was released, Congress in October 1992 passed the Kennedy Assassination Records Collection Act. It sought to guarantee "expeditious . . . public disclosure" at a time when more than 80 percent of the public did not believe the Warren Commission's conclusion that Lee Harvey Oswald had acted alone. The law required that each government agency identify and organize all of its records about the assassination and send them to the National Archives, which was required to make them available to the public thirty days after receipt.

To fight the culture of secrecy, Congress established an independent Assassination Records Review Board (ARRB) with extraordinary power—it had access to every record of every federal agency and the power to order release of documents over the objections of the agencies; only the president had the power to overrule the review board. Public access to the Kennedy assassination records thus has much stronger protection than the FOIA provides for other government documents.

Under the Kennedy Assassination Records Collection Act, the entire process of identifying relevant documents, depositing them at the National Archives, and processing them for release was to be completed in 300 days. But the culture of secrecy delayed implementation of the new law. President Bush failed to appoint the review board members before leaving office. Although Congress had required their appointment before the end of January 1993, the Clinton administration delayed making nominations for almost a full year. The Senate confirmation hearings caused further delays, so the board was not sworn in until April 1994, eighteen months after passage of the act—and eight months after the date Congress had set as the deadline.

No federal agency met the congressional deadline for reviewing documents and conveying them to the National Archives, with the exception of the National Archives itself. Congress and the White House failed to appropriate funds for the review board for another seven months. No documents could be reviewed by the board staff until office space could be found with secure vaults for classified documents—vaults approved by the CIA. And the staff of twenty-five could not go to work until members had received security clearances from the FBI.

Although Congress gave the ARRB the unprecedented power to release classified documents, something courts cannot do under the FOIA, the FBI and CIA argued strenuously against release. According to Anna K. Nelson, a historian at George Washington University who served on the review board, both the FBI and the CIA contended that the information they had gathered thirty years ago was as sensitive as information gathered three days ago. Both claimed that all their sources had to be protected, whether they were alive or dead, high-level spies or citizens volunteering information. Both agencies, Nelson writes, "expected the board to accept without question the rather generic explanations they offered" for withholding documents. Board members were "appalled at the agencies' seemingly irrational obsession" with protecting sources.[6]

The CIA, Nelson writes, told the board that releasing its information about the Kennedy assassination would have dire consequences: "governments would fall, allies would be lost, and cooperation with other intelligence organizations would come to an end." Despite board members' protests, agency officials argued that "the accidental release of one word or phrase will not only kill countless people but also send the country to its knees." CIA and FBI officials required a line-by-line review of each of their documents. Almost four million pages were included in the collection when it was finally completed in 1998.[7]

Although the 300-odd pages of Lennon files don't approximate the historical significance of the Kennedy assassination records, it should be obvious that the issues involved in the release of both are similar and that the arguments are the same. There's nothing special about the Lennon files, except that John Lennon is the subject; the FBI and CIA made the same justifications detailed in this book as they did about the Kennedy assassination files. The Lennon case thus provides a microcosm of the battle against the culture of secrecy in government.

What is to be done? Citizens ought to challenge government secrecy by asking officials questions and insisting on answers. Journalists and scholars have a special responsibility to expose government secrecy whenever it seems unjustified and fight it. The principle of the FOIA is the right one: democracy works best when the maximum amount of information is available to the public for review and debate. Genuine "national security" requires a vibrant democracy and a well-informed citizenry, not a culture of secrecy.

In the meantime, foes of the FOIA within the government are developing new strategies. A memo circulating within NASA, titled "Suggestions for Anticipating Requests under Freedom of Information Act," recommended that officials not make annotations directly on their copies of documents, since an annotated copy is regarded under the FOIA as a separate document potentially subject to release. Instead, officials were advised to use "stick-on" notes for annotations; the Post-it notes would be subject to release, but "since there is no obligation under FOIA to provide documents in any particular order or relationship to one another, furnishing out-of-context copies of stick-ons can render the information significantly less meaningful."[8] There is no reason to think that NASA is the only government agency taking such steps to subvert the FOIA.

Alongside new initiatives to undermine freedom of information, old patterns of secrecy remain entrenched. CIA Director Robert Gates declared in 1991 that, with the end of the Cold War, the agency would reduce secrecy and "make CIA and the intelligence process more visible and understandable" to the public. To accomplish this worthy goal, Gates established a CIA Openness Task Force. Shortly thereafter, the Center for National Security Studies in Washington, D.C. filed an FOIA request for documents relating to the CIA's Openness Task Force. Max Weber, the theorist of official secrecy, would not have been surprised by the CIA's reply:

> We recently completed a thorough search for material pertaining to your request for records regarding the "recommendations of the Openness Task Force set up by Director Gates" and located one document, a report dated 20 December 1991, which we have determined must be withheld in its entirety.
>
> You have a right to appeal this determination. Address your appeal to the CIA Information Review Committee. Should you decide to do this, please explain the basis of your appeal.[9]

John Lennon offered a reply to this mentality in a song on his *Imagine* album: he titled it "Gimme Some Truth."

Part Two

THE FILES

FBI documents are written with an intimidating array of code words, abbreviations, acronyms, and neologisms arranged and classified in complicated and confusing ways. Herewith, a brief introductory guide.

FBI files are organized around field offices, which conduct investigations, and headquarters in Washington, D.C., to which the field offices transmit summaries. The "OO" (Office of Origin) is the field office with primary responsibility for an investigation — in Lennon's case it was New York. The head of a field office is called the "SAC" (special agent in charge). Several other FBI field offices — Detroit, Miami, and Houston — participated in the Lennon investigation and thus maintained their own files on him. The New York file contains the most complete documents and should contain virtually all original investigative materials, the primary source material for the investigation.

Headquarters or "HQ" files have a different significance: they contain crucial material not found in field office files, especially reports to other agencies and officials — in Lennon's case, memos from J. Edgar Hoover to President Nixon's Chief of Staff H. R. Haldeman and memos prepared for other government agencies, especially the CIA and INS. Evidence of the political significance of the Lennon files is found in the HQ file.

Lennon's main file in the FBI Central Records System in Washington, D.C. is a "100 case file." "100" is the classification number for "domestic security" investigations. Documents in the Lennon file are identified by a number beginning with "100-," followed by the individual case number for a particular field office or headquarters. Case numbers are assigned in chronological order; Lennon's New York case number is 100–469910, indicating the FBI had opened 469,909 domestic security investigations in New York City before his. His headquarters ("HQ") file is numbered 100–175319.

After the file number and the case number comes the serial or document number, indicating the order in which the document was placed in the file.

In addition to this long number, the first page of each document in this volume has a designation at the bottom right, not appearing on the original document, assigned by the FBI as part of the FOIA release of pages. These consist of an abbreviation for the office of origin (e.g., "HQ" or "NY" or "INS") followed by a document number. The FOIA release put the HQ file first, followed by the files from New York, then the Washington field office, then Detroit, and so on. This system of numbering the pages of the Lennon file does not always coincide with their chronological order. In this volume the pages have been arranged in strict chronological order without regard to the FOIA document numbers that appear at the bottom.

The FBI file contains several types of documents: a "teletype" is a secret message requiring complicated encrypting and decrypting sent over the bureau's own communications network; an "airtel" is an internal message urgent enough that it must be sent the same day it is created but routine enough to be sent by airmail rather than by teletype. Letterhead memoranda (LHMs) are documents prepared by the FBI for dissemination to other government agencies. In Lennon's case LHMs were distributed to the CIA, the Secret Service, military intelligence, the State Department, and the Immigration and Naturalization Service (INS).

In the FBI files J. Edgar Hoover is never referred to by name, but only by his title, "The Director," which takes on an Orwellian ring.

A glossary follows the annotated documents, providing definitions for other codes, acronyms, and abbreviations that appear in the Lennon file.

JOHN SINCLAIR FREEDOM RALLY   Lennon performed in Ann Arbor, Michigan, on December 10, 1971, at the "John Sinclair Freedom Rally" before an audience of 15,000. It was his first live concert in the U.S. since the Beatles had waved farewell at Candlestick Park in San Francisco in 1966. FBI informers in the audience carefully monitored the event, as reported in Lennon file document DE-4, of which page one is the cover sheet for the confidential informant report, addressed to J. Edgar Hoover.

Sinclair was a local activist leader who had been sentenced to ten years in the state prison for selling two joints of marijuana to an undercover agent. The rally had a huge program lasting eight hours; the speakers included Allen Ginsberg, Bobby Seale, and Jerry Rubin, and the performers included Stevie Wonder, Archie Shepp, and Phil Ochs as well as John Lennon and Yoko Ono. The FBI was interested because Lennon considered his appearance at the rally a trial run for a national anti-Nixon tour, on which he would bring rock 'n' roll together with radical politics in a dozen cities. At each stop, local organizers would give speeches, and young people would be urged to register to vote and vote against the war. Lennon had talked about ending the tour in August 1972 at a giant protest rally and counterculture festival outside the Republican National Convention, where Richard Nixon was to be renominated. The rest of Lennon's FBI file documents the Nixon administration's efforts to stop him from setting off on this tour, to silence him as a voice of the antiwar movement and critic of the president.

This FBI cover sheet is captioned "SM—New Left" ("SM" is FBI shorthand for "Security Matter") and "IS—White Panther Party" ("IS" is shorthand for "Internal Security"). The distribution list is impressive: FBI field offices in seven cities received copies.

12/27/71

AIRTEL

TO: DIRECTOR, FBI

FROM: SAC, DETROIT (100-40422) (C)

FREEDOM RALLY, UNIVERSITY OF MICHIGAN,
ANN ARBOR, MICHIGAN, 12/10/71,
SPONSORED BY COMMITTEE TO FREE
JOHN SINCLAIR
SM - NEW LEFT; TRAVEL OF DEFENDENTS;
IS - WHITE PANTHER PARTY

FOIA/PA

DO NOT DESTROY SERIAL _20_
PRIOR TO_____ ~186

          Re Detroit teletype to Bureau, 12/11/71.

          Enclosed for the Bureau are five (5) copies of
a LHM setting forth information regarding captioned rally.
Copies of LHM being furnished to below-listed offices for
information purposes: (U)

          LHM classified confidential to protect the identity
of sources utilized therein whose identities if disclosed
could be detrimental to the national defense interests
of this nation. (U)

          Sources identified as follows:

          Source one is ▓▓▓▓▓▓▓▓
          Source two is Intelligence Unit, Mich. State
              Police

     2 - Bureau (Enc. 5) (RM)
     2 - Boston (Enc. 2) (RM)
     2 - Chicago (Enc.2)(RM)
          (1 - 176-5) (1 - 157-3315)(RM)
     2 - Milwaukee (157-1785) (Enc. 2)(RM)
     2 - New York (100-174910) (Enc. 2)(RM)
     2 - San Francisco (176-2) (Enc. 2) (RM)
     2 - WFO (1 - 100-▓▓▓▓▓▓▓ (Enc. 2) (RM)
          (1 - NATIONAL STUDENT ASSOCIATION)
     5 - Detroit (2 - 100-40422) (1 - 100-40452)
          (1 - 176-219) (1 - 176-68)
JBR:js
(19)   9-22-78

DO NOT DESTROY
PENDING LITIGATION

Level of Classification
Classified a
Reason for
Date of Re

DE-4

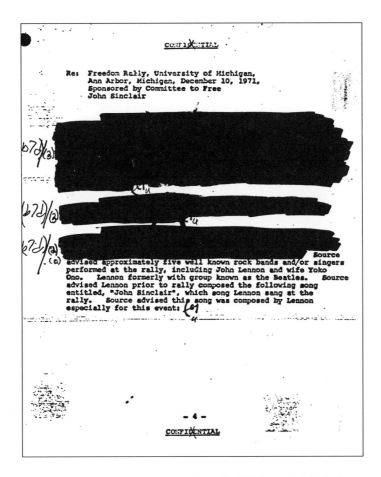

Re: Freedom Rally, University of Michigan,
Ann Arbor, Michigan, December 10, 1971,
Sponsored by Committee to Free
John Sinclair

Source
advised approximately five well known rock bands and/or singers
performed at the rally, including John Lennon and wife Yoko
Ono. Lennon formerly with group known as the Beatles. Source
advised Lennon prior to rally composed the following song
entitled, "John Sinclair", which song Lennon sang at the
rally. Source advised this song was composed by Lennon
especially for this event:

- 4 -

Figure 5a. DE-4 page 3, initial release.

"GROUP KNOWN AS THE BEATLES"　　In the FBI's original release of documents, large sections of the informer's report on the John Sinclair Freedom Rally were withheld on the grounds that they contained confidential source information (DE-4 page 3). The FBI claimed that releasing them would reveal the identity of sources who had obtained a promise of confidentiality. After years of litigation, those passages were released: they gave the number of people attending the concert—15,000—and the fact that it "terminated in the early morning hours."

The sentence "Lennon formerly with group known as the Beatles" is a remarkable one: oh, *that* Lennon!

Re: Freedom Rally, University of Michigan,
    Ann Arbor, Michigan, December 10, 1971,
    Sponsored by Committee to Free
    John Sinclair

       Source five advised December 13, 1971, rally
was attended by an estimated 15,000 persons and terminated
in the early morning hours of December 11, 1971, without
any incidents. Source advised 10 off-duty Ann Arbor
police officers patroled the area near the rally hall. Source
advised the services of the off-duty police officers were
obtained and paid for at a cost of $150.00 by the WPP at
Ann Arbor, Michigan. Source advised police officers patroled
only on the outside of the rally hall and were not permitted
to enter rally.

       Source advised the entire portion of the rally
hall was patroled by so-called WPP Rangers, also known as
The Psychedelic Rangers.

       Source six advised December 13, 1971, University
of Michigan facilities for captioned rally were obtained by
unknown persons on or about November 30, 1971, at a cost of
$4,000.00, which was paid for in cash and in advance. Source
advised approximately five well known rock bands and/or singers
performed at the rally, including John Lennon and wife Yoko
Ono. Lennon formerly with group known as the Beatles. Source
advised Lennon prior to rally composed the following song
entitled, "John Sinclair", which song Lennon sang at the
rally. Source advised this song was composed by Lennon
especially for this event:

Figure 5b. DE-4 page 3, after settlement.

"IT AIN'T FAIR, JOHN SINCLAIR"   The confidential informant report on the John Sinclair concert included a transcription of the words to "John Sinclair," "which song Lennon sang at the rally. Source advised this song was composed by Lennon especially for this event" (DE-4 page 3). The FBI classified this transcription as "confidential" and kept it secret for twelve years, even though Lennon printed the same lyrics on the back jacket of his next album, *Some Time in New York City*. The ACLU cited this page in court arguments as evidence that the FBI lacked a legitimate law enforcement purpose in its investigation of Lennon, pointing out that it was not a crime to sing a song about John Sinclair—it was a form of political expression protected by the First Amendment.

Re: Freedom Rally, University of Michigan
Ann Arbor, Michigan, December 10, 1971
Sponsored by Committee to Free
John Sinclair

It ain't fair, John Sinclair
In the stir for breathing air
Won't you care, for John Sinclair
In the stir for breathing air.
Let him be, let him free
Let him be like you and me

They gave him 10 for 2
What more can the judges do
Gotta, gotta, gotta, gotta, gotta
Gotta, gotta, set him free.

If he'd been a soldier man
Shooting gooks in Vietnam
If he was a flying man
Dropping dope in old Siam
He'd be free, they'd let him be,
Breathing air, like you and me.

They gave him 10 for 2
What more can Judge Colombo do
Gotta, gotta, gotta, gotta, gotta
Gotta, gotta, set him free.

Was he jailed for what he done
Representing everyone
Free John Now if we can
From the dlutches of the man
Let him free, lift the lid
Bring him to his wife and kids

They gave him 10 for 2
What more can Colombo, Nixon, Rockefeller, Agnew do
Gotta, gotta, gotta, gotta, gotta
Gotta, gotta, set him free.

(C)

On December 13, 1971, source six advised he learned
from Lennie Sinclair, Officer WPP, that the Detroit Committee
to Free John Sinclair netted a total of $26,000.00 from the
rally. (C)

Following are verbatim speeches of William Kuntzler,
Rennie Davis, Jerry Rubbin and others as indicated: (C)

- 5 - 4

Figure 6. DE-4 page 4.

WILLIAM KUNSTLER'S SPEECH   The informer at the John Sinclair Freedom
Rally carefully transcribed the speeches, starting with the MC's announcement
of the location of the "drug help" center (DE-4 page 5). Then a tape was played
of William Kunstler's logical and fact-filled speech. The "John" referred to here
is John Sinclair, not John Lennon. Kunstler's speech, appropriately enough, is
all about John Sinclair.

BOB RUDNICK - MC

People have come from various parts of the planet
to help get JOHN out. All right, BOBBY SEALE will be here, PHIL
OAKS, JERRY RUBIN, SHEILA MURPHY, the UP, ED SANDERS, Commander
CODY, RENNIE DAVIS, LENI SINCLAIR, ARCHIE SHEPP (phonetic),
Father GROPPI, a special guest and then DAVID PEALE with JOHN
LENNON and YOKO ONO.

The lost and found and drug help is in the north
west, I think that's over there if you need it. Right now
we're gonna have a tape. Ok, this is gonna be an all night
long hassle, we gotta keep the aisles clear, the firemen are
running around so if possible we're gonna have to keep
announcing, just keep the lanes as clear as you can.

WILLIAM KUNSTLER is a little busy with a new case.
He's trying to get someone else out of jail and couldn't be
here, so to send a message he put it on tape and we're gonna
have that in about ten seconds.

WILLIAM KUNSTLER (taped message)

I have tried everything I could to be in Ann Arbor
tonight but it is impossible. But I know that so many of
JOHN SINCLAIR's friends will be with you that my absence
will be more keenly felt by me than by anyone else. Yet I
could not let the night go by without at least making this
tape, unsatisfactory as it is, to give some concrete form to
my devotion to JOHN and the cause which he symbolizes and
represents.

JOHN is in jail for two essential reasons; first of
all he is a political person who calls into question the
validity of the super state which seeks to control all of us
and destroys those it cannot readily dominate. Secondly, his
harsh sentence dramatizes the absurdity of our marijuana laws
which are irrational, unjust and indefensible. Recently, the
National Institute of Mental Health submitted to the Congress
its hundred and seventy six page report "Marijuana and Health"
which comes to the conclusion that quote For the bulk of
smokers, marijuana does not seem to be harmful, end quote.
Yet it is made a crime in every state with penalties ranging
in severity from life to six months in jail. On the other
hand, conventional cigarettes can be legally sold as long as
they bear a legend on the package that they can cause serious
illness or death.

Figure 7. DE-4 page 5.

"REALLY UNITE MUSIC AND REVOLUTIONARY POLITICS"   The informer's transcription of the John Sinclair Freedom Rally proceedings included Jerry Rubin's speech, transcribed without paragraph breaks, which makes it difficult to read (DE-4 page 7). Here, Rubin waxes eloquent about "a whole cultural renaissance" that Lennon was about to initiate — one that would "really unite music and revolutionary politics."

In his speech Rubin also called for "a million of you to turn up at the Republican national convention to humiliate and defeat Richard Nixon"—that's what the FBI was most interested in.

This document provides an example of the invaluable role the FBI played in creating and preserving unique historical records. There's nowhere else you can go to find speeches like this; no one else had the resources, or the motivation, to produce and save verbatim transcripts of political rallies.

very involved in music, who are identifying to the culture you
and I are part of.   The family that you and I are part of
and for them to come on this stage, and for JOHN to sing his
song it ain't fair JOHN SINCLAIR and for JOHN and YOKO to
sing a song about the IRA and Attica state.   Its really
incredible.   It shows that right now we can really unite
music and revolutionary politics and really build the movement
all across the country. (applause).   It's like a whole, it's
like a whole cultural renaissance, is about to begin and if
JOHN and YOKO can come here we really have to go back to high
school and colleges and communitites and rebuild the movement
to rebuild the revolution because all the people who say the
movement and the revolution is over should see what's going on
right here, because it doesn't look over to me.   But there are,
there are a lot of problems, for example the amount of heroin
and dope that is smoked in the black and white youth communities
is really serious so many young, 15, 16, 17 year old kids
who are totally wiped out on downers, cause they have to find
some way to get through the prison of high school and college
and someway out of the prison of America, instead of building
a revolutionary movement the amount of heroin that is floating
around our communities, we have to drive the heroin pushers
out of our communities and build (pplause).   So heroin is
poison and you know it gets its source from Southeast Asia, Laos,
and then, it's shipped by the CIA back to the U.S. as a poison
to poison us so we don't make a revolution, that's why they
are pushing all this heroin into us.   (applause).   Also, there
is like a very strange spirit among young people today, a spirit
of tremendous mistrust, a spirit of which anybody who takes
an action, calls a demonstration, comes forward with something
is attacked by someone else, in the movement for being an ego-
tripper or media freak or doing something wrong, its a total
anti-leadership spirit, so the people are afraid take the
initiative or afraid to take actions, not because of what the
pig might do, but afraid to take, take action because of
what their own brothers and sisters might say about them.
Its a very strange thing that people are afraid to speak out
and that's why there's such a quiet across the country, cause
the moment somebody does something someone else right next to
him says, I didn't like what you did.   We have to give each
other a chance to make mistakes, we have to give each other a
chance (inaudible) because if we are our own worst critics, no
one is going to do anything, we are going to be paralyzed in
fear, and all the violence and hostilities that we felt against

18

7 CONFIDENTIAL

Figure 8. DE-4 page 7.

A NEW SONG "LACKING LENNON'S USUAL STANDARDS" The FBI also monitored and archived press coverage of targets of investigations. Lennon's Detroit file contains this newspaper clipping of a review of the John Sinclair Freedom Rally published in the *Detroit News* on December 13, 1971 (DE-3). In this one, the writer reports that the song "John Sinclair" "probably will become a million seller," even though it was "lacking Lennon's usual standards." The piece also complains that "Yoko can't even remain on key."

The ACLU cited this passage in court arguments as evidence that the FBI lacked a legitimate law enforcement purpose in investigating Lennon, arguing that the released information did not concern criminal activities. Singing off key, the ACLU argued, is not a federal offense.

(Mount Clipping in Space Below)

Lennon let his followers down

BY BILL GRAY
News Amusement Writer

If anyone went to the John Sinclair rally Friday night in Ann Arbor for the sole purpose of seeing a rare John Lennon performance, he had to go away disappointed.

Lennon was the drawing card that brought many, if not most, of the 15,000 young people to Crisler Arena.

But almost eight hours of speeches by radical leaders, poetry by Allen Ginsberg, country rock by Commander Cody and rhythm and blues by Stevie Wonder preceded the former Beatle's appearance.

WHEN HE DID, it was brief and one major factor nearly spoiled the whole thing.

He brought Yoko.

Mrs. Lennon may be the genius that John keeps insisting she is. Possibly, if he keeps heavily hyping her, someone might believe it.

But before a singer can be judged, she must first be able to carry a tune. Yoko can't even remain on key.

This was evidenced clearly when she sang "O Sisters, O Sisters," A Women's Lib tune she claimed she wrote for the "Sisters of Ann Arbor" the day before the rally.

STANDING beside her, Lennon managed not to wince. He even kissed her when it was over.

Lennon's portion of the show was hardly worth the wait — three songs, all of which were unfamiliar to the crowd.

They were so new that Lennon had to read the lyrics from a music stand as he sang.

His tribute to Sinclair, which began, "John Sinclair, in the stir for breathing air," was played on steel guitar.

BECAUSE of the name attached to it, the song probably will become a million seller and should make Detroit Recorder's Court Judge Robert J. Colombo an antihero in the subculture. "He gave him (Sinclair) 10 (years) for two (marijuana cigarets) what else can Judge Colombo do?")

It was an interesting piece, but lacking Lennon's usual standards.

Lennon and Yoko were dressed in matching black leather jackets, unzipped to reveal "Free John Now" T-shirts. Lennon wore small circular sunglasses. He was flippant and tried to give the crowd the impression that they weren't watching a superstar, but simply the working-class hero.

PRECEDING the Lennons were David Peel and the Lower East Side, positively the worst act I've ever seen. The greasy-looking Peel sang like a deranged gorilla. The lyrics of one song consisted solely of repeating "mara-wanna" about 50 times.

The best rock 'n' roll of the evening was provided by some local artists. Bob Seger (formerly with the System) and Teegarden and VanWinkle combined for the evening's musical highlight.

Seger's "Looking Back" may be only a four-chord progression piece, but it's well-performed, and the lyrics should go down as the subculture's national anthem.

Figure 9. DE-3.

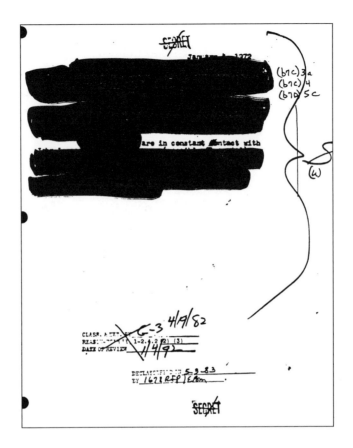

Figure 10a. NY-81, initial release.

CONFIDENTIAL INFORMANT REPORT   Three weeks after the John Sinclair Freedom Rally, FBI undercover agents in New York began filing reports on Lennon and his friends in the antiwar movement. These "Confidential Informant Reports" mostly describe mundane comings and goings. Here, in one dated January 4, 1972 (NY-81), no illegal activities or plans are reported; instead, FBI officials were told that "Stu and Jerry are in constant contact with John Lennon. Reasons unknown (possibly financial)."

This is the first of several mentions in the Lennon file of Stewart Albert. In 1993 he explained that Lennon "stated very firm guidelines" for any protest events in which he would participate: they would have to be legal and "within the framework of pacifism." "At no time in this or any other meeting on this matter," Albert declared, "was there ever any discussion or advocacy of illegal activities."

January 4, 1972

George Vicers was in the office today. So was Mike Drebineer, Carol Cullen, Alex, Chris and Tom, and Stu Albert. All of the above, except for the first two, are members of the Alamuchie Group.

Stu Albert is living with Jerry Rubin when he's in New York. Stu, Carol and Mike are leaving for Washington on Thursday where they will stay in Carol Cullen's apartment.

Stu and Jerry are in constant contact with John Lennon. Reasons unknown (possibly financial). There will be an interim committee meeting Wednesday at 4:00 PM.

Stu will be traveling to Washington in Mike Drebineer's parents car.

(u)

Figure 10b. NY-81, *after settlement.*

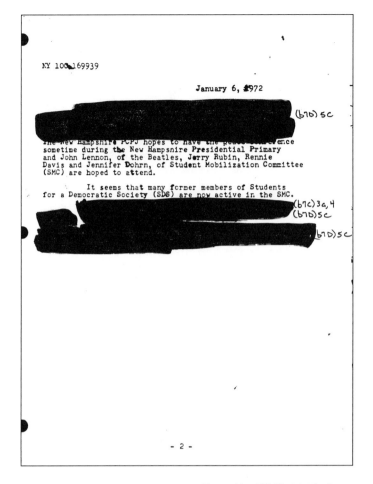

NY 100-169939

January 6, 1972

(b7D) 5c

The New Hampshire PCPJ hopes to have the peace conference sometime during the New Hampsnire Presidential Primary and John Lennon, of the Beatles, Jerry Rubin, Rennie Davis and Jennifer Dohrn, of Student Mobilization Committee (SMC) are hoped to attend.

It seems that many former members of Students for a Democratic Society (SDS) are now active in the SMC.

(b7c) 3a, 4
(b7D) 5c

(b7D) 5c

- 2 -

Figure 11a. NY-82, initial release.

NEW HAMPSHIRE "PEACE CONFERENCE"   Another confidential informant report, dated January 6, 1972, describes planning for a "peace conference" to be held in New Hampshire during the presidential primary in that state (NY-82). This is one of the pages withheld by the FBI for fourteen years until the 1997 settlement. Previously the government had withheld it under the claim that it contained law enforcement information provided by an individual who received an express guarantee of confidentiality.

The ACLU cited this passage in court arguments as evidence that the FBI lacked a legitimate law enforcement purpose in investigating Lennon. It was not a crime to plan a "peace conference"; it was constitutionally protected dissent.

January 6, 1972

The New Hampshire Peoples Coalition for Peace
and Justice (PCPJ) is planning a peace conference in
March, time and place not yet determined. At this time,
the Peach March is planned to resemble a mule train.
The New Hampshire PCPJ hopes to have the peace conference
sometime during the New Hampshire Presidential Primary
and John Lennon, of the Beatles, Jerry Rubin, Rennie
Davis and Jennifer Dohrn, of Student Mobilization Committee
(SMC) are hoped to attend.

It seems that many former members of Students
for a Democratic Society (SDS) are now active in the SMC.

Mike Drobenare is now using his parent's car
again.

The May Day Collective has an office in Washington,
D.C. (exact address unknown).

Figure 11b. NY-82, after settlement.

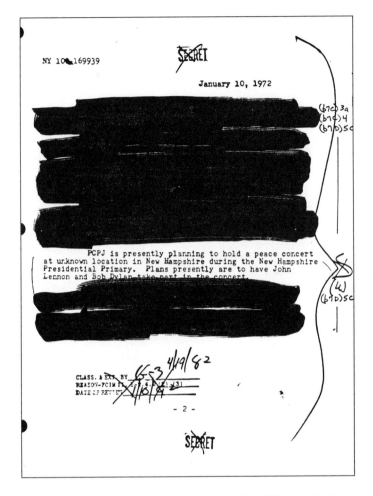

NY 100-169939

~~SECRET~~

January 10, 1972

(b7c) 3a
(b7d) 4
(b7D) 5c

[blacked out]

PCPJ is presently planning to hold a peace concert
at unknown location in New Hampshire during the New Hampshire
Presidential Primary. Plans presently are to have John
Lennon and Bob Dylan take part in the concert.

[blacked out]

(4)
(b7D) 5c

CLASS. & EXT. BY [handwritten] 4/19/82
REASON-FCIM II 2,6, 4. B (1,3)
DATE OF REVIEW 7/10/8

- 2 -

~~SECRET~~

Figure 12a. NY-83, initial release.

LENNON AND DYLAN   This confidential informant report dated January 10, 1972 (NY-83) was withheld in its entirety for fourteen years to protect the identity of the informant and then was released in the 1997 settlement of the case. It provides a vivid example of the kinds of trivial information the FBI collected and filed. It also includes erroneous information—in this case, that John Lennon and Bob Dylan are to "take part" in "a peace concert at unknown location in New Hampshire during the New Hampshire Presidential Primary."

The ACLU cited this passage in court arguments as evidence that the FBI lacked a legitimate law enforcement purpose in investigating Lennon. It was not a crime for anyone to take part in a peace concert.

SECRET

January 10, 1972

Tom Hayden is expected to be in New York City January 19 through 21, 1972. Alex Hladsky is making efforts to find speaking engagements for Hayden.

Mike Drobenare and Carrol Kitchens are presently in New York City.

Robert Greenblatt presently pays $75 per month to the New York Peoples Coalition for Peace and Justice (PCPJ) for use of one of the rooms at PCPJ Headquarters which he uses as his office. Recently Greenblatt has been spending much time at the PCPJ Office.

A male North Vietnamese exchange student at MIT named Dwon (ph) has contacted the New York PCPJ and wants to take part in anti-war activities. PCPJ has begun efforts to schedule speaking engagements for the student in New Hampshire.

PCPJ is presently planning to hold a peace concert at unknown location in New Hampshire during the New Hampshire Presidential Primary. Plans presently are to have John Lennon and Bob Dylan take part in the concert.

A peace concert has also been planned for the Boston area after the New Hampshire concert.

It appears that all of the equipment from the Washington, DC PCPJ Headquarters has now been transferred to the New York Office.

CLASS. & EXT. BY _____ 4/19/82
REASON-FCIM I, 1.4.2 (2) (3)
DATE OF REVIEW _____

- 2 -

SECRET

Figure 12b. NY-83, after settlement.

"ALL EXTREMISTS SHOULD BE CONSIDERED DANGEROUS" An "SA," or FBI "Special Agent," sent a handwritten memo to the "SAC," "Special Agent in Charge" of the New York FBI office, dated January 12, 1972 (NY-78). After reporting that Jerry Rubin appeared with John and Yoko at a press conference shown on local TV news, the agent added for his superior the message underlined and in large caps at the bottom of the page.

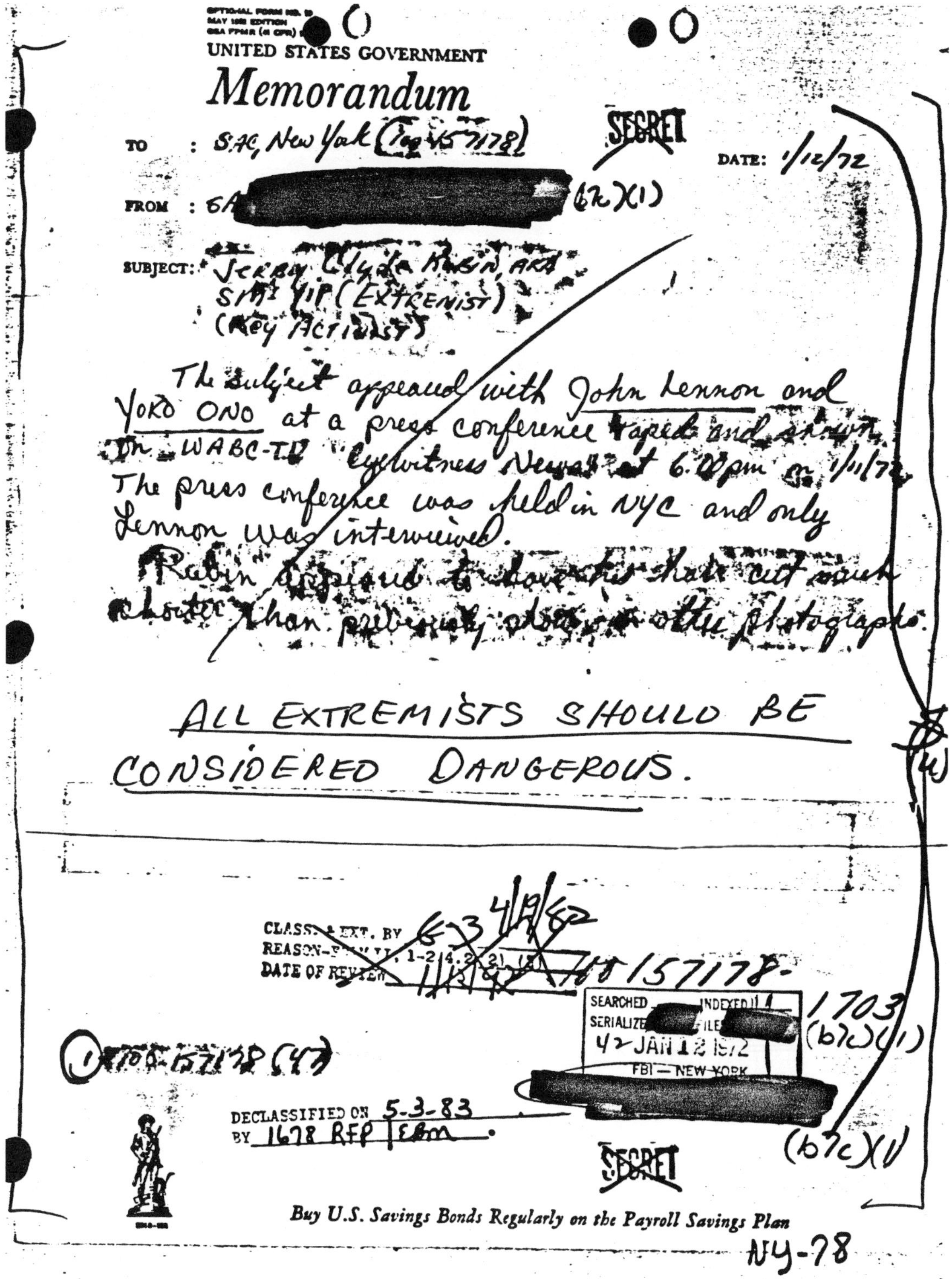
OPTIONAL FORM NO. 10
MAY 1962 EDITION
GSA FPMR (41 CFR)

UNITED STATES GOVERNMENT

Memorandum

SECRET

TO : SAC, New York (100-157178)

DATE: 1/12/72

FROM : SA [redacted] (b7c)(1)

SUBJECT: Jerry Clyde Rubin, AKA
SM - YIP (EXTREMIST)
(Key Activist)

The subject appeared with John Lennon and Yoko Ono at a press conference taped and shown on WABC-TV "Eyewitness News" at 6:00pm on 1/11/72. The press conference was held in NYC and only Lennon was interviewed.

Rubin appeared to have his hair cut much shorter than previously observed in other photographs.

ALL EXTREMISTS SHOULD BE CONSIDERED DANGEROUS.

(S)(U)

CLASS. & EXT. BY 6-3 4/19/82
REASON-FCIM II, 1-2.4.2 (2) (3)
DATE OF REVIEW 1/13/92

100-157178-

SEARCHED [redacted] INDEXED
SERIALIZED [redacted] FILED
42 JAN 12 1972
FBI — NEW YORK

1703 (b7c)(1)

(1) 100-157178 (47)

[redacted]

DECLASSIFIED ON 5-3-83
BY 1678 RFP | EBM

(b7c)(1)

SECRET

Buy U.S. Savings Bonds Regularly on the Payroll Savings Plan

NY-78

Figure 13. NY-78.

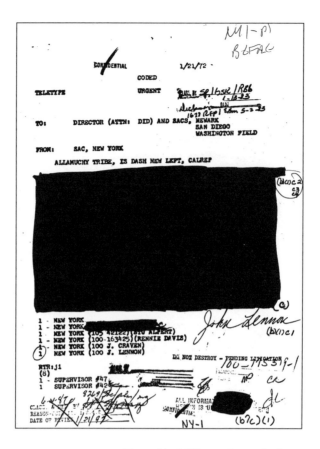

Figure 14a. NY-1 page 1, initial release.

"NATIONAL SECURITY" MATTERS: OPENING A NEW YORK OFFICE   The first item listed in Lennon's New York FBI file (NY-1) is an urgent coded teletype addressed to J. Edgar Hoover, dated January 21, 1972, the entire body of which had been withheld on national security grounds. The codes in the right margin of the initial release refer to different subcategories of the national security exemption to the FOIA: (b)(1)c2 to "intelligence source data collection capability"; (b)(1)c3 to information provided by an intelligence source; (b)(1)c4 to dates information furnished by an intelligence source.

The FBI originally claimed disclosure of this information could "enable a hostile analyst to unravel the cloak of secrecy that protects the intelligence source's identity," "allow hostile entities' assessment . . . of areas and targets which may have been compromised," and "result in termination of the source . . . and possible loss of life."

DECLASSIFIED BY 1678 RFP/EBM CONFIDENTIAL
ON 5/7/84

2/21/72

CODED

TELETYPE URGENT

CLASS. BY SP. NDSR/RBB 1-13-83
Declassify 1678 RFP/EBM 5-2-83

TO: DIRECTOR (ATTN: DID) AND SACS, NEWARK
SAN DIEGO
WASHINGTON FIELD

FROM: SAC, NEW YORK

ALLAMUCHY TRIBE, IS DASH NEW LEFT, CALREP

INSTANT DATE, SOURCE, WHO HAS FURNISHED RELIABLE INFORMATION IN THE PAST, ADVISED THAT THE ALLAMUCHY TRIBE IS TO OPEN AN OFFICE IN NYC DURING THE NEXT TWO WEEKS. SOURCE STATED THIS GROUP WAS FORMED FROM MEETINGS HELD AT THE PETER STUYVESANT FARM, ALLAMUCHY, NJ, DURING THE LAST MONTH. MEMBERS OF THIS GROUP, HEADED BY RENNIE DAVIS, INCLUDE STU ALPERT, J. CRAVEN. SOURCE NOTED ALL INDIVIDUALS PARTICIPATING IN THIS ENITY WERE ~~HARD CORE NEW LEFT~~ ACTIVISTS FORMERLY ASSOCIATED WITH MAYDAY AND PEOPLES COALITION FOR PEACE AND JUSTICE (PCPJ). SOURCE FURTHER ADVISED THE PURPOSE OF THIS GROUP WAS TO DIRECT MOVEMENT ACTIVITIES DURING THE ELECTION YEAR TO CULMINATE WITH (X) John Lennon

b2
b7D

1 - NEW YORK
1 - NEW YORK [redacted]
1 NEW YORK (105 42122)(STU ALPERT)
1 - NEW YORK (100-163425)(RENNIE DAVIS)
1 NEW YORK (100 J. CRAVEN)
1 NEW YORK (100 J. LENNON)

DO NOT DESTROY - PENDING LITIGATION

NTR:jl
(8)
1 - SUPERVISOR #47
1 SUPERVISOR #42 [redacted]

100-175319-1
SEARCHED
SERIALIZED

b7C

6-14-84 8269/...
CLASS. & EXT. BY
REASON-FCIM II, 1-2.4.2
DATE OF REVIEW 1/21/97

ALL INFORMATION CONTAINED HEREIN IS UNCLASSIFIED [redacted]
CONFIDENTIAL

NY-1

Figure 14b. NY-1 page 1, after settlement.

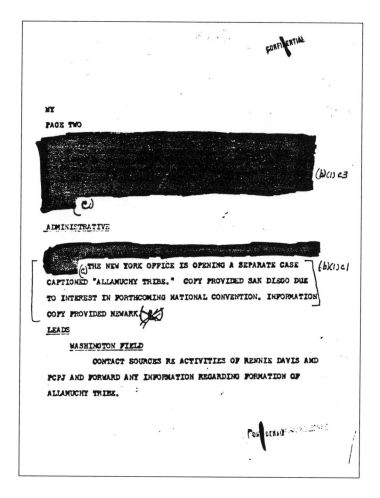

Figure 15a. NY-1 page 2, initial release.

"A LARGE SUM OF MONEY"   The January 21 teletype to Hoover continues with a report that the FBI is opening a case captioned "Allamuchy Tribe," named after a town in New Jersey where the founding meeting was reportedly held. Stew Albert, who is mentioned on the preceding page as one of the people participating in that meeting (misidentified as "Stu Alpert" here), later filed a sworn statement as part of the litigation over the Lennon files. In it he recalled attending "a retreat in a small community named Allamauchy," but declared that the group that developed the proposal for a political concert tour for Lennon in 1972 "never called itself the Allamauchy Tribe." Nevertheless the information reported here appears in several subsequent FBI memos.

DEMONSTRATIONS AT THE REPUBLICAN CONVENTION AUGUST NEXT.
SOURCE NOTED A LARGE SUM OF MONEY HAS BEEN GIVEN TO THIS
GROUP BY JOHN LENNON. JOHN LENNON IS IDENTIFIED AS FORMER
MEMBER OF THE BEATLES ROCK GROUP, WHO IS CURRENTLY RESIDING
IN NYC [R][U]

ADMINISTRATIVE

b2
b7D

[U] SOURCE IS IDENTIFIED AS ███████████
███████ THE NEW YORK OFFICE IS OPENING A SEPARATE CASE
CAPTIONED "ALLAMUCHY TRIBE." COPY PROVIDED SAN DIEGO DUE
TO INTEREST IN FORTHCOMING NATIONAL CONVENTION. INFORMATION
COPY PROVIDED NEWARK [U]

LEADS

WASHINGTON FIELD

CONTACT SOURCES RE ACTIVITIES OF RENNIE DAVIS AND
PCPJ AND FORWARD ANY INFORMATION REGARDING FORMATION OF
ALLAMUCHY TRIBE.

Figure 15b. NY-1 page 2, after court decision.

"TO: THE PRESIDENT"   J. Edgar Hoover sent a coded "priority" report on "Protest Activity and Civil Disturbances" to the president, the director of the CIA, and other top White House and military officials. This document, dated January 23, 1972, was released by the CIA. According to a letter from James K. Hall, chief of the Freedom of Information Section of the FBI, written a year after the FOIA suit was filed, the CIA "surfaced" this document and referred it to the FBI for review since the bureau was the source of the document. The list of addressees indicates the large number of government agencies and departments monitoring "protest activity," including the army, the navy, and the air force.

JB 02 01-23-72 12:1( ) KJB   8

CODE   PRIORITY

TO: THE PRESIDENT   SE**X**ET

TO: THE VICE PRESIDENT

TO: SECRETARY OF STATE

TO: DIRECTOR, CENTRAL INTELLIGENCE AGENCY

TO: DIRECTOR, DEFENSE INTELLIGENCE AGENCY

TO: DEPARTMENT OF THE ARMY

TO: DEPARTMENT OF THE AIR FORCE

TO: NAVAL INVESTIGATIVE SERVICE

TO: U. S. SECRET SERVICE (PID)

TO: ATTORNEY GENERAL   (BY MESSENGER)

                                          5 b1

FROM: DIRECTOR, FBI

~~CONFIDENTIAL~~

PROTEST ACTIVITY AND CIVIL DISTURBANCES.

    THE FOLLOWING IS A SUMMARY OF CURRENT INTELLIGENCE INFOR-
MATION RELATING TO DEMONSTRATIONS AND CIVIL DISTURBANCES GROWING
OUT OF PROTEST ACTIVITY.

END PAGE ONE

        ALL INFORMATION CONTAINED   8-19-80
        HEREIN IS UNCLASSIFIED   CLASS. & EXT. BY SP-1 GSK/DB/Cal-
        EXCEPT WHERE SHOWN   REASON-FCIM II, 1-2.4.2
        OTHERWISE   DATE OF REVIEW 1-23-92
                                   C-C22407

                    SEC**X**ET

Figure 16. CIA-X page 1.

"TO: THE PRESIDENT," CONTINUED   The second page of Hoover's memo "To: The President" includes John Lennon's name. The context is not completely clear but involves a report on the "Tribe," which, according to Hoover, "was organized to direct movement activities during the election year, which . . . will culminate with demonstrations at the Republican National Convention." It is notable that nothing in this document describes or refers to any plans for criminal activity or violations of the law.

CONFIDENTIAL   SECRET

ANOTHER SOURCE WHO HAS FURNISHED RELIABLE INFORMATION IN
THE PAST HAS ADVISED

67d

THE "TRIBE" IS TO BE HEADED BY RENNIE DAVIS, ONE OF
THE DEFENDANTS IN THE CHICAGO SEVEN TRIALS AND WILL INCLUDE
STU ALPERT AND J. CRAVEN, BOTH OF WHOM WERE ACTIVISTS IN MAY DAY
COLLECTIVES AND WHO PARTICIPATED IN THE ACTIVITIES OF THE PEOPLES
COALITION FOR PEACE AND JUSTICE. ACCORDING TO THE SOURCE,
THE "TRIBE" WAS ORGANIZED TO DIRECT MOVEMENT ACTIVITIES DURING
THE ELECTION YEAR, WHICH ACTIVITIES WILL CULMINATE WITH DEMON-
STRATIONS AT THE REPUBLICAN NATIONAL CONVENTION.

BEATLE SINGER JOHN LENNON.

END PAGE THREE

*Does not pertain
to the subject
of your request.*

SECRET

Figure 17. CIA-X page 2.

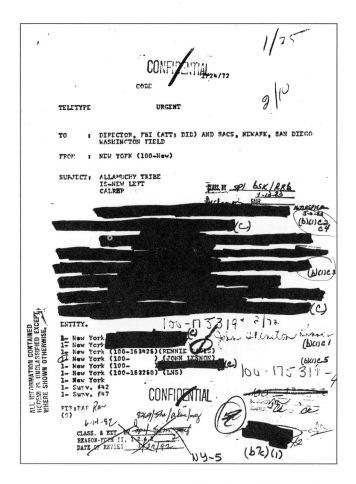

Figure 18a. NY-5, initial release.

"NATIONAL SECURITY" MATTERS: A $75,000 CONTRIBUTION   On January 24, 1972, the first document appears reporting that Lennon contributed $75,000 to the "Allamuchy Tribe" (NY-5), a report that would be repeated dozens of times in secret FBI communications in the months leading up to Nixon's reelection. It is an urgent coded teletype sent to Hoover and others by the New York FBI office. The original release deleted the entire body of this document under the claim that releasing it would endanger the national security. Parts of this document were withheld through fourteen years of litigation and then released as part of the 1997 settlement. The FBI continues to withhold a small part of this document under the national security exemption, next to the "(b)(1)" at the bottom left. That redaction remains in litigation.

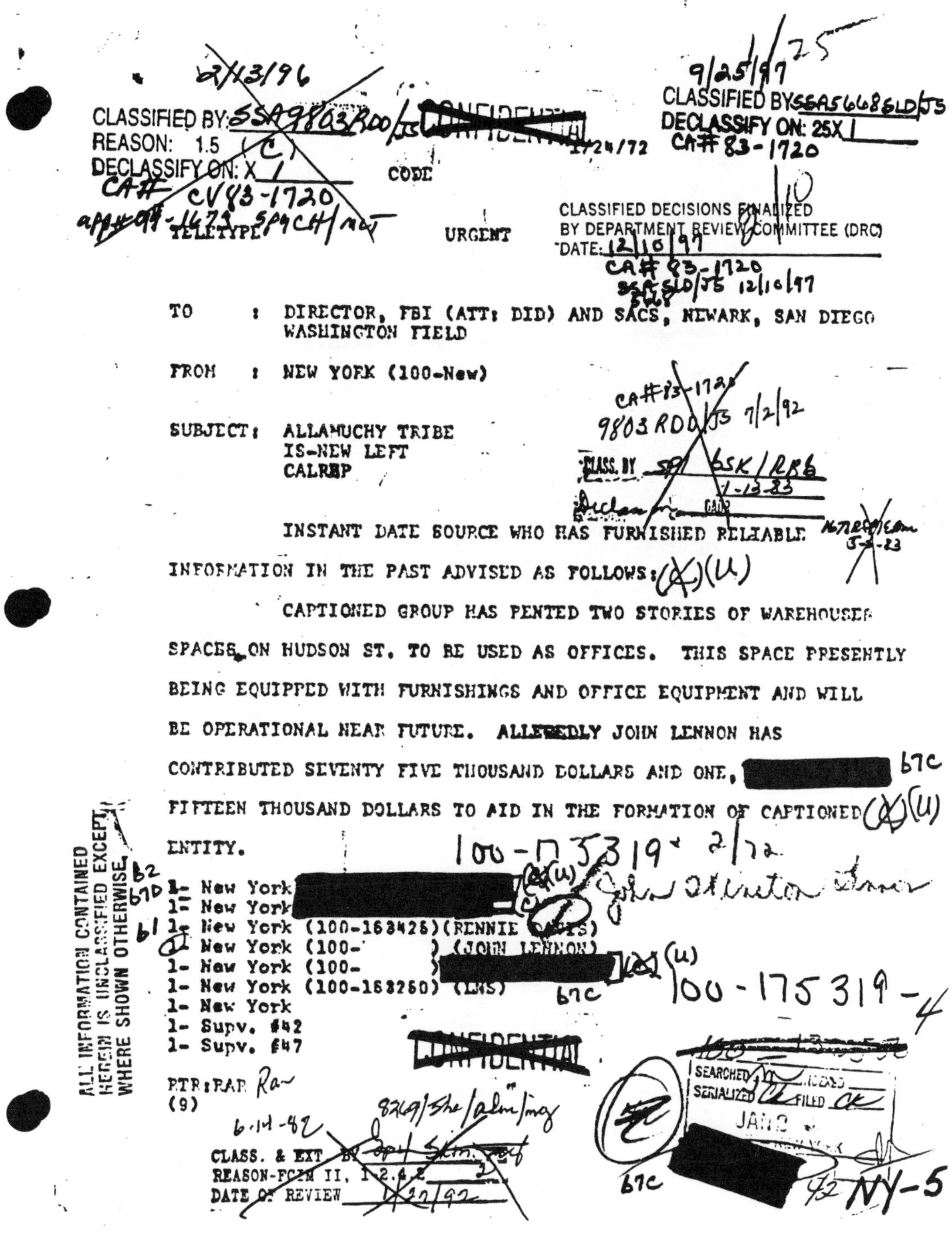

TO : DIRECTOR, FBI (ATT: DID) AND SACS, NEWARK, SAN DIEGO
WASHINGTON FIELD

FROM : NEW YORK (100-New)

SUBJECT: ALLAMUCHY TRIBE
IS-NEW LEFT
CALREP

CA#83-172X
9803RD0/JS 7/2/92
CLASS. BY SP 65K/RRB
1-13-83

INSTANT DATE SOURCE WHO HAS FURNISHED RELIABLE

INFORMATION IN THE PAST ADVISED AS FOLLOWS: (X)(U)

CAPTIONED GROUP HAS RENTED TWO STORIES OF WAREHOUSE

SPACES ON HUDSON ST. TO BE USED AS OFFICES. THIS SPACE PRESENTLY

BEING EQUIPPED WITH FURNISHINGS AND OFFICE EQUIPMENT AND WILL

BE OPERATIONAL NEAR FUTURE. ALLEGEDLY JOHN LENNON HAS

CONTRIBUTED SEVENTY FIVE THOUSAND DOLLARS AND ONE, ████████ b7C

FIFTEEN THOUSAND DOLLARS TO AID IN THE FORMATION OF CAPTIONED (X)(U)

ENTITY.

100-N5319 2/72

1- New York ████████
1- New York ████████
1- New York (100-163425)(RENNIE DAVIS)
1- New York (100-)(JOHN LENNON)
1- New York (100-)
1- New York (100-163260) (LMS) b7C
1- New York
1- Supv. #42
1- Supv. #47

RTR:RAR Raw
(9)

6-14-92   8269/She/alm/img

CLASS. & EXT BY SP Skin Sof
REASON-FCIM II, 1.2.4.2
DATE OF REVIEW 6/22/92

100-175319-4

SEARCHED _____ INDEXED _____
SERIALIZED _____ FILED OK
JAN 3

b7C

42 NY-5

Figure 18b. NY-5, after settlement.

Figure 19a. NY-23 *page 1, initial release.*

INFORMANT REPORT COVER SHEET   An example of the excesses of "national security" classification can be found in the cover sheet prepared March 7 for a confidential informant report dated January 25 (NY-23 page 1). Originally released as a completely black page except for file numbers and classification stamps, it was given five different national security exemptions, including "intelligence source information," "channelization/dissemination instructions for intelligence source information," and "identity of an intelligence source's contact." When the bulk of the page was finally released in the 1997 settlement, it turned out to be the FBI's FD306 informant report cover sheet form, with checked boxes.

2/13/96

CLASSIFIED BY: SSA9803RDO/JS ~~CONFIDENTIAL~~ 1/24/72
REASON: 1.5 (C)
DECLASSIFY ON: X 1
CA# CV83-1720
app#97-1673 SP4CH/MT

CODE

TELETYPE URGENT

9/25/97 25
CLASSIFIED BY SSA5668SLD/JS
DECLASSIFY ON: 25X 1
CA# 83-1720

CLASSIFIED DECISIONS FINALIZED
BY DEPARTMENT REVIEW COMMITTEE (DRC)
DATE: 12/10/97
CA# 83-1720
SSA5668SLD/JS 12/10/97

TO : DIRECTOR, FBI (ATT: DID) AND SACS, NEWARK, SAN DIEGO
WASHINGTON FIELD

FROM : NEW YORK (100-New)

SUBJECT: ALLAMUCHY TRIBE
IS-NEW LEFT
CALREP

CA#83-1720
9803RDO/JS 7/2/92
CLASS. BY SP1 BSK/RRB
1-12-83
Declass on OADR

INSTANT DATE SOURCE WHO HAS FURNISHED RELIABLE INFORMATION IN THE PAST ADVISED AS FOLLOWS: (X)(U)

CAPTIONED GROUP HAS RENTED TWO STORIES OF WAREHOUSE SPACES ON HUDSON ST. TO BE USED AS OFFICES. THIS SPACE PRESENTLY BEING EQUIPPED WITH FURNISHINGS AND OFFICE EQUIPMENT AND WILL BE OPERATIONAL NEAR FUTURE. ALLEGEDLY JOHN LENNON HAS CONTRIBUTED SEVENTY FIVE THOUSAND DOLLARS AND ONE, [redacted] b7C FIFTEEN THOUSAND DOLLARS TO AID IN THE FORMATION OF CAPTIONED (X)(U) ENTITY.

100-175319 - 2/72

ALL INFORMATION CONTAINED HEREIN IS UNCLASSIFIED EXCEPT WHERE SHOWN OTHERWISE

b2 b7D 1- New York [redacted] (X)(U)
1- New York [redacted]
b1 1- New York (100-163426)(RENNIE DAVIS)
1- New York (100-) (JOHN LENNON)
1- New York (100- [redacted] (X)(U)
1- New York (100-163260) (LNS) b7C
1- New York
1- Supv. #42
1- Supv. #47

100-175319-4

~~CONFIDENTIAL~~

RTR:RAR
(9)

6-14-82

CLASS. & EXT. BY
REASON-FCIM II, 1-2.4.2
DATE OF REVIEW

SEARCHED INDEXED
SERIALIZED FILED
JAN 2
NEW YORK

b7C

NY-5

Figure 18b. NY-5, after settlement.

Figure 19a. NY-23 page 1, initial release.

INFORMANT REPORT COVER SHEET   An example of the excesses of "national security" classification can be found in the cover sheet prepared March 7 for a confidential informant report dated January 25 (NY-23 page 1). Originally released as a completely black page except for file numbers and classification stamps, it was given five different national security exemptions, including "intelligence source information," "channelization/dissemination instructions for intelligence source information," and "identity of an intelligence source's contact." When the bulk of the page was finally released in the 1997 settlement, it turned out to be the FBI's FD306 informant report cover sheet form, with checked boxes.

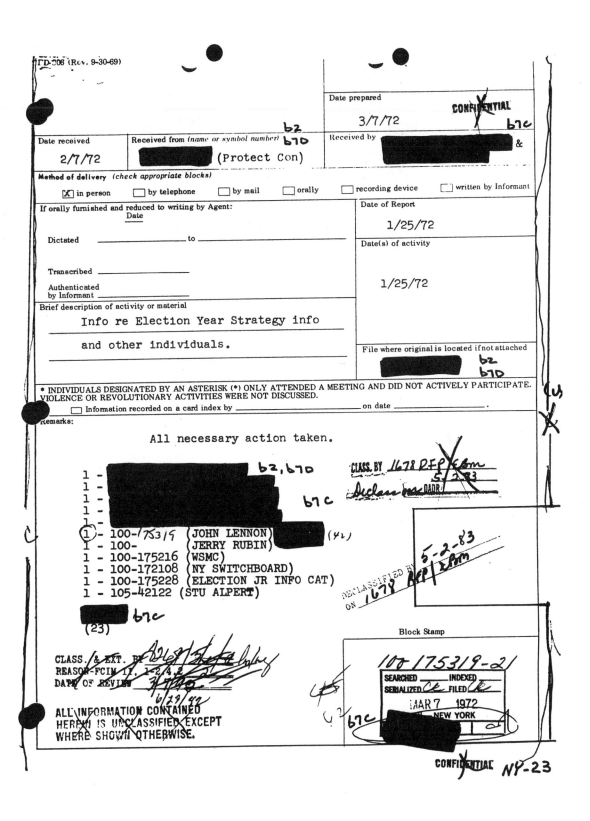

FD-306 (Rev. 9-30-69)

Date prepared
3/7/72   CONFIDENTIAL

Date received   Received from (name or symbol number)   Received by
2/7/72   ▮▮▮▮▮▮▮ (Protect Con)   ▮▮▮▮▮▮ &

Method of delivery (check appropriate blocks)

[X] in person   [ ] by telephone   [ ] by mail   [ ] orally   [ ] recording device   [ ] written by Informant

If orally furnished and reduced to writing by Agent: Date of Report
Date   1/25/72

Dictated _____ to _____   Date(s) of activity

Transcribed _____

Authenticated   1/25/72
by Informant _____

Brief description of activity or material
    Info re Election Year Strategy info
    and other individuals.   File where original is located if not attached
                                                             ▮▮▮▮▮▮▮

* INDIVIDUALS DESIGNATED BY AN ASTERISK (*) ONLY ATTENDED A MEETING AND DID NOT ACTIVELY PARTICIPATE.
VIOLENCE OR REVOLUTIONARY ACTIVITIES WERE NOT DISCUSSED.
[ ] Information recorded on a card index by _____ on date _____.

Remarks:
                    All necessary action taken.

    1 - ▮▮▮▮▮▮▮▮▮▮▮▮▮▮▮▮▮
    1 - ▮▮▮▮▮▮▮▮▮▮▮▮▮▮▮▮▮
    1 - ▮▮▮▮▮▮▮▮▮▮▮▮▮▮▮▮▮
    1 - ▮▮▮▮▮▮▮▮▮▮▮▮▮▮▮▮▮
    1 - 100-175319 (JOHN LENNON)
    1 - 100-   (JERRY RUBIN)
    1 - 100-175216 (WSMC)
    1 - 100-172108 (NY SWITCHBOARD)
    1 - 100-175228 (ELECTION JR INFO CAT)
    1 - 105-42122   (STU ALPERT)

    ▮▮▮▮▮▮
    (23)

CLASS. & EXT. BY _____
REASON-FCIM II, 1-2, 4.2
DATE OF REVIEW _____

ALL INFORMATION CONTAINED
HEREIN IS UNCLASSIFIED EXCEPT
WHERE SHOWN OTHERWISE.

CLASS. BY 1678 DFP/EBM

Block Stamp

100-175319-21

SEARCHED _____ INDEXED _____
SERIALIZED _____ FILED _____
MAR 7 1972
NEW YORK

CONFIDENTIAL   NY-23

Figure 20a. NY-23 page 3, initial release.

"FRONT MAN FOR . . . JOHN LENNON"　　This FBI informant report (NY-23 page 3) was withheld in its entirety for fourteen years, originally as national security intelligence source information. Disclosure could endanger the national security, the FBI argued, because it "would enable a hostile analyst to unravel the cloak of secrecy that protects the intelligence source's identity." The FBI abandoned that claim and released it as part of the 1997 settlement.

　　The final released version contains a deceptive white-out in the last line of the middle paragraph, following "The bulk of the . . . ". The FBI is supposed to black-out, rather than white-out, deleted words. In this case the missing word is probably "$75,000," the figure that is often cited in these files.

[Tuesday January 25, 1972]

b1D

                                                                This
is the first sign of tightening in the open house procedure
that has prevailed.

    One Michael LNU, acting as front man for Rennie
Davis, John Lennon and Jerry Rubin, came to Washington
Square Meth to the NY Office and had a long discussion with
William Kittredge about what was going down. The office
will be opened in 2 weeks - 1 month at Hansson and 10th
Street and will occupy 2 floors there. The staff that was
brought from Washington, DC appear to have some problems
with the middle leadership (Stu Alpert and Jay Craven in
particular). The staff salaries are said to be $125 per
week, and Rubins pressence in the top echelon in confirmed.
The bulk of the   is coming from Lennon-One.

    Renner and Kittredge went to the NYLC loft to
see William Smith about 8:00 p.m. and later went to Larry
Levy's returning to the church at 1:30 a.m. (1/26/72)
Joseph Pissarevsky was in touch with Revolutionary Union,
Dia Cooper with LNS, and C. Donham with AIO. The purpose
of all these meetings was to discuss a conference format
that this group has cooked up and to feel out the various
groups vis a vis the Red Balloon people.

Figure 20b. NY-23 page 3, after settlement.

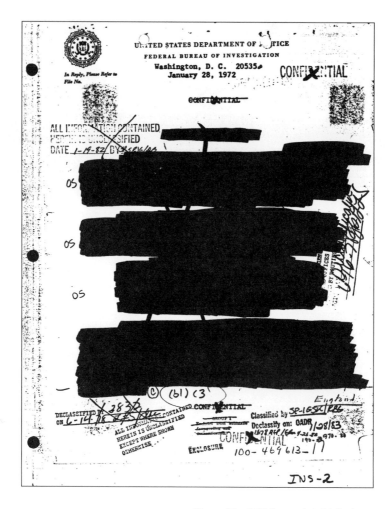

Figure 21a. INS-2 page 1, initial release.

ANTIWAR PLANNING   The entire text of this letterhead memo from FBI head-quarters in Washington to the INS, dated January 28, 1972, was originally with-held (INS-2 page 1). The FBI claimed portions did not concern Lennon ("O/S" means "outside the scope of request"), while the Lennon portions were with-held under the national security-intelligence source exemption. The full text was withheld through fourteen years of litigation and then released as part of the 1997 settlement.

Regarding "Stu Alpert," who is mentioned in this document as one of the members of the "Allamuchy Tribe," see p. 122.

UNITED STATES DEPARTMENT OF JUSTICE

FEDERAL BUREAU OF INVESTIGATION

Washington, D. C. 20535

January 28, 1972

~~CONFIDENTIAL~~

In Reply, Please Refer to File No.

APPROPRIATE AGENCIES
AND FIELD OFFICES
ADVISED BY ROUTING
SLIP (S) BY RW
DATE 8/2/84

DECLASSIFIED ON 4-27-84
1678 Rep 1eBrm
I Agree 1565 SDP/OH 3/4/89
Appeal # 83-1890(190-17725)

ALLAMUCHY TRIBE

On January 21, 1972, a confidential source advised that a group called the "Allamuchy Tribe" was planning to open an office in New York City, New York, during the following two weeks. The source stated that this group was formed from meetings held at the Peter Stuyvesant Farm, Allamuchy, New Jersey, during the Month of December, 1971.

Members of this group, headed by Rennard Cordon Davis, also known as Rennie Davis, include Stu Alpert and Jay Craven. The source noted that all of these individuals have been, or are currently affiliated with the People's Coalition for Peace and Justice (PCPJ).

The PCPJ in a press release dated March 1, 1971, described itself as being headquartered in Washington, D. C., and consisting of over one hundred organizations which are using massive civil disobedience to combat racism, poverty, repression, and war.

The source further advised that the purpose of this group was to direct New Left movement activities during the 1972 National Election Year, with plans to culminate with demonstrations at the Republican National Convention scheduled to be held at San Diego, California, during August, 1972. The source concluded by noting that a large sum of money has been given to this group by John Lennon, a former member of the Beatles rock group, and who is currently residing in New York City, New York.

DECLASSIFIED BY 2838

ON 6-14-78

~~CONFIDENTIAL~~

GROUP 1
Excluded from automatic
downgrading and
declassification

Classified by SP/GSX/RBG
Declassify on OADR 1/28/83
1678 Rfp/6

ENCLOSURE

100- 469 613 - 17

INS-2

Figure 21b. INS-2 page 1, after court decision.

Figure 22a. INS-2 page 2, initial release.

"ALLAMUCHY TRIBE"   The FBI originally withheld the top paragraph of this INS document (INS-2 page 2) under the national security exemption, claiming it contained "detailed information pertaining to or provided by an intelligence source." The second paragraph was originally withheld on the grounds that it was "outside the scope" ("OS") of a request for information about Lennon, and the bottom paragraph was originally withheld as "investigatory records compiled for law enforcement purposes which would disclose the identity of a confidential source who has received an explicit guarantee of confidentiality." The full text was withheld through fourteen years of litigation and then released as part of the 1997 settlement.

ALLAMUCHY TRIBE

On January 24, 1972, the same source advised that the Allamuchy Tribe has rented two stories of warehouse space on Hudson Street, New York City, and anticipates utilizing this space for offices. This space is presently being equipped with furnishings and office equipment, and will be operational in the near future. Allegedly, John Lennon has contributed $75,000.00 to aid in the formation of the Allamuchy Tribe.

On January 28, 1972, a second source advised that the Allamuchy Tribe is a name coined by individuals that attended the Allamuchy, New Jersey, meetings, previously described. This second source advised that any meetings called by New Left Activists associated with Rennie Davis in the future, that deal with the topic of demonstrations surrounding the Republican National Convention, 1972, would call the participants, members of "The Allamuchy Tribe."

This second source further advised that while individual meetings concerning the Republican National Convention would be known as Allamuchy Tribe meetings, previously mentioned Rennie Davis, Stu Alpert, Jay Craven, with the additions of John Lennon, his wife, Yoko Ono Lennon, and Jerry Rubin, convicted Chicago Seven Conspiracy Trial Defendant, were getting up office space in New York City, under the name "International News Service." The alleged purpose of the group would be to spear-head tours throughout the major states holding primary elections during 1972, presenting New Left movement messages, and attempting to encourage large numbers of individuals to demonstrate at the Republican National Convention at San Diego. This second source indicated that the office space being rented in New York City has been negotiated by the previously mentioned individuals, and that while, depending upon the situation, they call themselves "The Allamuchy Tribe" or "International News Service," these two terms are often used interchangably by individuals closely involved with Rennie Davis and his current plans.

Figure 22b. INS-2 page 2, after court decision.

Within the redacted document, partially visible text reads:

John Lennon is working very closely within May
Day and there may be a ~~~~~~~~~~~ the
Boston Garden

Marginal notations: (b7D)5c, (b7C)3a, (b7C)4, (b7D)5c

Figure 23a. NY-28, initial release.

A PEACE CONCERT IN THE BOSTON GARDEN   In this confidential informant report (NY-28), dated February 1, 1972, sent by the New York FBI office to its counterpart in Boston, an informer provides the names of "key contacts" who have signed a pledge stating they "will not support a war candidate." It was withheld virtually in its entirety through fourteen years of litigation and then released as part of the 1997 settlement. Clearly the FBI here was monitoring political activity protected by the First Amendment. Lennon, the informant reports, may perform at "a Peace Concert next month in the Boston Garden." Lennon never did perform in the Boston Garden, but even if he had, the FBI had no legitimate law enforcement purpose in collecting that information.

February 1, 1972] ∉(u)

b7D

∉(u)

Renne Davis is staying at Jerry Rubin's house.
May Day is at Odds with PCPJ. ∉(u)

Dave Dellinger is still in a hospital in Boston.
Some people in Harrisburg Committee said last Friday some
government agents were around. Please find some 3" x 5"
cards of key contacts in the Southwest. PCPJ is conducting
a campaign of Pledge signing. The Pledge states that the
signee will not support a war candidate. May Day promises
that San Diego will be like Washington, but with 100 times
the people. ∉(u)

Davis and Rubin still run May Day, but do not
wish the public eye to be cast upon them so they are running
the party from the background. ∉(u)

John Lennon is working very closely within May
Day and there may be a Peace Concert next month in the
Boston Garden. PCPJ refuses to pay any taxes, including
the phone excise tax. ∉(u)

Barbara Webster will most likely be in the office
Thursday (Wait for my call) ∉(u)

Figure 23b. NY-28, after settlement.

THE WRONG ADDRESS FBI confusion is evident on this page (WFO-2 page 2) of an urgent coded teletype to Hoover by the New York FBI office on February 2, 1972. It reports Lennon's residence as "Saint Regis Hotel, One Fifty Bank Street." Every cop and cabbie in New York knows the Saint Regis is on Central Park South, while Bank Street is in Greenwich Village. Lennon did live on Bank Street, and had for the previous four months, but not at number 150— that was a humble typo. His correct address was 105 Bank Street.

The New York FBI here requests a "photo of subject." Was this from a fan? Lennon was among the best-known people in the world, but apparently the FBI wasn't sure their agents could recognize him. The only photos appearing in the FBI files (aside from newspaper clippings) are in NY-7, FBI Current Intelligence Analysis, February 11, (see p. 164) and in HQ-24, the "wanted poster," (see p. 291).

HE IS PRESENTLY MARRIED TO YOKO ONO LENNON,

██████████████████████████████████

██████████████████████████████████   (b7c)(3)(x6)

██████████████████████████████████

█████████████████████

     INS LIST NYC RESIDENCE AS SAINT REGIS HOTEL,
ONE FIFTY BANK STREET. LENNON HAS SINCE MOVED TO UNKNOWN
ADDRESS.

LEAD

    WASHINGTON FIELD OFFICE IMMEDIATELYREVIEW INS
FILE REGARDING LENNON, AND FORWARD BACKGROUND INCLUDING
PHOTO OF SUBJECT TO NYO.

END

CORR IN CAPTION SHOLD BE (CALREP)

ASW WF FBI FOR FOUR

Figure 24. WFO-2 page 2.

THE CIA "CACTUS CHANNEL" MEMO   The first item in Lennon's file at FBI headquarters (HQ-1) is a memorandum to the FBI from the CIA. Dated February 3, 1972, it requests additional information about "LENNON's relationship with the 'Allamuchy Tribe.'" The word "Cactus" appearing in the last sentence on the page, "Please transmit reply via CACTUS channel," was withheld by the CIA through twelve years of litigation, until it was released under the FOIA in January 1993. CIA Information Review Officer Louis J. Dube declared in a 1983 affidavit that a "one word CIA cryptonym" was being withheld under both the (b)(1) national security exemption and the (b)(3) "sources and methods" exemption. The disclosure of cryptonyms, he explained, "would make it possible for . . . the intelligence service of a hostile foreign power" to "divine the nature and purpose of the CIA activity with respect to which the cryptonym is employed." This qualified as "damage to the national security" in terms of the FOIA.

The CIA explained its decision to release the document in a sworn statement from Lee E. Carle, the information review officer of the Directorate of Operations, and the successor to Louis J. Dube, whose earlier affidavit had justified withholding the cryptonym. "CACTUS," Carle declared, "had recently been released in another litigation," so he was releasing it in this litigation as well.

RECEIVED FROM

FEB 3 1972

CIA VIA COURIER

I- 360
3 FEB 1972

SUBJECT: John LENNON;
Allamuchy Tribe (NL)

1. Reference is made to your teletype 003, dated 24 January 1972, Subject: Protest Activity and Civil Disturbances, reporting that former Beatles singer John LENNON had contributed a large sum of money to the "Allamuchy Tribe", headed by Rennie DAVIS. (U)

2. It is requested that you furnish this office with any additional pertinent information concerning LENNON's relationship with the "Allamuchy Tribe" (b7D) 5c

(U)

Please transmit reply via [CACTUS] channel

classified per CIA letter
dtd 1/16/84 and affidavit

Declassified per CIA declaration
dtd 10/16/87 spt clo/msg 11/19/90 #20261

SPt clo/msg
1-25-84

105-222166

100-469910 - X
16 FEB 10 1972

5 - P3-2

FEB 14 1972 745

51 FEB 22 1972 ~~SECRET~~ b3 (CIA)

b3 (CIA)

HQ-1

_____

Figure 25. HQ-1.

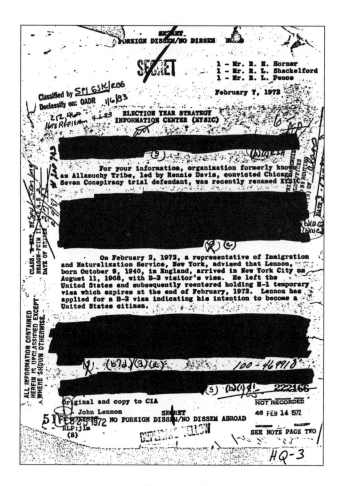

Figure 26a. HQ-3 page 1, initial release.

REPLY TO THE CIA The FBI replied to the CIA's request for information in a letterhead memorandum (HQ-3) dated February 7, 1972. In the original release of this document, several paragraphs were withheld under the national security exemption as intelligence source information. The FBI originally claimed disclosure of this information could reveal the identity of the source, which could result in "possible loss of life." The last paragraph, in which the FBI states that it has "no additional pertinent information" to report, was originally withheld under a different national security claim: foreign government information. According to the FBI's codebook, the disclosure of this sentence "can reasonably be expected" to lead to "foreign military retaliation against the United States." Nevertheless after fourteen years of litigation the FBI released the full text as part of the 1997 settlement.

154

SECRET
NO FOREIGN DISSEM/NO DISSEM ABROAD

SECRET

1 - Mr. R. H. Horner
1 - Mr. R. L. Shackelford
1 - Mr. R. L. Pence

I Appeal 1565 SDP/
Appeal # 83-1890
(190-17725) Page RFP/KJ 1-15-86

Classified by SP1 6JR/RBG
Declassify on: OADR 1/6/83

212,460
1678 RFP/EBm 4-6-83

CLASSIFIED DECISIONS FINALIZED
BY DEPARTMENT REVIEW COMMITTEE (DRC)
DATE: JUN 23 1989 1565 SDP/ 8/23/89

February 7, 1972

ELECTION YEAR STRATEGY
INFORMATION CENTER (EYSIC)

DECLASSIFIED BY SP4
ON 11/9/90 #208161

Reference is made to your memorandum captioned "John Lennon; Allamuchy Tribe (NL)," dated February 3, 1972, your reference I-360.

For your information, organization formerly known as Allamuchy Tribe, led by Rennie Davis, convicted Chicago Seven Conspiracy trial defendant, was recently renamed EYSIC.

A confidential source, who has furnished reliable information in the past, has advised that John Lennon, former member of The Beatles singing group, has contributed $75,000 to assist in the formation of EYSIC, formed to direct movement activities during the coming election year to culminate with demonstrations at the Republican National Convention during August, 1972. This source advised that other leaders of EYSIC are in constant contact with Lennon.

On February 2, 1972, a representative of Immigration and Naturalization Service, New York, advised that Lennon, born October 9, 1940, in England, arrived in New York City on August 11, 1968, with B-2 visitor's visa. He left the United States and subsequently reentered holding H-1 temporary visa which expires at the end of February, 1972. Lennon has applied for a B-2 visa indicating his intention to become a United States citizen.

On February 2, 1972, a second confidential source, who has furnished reliable information in the past, advised that Lennon and his wife, Yoko Ono Lennon, are currently vacationing in the Virgin Islands for health reasons and most EYSIC planning meetings will be postponed until their return to New York City, possibly during the second week in February, 1972.

100-469910

At this time, this Bureau has no additional pertinent information concerning other foreign sources of funds for the activities of EYSIC or Rennie Davis.

105 ~~222166~~

Original and copy to CIA

NOT RECORDED
46 FEB 14 1972

1 - John Lennon

51 FEB 25 1972

SECRET
NO FOREIGN DISSEM/NO DISSEM ABROAD

RLP:jlm
(8)

SEE NOTE PAGE TWO

HQ-3

CLASS. & EXT. BY SP4
REASON-FCIM II, 1-2.4.2
DATE OF REVIEW

ALL INFORMATION CONTAINED
HEREIN IS UNCLASSIFIED EXCEPT
WHERE SHOWN OTHERWISE.

Figure 26b. HQ-3 page 1, after settlement.

THE CIA "CHAOS" MEMO   The CIA released this teletype dated February 8, 1972 (CIA-3). The heading has been withheld except for the word "MHCHAOS." "MHCHAOS" was a secret, illegal CIA program of surveillance of domestic political dissent, a violation of the CIA charter. The program was launched in August 1967 under Director Richard Helms. The CIA sent Operation CHAOS domestic intelligence reports on political dissent first to President Johnson and later to Nixon, as well as to Henry Kissinger and John Dean, counsel to the president. Under Nixon, the CHAOS program was expanded to sixty agents, who, according to Angus MacKenzie, "became the Nixon administration's primary source of intelligence about the antiwar leadership."[*]

CIA Operation CHAOS was revealed in 1976 by Congresswoman Bella Abzug's House Subcommittee on Government Information and Individual Rights. The CIA director at the time was George Bush, who conceded in congressional testimony that "the operation in practice resulted in some improper accumulation of material on legitimate domestic activities."

Katherine M. Stricker, Information Review Officer for the Directorate of Operations of the CIA, answered questions about this document under oath in a deposition conducted by Mark Rosenbaum of the ACLU. He asked, "Do you have any information . . . that Mr. Lennon had any connections with a foreign government or a foreign nation with respect to his political activities?" "I have no information," she answered. Nevertheless in her affidavit she wrote that the withheld information on this page "consists of detailed reporting from a sensitive and reliable CIA intelligence source concerning certain activities of John Lennon and his affiliation with a particular group."

[*] Angus MacKenzie, *Secrets: The CIA's War at Home* (Berkeley: University of California Press, 1997), 30.

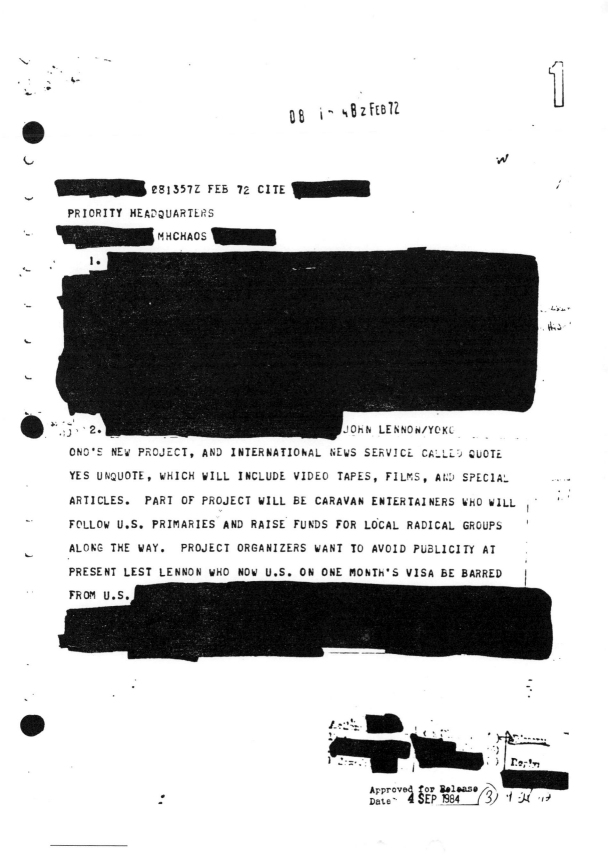

DB 1-48zFEB72

281357Z FEB 72 CITE ▮▮▮▮

PRIORITY HEADQUARTERS

▮▮▮▮ MHCHAOS ▮▮▮▮

1. ▮▮

2. ▮▮▮▮▮▮▮▮▮▮▮▮▮▮▮▮▮▮ JOHN LENNON/YOKO
ONO'S NEW PROJECT, AND INTERNATIONAL NEWS SERVICE CALLED QUOTE
YES UNQUOTE, WHICH WILL INCLUDE VIDEO TAPES, FILMS, AND SPECIAL
ARTICLES. PART OF PROJECT WILL BE CARAVAN ENTERTAINERS WHO WILL
FOLLOW U.S. PRIMARIES AND RAISE FUNDS FOR LOCAL RADICAL GROUPS
ALONG THE WAY. PROJECT ORGANIZERS WANT TO AVOID PUBLICITY AT
PRESENT LEST LENNON WHO NOW U.S. ON ONE MONTH'S VISA BE BARRED
FROM U.S.

Approved for Release
Date 4 SEP 1984

Figure 27. CIA-3.

"FROM: DIRECTOR, CENTRAL INTELLIGENCE AGENCY"   CIA Director Richard Helms sent this coded teletype to Hoover on February 10, 1972 (CIA-4 page 1). The subject is "John Lennon and Project 'Yes.'" Here, the CIA reports that Lennon is involved in a project "which will include the use of video tapes, films, and special articles"—not exactly a crime in America—and participation by "a caravan of entertainers." It's hard to see why any law enforcement agency, much less the CIA, had a legitimate reason for monitoring "a caravan of entertainers."

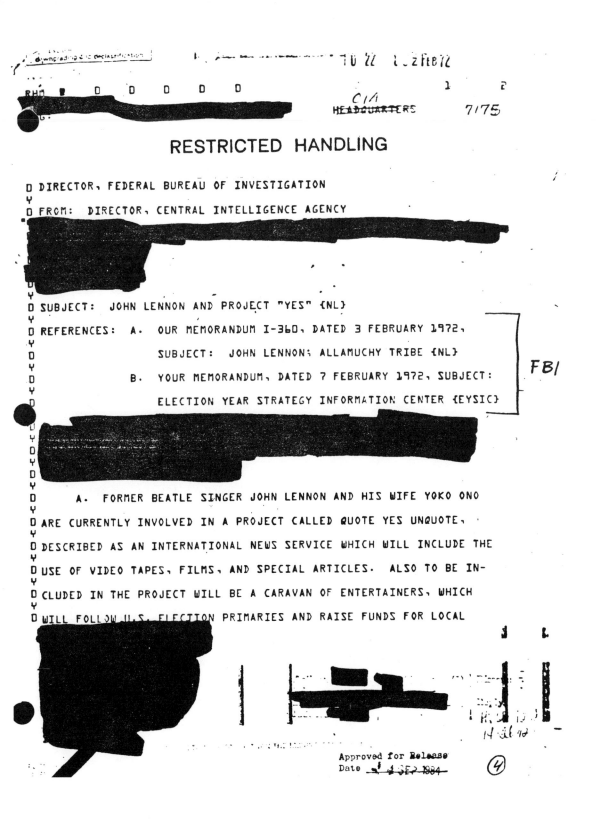

CIA HEADQUARTERS   7175

D DIRECTOR, FEDERAL BUREAU OF INVESTIGATION

D FROM: DIRECTOR, CENTRAL INTELLIGENCE AGENCY

D SUBJECT: JOHN LENNON AND PROJECT "YES" {NL}

D REFERENCES: A. OUR MEMORANDUM I-360, DATED 3 FEBRUARY 1972,

SUBJECT: JOHN LENNON; ALLAMUCHY TRIBE {NL}

B. YOUR MEMORANDUM, DATED 7 FEBRUARY 1972, SUBJECT:

ELECTION YEAR STRATEGY INFORMATION CENTER {EYSIC}

FBI

A. FORMER BEATLE SINGER JOHN LENNON AND HIS WIFE YOKO ONO

D ARE CURRENTLY INVOLVED IN A PROJECT CALLED QUOTE YES UNQUOTE,

D DESCRIBED AS AN INTERNATIONAL NEWS SERVICE WHICH WILL INCLUDE THE

D USE OF VIDEO TAPES, FILMS, AND SPECIAL ARTICLES. ALSO TO BE IN-

D CLUDED IN THE PROJECT WILL BE A CARAVAN OF ENTERTAINERS, WHICH

D WILL FOLLOW U.S. ELECTION PRIMARIES AND RAISE FUNDS FOR LOCAL

Approved for Release
Date _____ 1984   (4)

Figure 28. CIA-4 page 1.

RICHARD OBER   CIA-4 page 2 is the continuation of the coded teletype from CIA Director Helms to Hoover. Most of this page is blacked out, but the unredacted portion notes Lennon's precarious visa situation. This memo is dated six days after the Strom Thurmond memo proposing that Lennon's visa be terminated to prevent him from undertaking the protest activities described here.

The name "Richard Ober" appears at the bottom left. Ober was a counterintelligence specialist in the CIA's Directorate of Plans, which, according to Angus MacKenzie's history of CIA monitoring of domestic dissent, was "sometimes known as the dirty tricks department." Ober's work in counterintelligence included "stopping American publications from printing articles about questionable CIA operations," such as *Ramparts* magazine. Ober headed CIA Operation CHAOS; his team of sixty agents became the Nixon administration's primary source of intelligence about the antiwar leadership.[*]

[*] Angus MacKenzie, *Secrets: The CIA's War at Home* (Berkeley: University of California Press, 1997), 19.

RESTRICTED HANDLING

RADICAL GROUPS ALONG THE WAY.

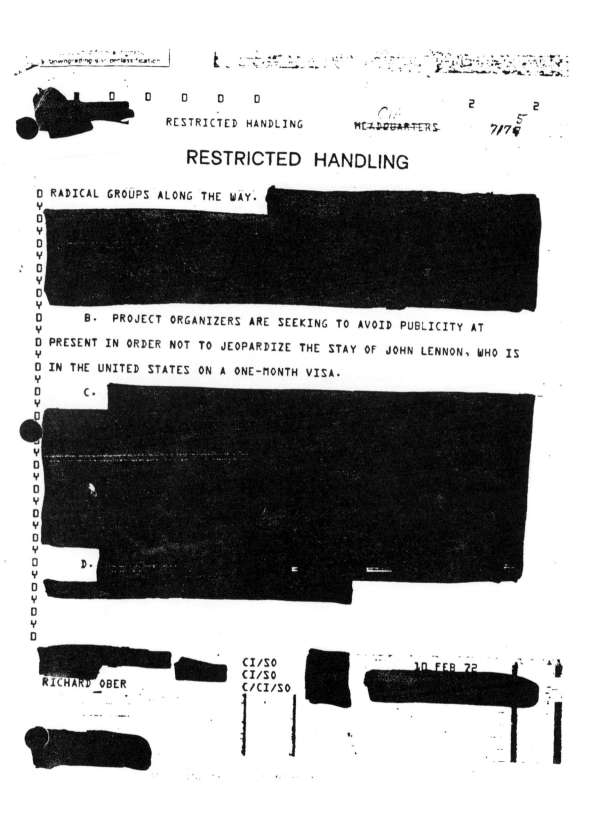

B. PROJECT ORGANIZERS ARE SEEKING TO AVOID PUBLICITY AT PRESENT IN ORDER NOT TO JEOPARDIZE THE STAY OF JOHN LENNON, WHO IS IN THE UNITED STATES ON A ONE-MONTH VISA.

C.

D.

RICHARD OBER

CI/SO
CI/SO
C/CI/SO

10 FEB 72

Figure 29. CIA-4 page 2.

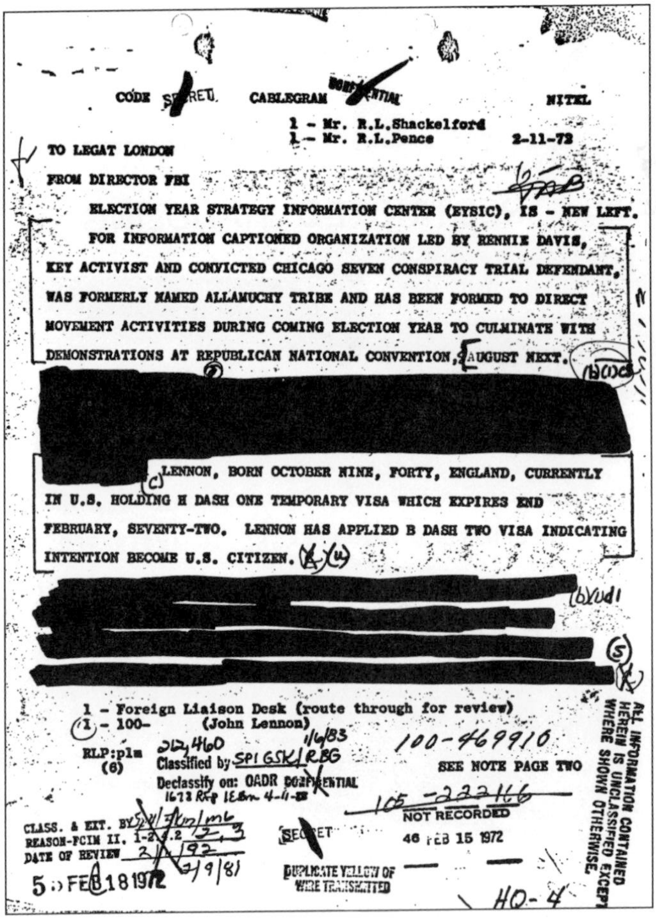

Figure 30a. HQ-4, initial release.

NATIONAL SECURITY DELETION: "MILITARY RETALIATION AGAINST THE UNITED STATES"

This coded cablegram (HQ-4), sent by Hoover to "Legat," the U.S. "Legal Attaché" in London, dated February 11, 1972, contains a national security deletion. The last four lines contain "intelligence information gathered by the United States about or from a foreign country, group or individual." The FBI claims disclosure of these four lines "can reasonably be expected to . . . lead to foreign diplomatic, economic and military retaliation against the United States . . . endanger citizens of the United States who might be residing or traveling in the foreign country involved." This claim remains in litigation.

CLASSIFIED BY ~~SSA9PB 3RDD/JS~~
REASON: 1 CODE O ~~SECRET~~
DECLASSIFY ON: X 6
CAF CV83-1220

CLASSIFIED BY ~~SSA 5668 SLD/JS~~
DECLASSIFY ON: 25X 6
CAF 83-1220 Rmt
NITEL

CABLEGRAM ~~CONFIDENTIAL~~

1 - Mr. R.L.Shackelford
1 - Mr. R.L.Pence   2-11-72

TO LEGAT LONDON

FROM DIRECTOR FBI

ELECTION YEAR STRATEGY INFORMATION CENTER (EYSIC), IS - NEW LEFT.

FOR INFORMATION CAPTIONED ORGANIZATION LED BY RENNIE DAVIS,

KEY ACTIVIST AND CONVICTED CHICAGO SEVEN CONSPIRACY TRIAL DEFENDANT,

WAS FORMERLY NAMED ALLAMUCHY TRIBE AND HAS BEEN FORMED TO DIRECT

MOVEMENT ACTIVITIES DURING COMING ELECTION YEAR TO CULMINATE WITH

DEMONSTRATIONS AT REPUBLICAN NATIONAL CONVENTION, AUGUST NEXT.

SOURCES ADVISE JOHN LENNON, FORMER MEMBER OF THE BEATLES SINGING

GROUP, HAS CONTRIBUTED SEVENTY-FIVE THOUSAND DOLLARS TO ASSIST IN

FORMATION OF EYSIC. SOURCES ADVISE EYSIC LEADERS IN CONSTANT CONTACT

WITH LENNON. LENNON, BORN OCTOBER NINE, FORTY, ENGLAND, CURRENTLY

IN U.S. HOLDING H DASH ONE TEMPORARY VISA WHICH EXPIRES END

FEBRUARY, SEVENTY-TWO. LENNON HAS APPLIED B DASH TWO VISA INDICATING

INTENTION BECOME U.S. CITIZEN.

b1

BULHM WITH AIRTEL COVER. REQUEST PERMISSION FROM SOURCES

1 - Foreign Liaison Desk (route through for review)
1 - 100-   (John Lennon)

RLP:plm   1-16-86/6/83   100-469910
(6)   Classified by SPI GSK/RBG 9803 RDD/JS SEE NOTE PAGE TWO
          Declassify on: OADR CONFIDENTIAL 7/2/92
                                        NOT RECORDED
CLASS. & EXT. BY
REASON-FCIM II, 1-2.4.2
DATE OF REVIEW   46 FEB 15 1972

5 FEB 18 1972   DUPLICATE YELLOW OF
                      WIRE TRANSMITTED   HQ-4

ORIGINAL FILED IN 100

ALL INFORMATION CONTAINED HEREIN IS UNCLASSIFIED EXCEPT WHERE SHOWN OTHERWISE.

CLASSIFIED DECISIONS FINALIZED BY DEPARTMENT REVIEW COMMITTEE (DRC) DATE

Figure 30b. HQ-4, after court decision.

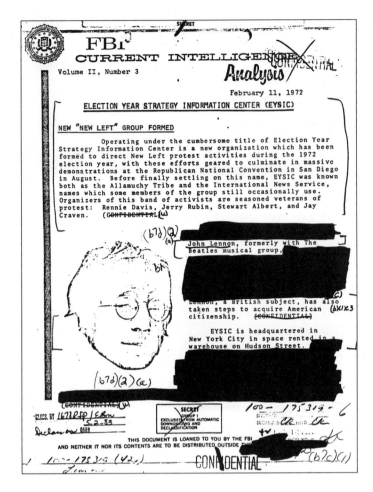

FBI
CURRENT INTELLIGENCE ~~CONFIDENTIAL~~
Analysis

Volume II, Number 3

February 11, 1972

ELECTION YEAR STRATEGY INFORMATION CENTER (EYSIC)

NEW "NEW LEFT" GROUP FORMED

         Operating under the cumbersome title of Election Year
Strategy Information Center is a new organization which has been
formed to direct New Left protest activities during the 1972
election year, with these efforts geared to culminate in massive
demonstrations at the Republican National Convention in San Diego
in August. Before finally settling on this name, EYSIC was known
both as the Allamuchy Tribe and the International News Service,
names which some members of the group still occasionally use.
Organizers of this band of activists are seasoned veterans of
protest: Rennie Davis, Jerry Rubin, Stewart Albert, and Jay
Craven. (~~CONFIDENTIAL~~)

John Lennon, formerly with The
Beatles musical group,

Lennon, a British subject, has also
taken steps to acquire American
citizenship. (~~CONFIDENTIAL~~)

EYSIC is headquartered in
New York City in space rented in a
warehouse on Hudson Street.

(~~CONFIDENTIAL~~)

THIS DOCUMENT IS LOANED TO YOU BY THE FBI
AND NEITHER IT NOR ITS CONTENTS ARE TO BE DISTRIBUTED OUTSIDE

CONFIDENTIAL

Figure 31a. NY-7, initial release.

"FBI CURRENT INTELLIGENCE ANALYSIS"   The issue of the FBI's classified publication "FBI Current Intelligence Analysis" dated February 11, 1972, has
Lennon on the cover (NY-7). The original release of this page deleted significant
sections as national security intelligence source information and as law enforcement confidential source information. It is not clear to whom or how widely
this publication was distributed.

February 11, 1972

ELECTION YEAR STRATEGY INFORMATION CENTER (EYSIC)

NEW "NEW LEFT" GROUP FORMED

Operating under the cumbersome title of Election Year Strategy Information Center is a new organization which has been formed to direct New Left protest activities during the 1972 election year, with these efforts geared to culminate in massive demonstrations at the Republican National Convention in San Diego in August. Before finally settling on this name, EYSIC was known both as the Allamuchy Tribe and the International News Service, names which some members of the group still occasionally use. Organizers of this band of activists are seasoned veterans of protest: Rennie Davis, Jerry Rubin, Stewart Albert, and Jay Craven. (CONFIDENTIAL) (U)

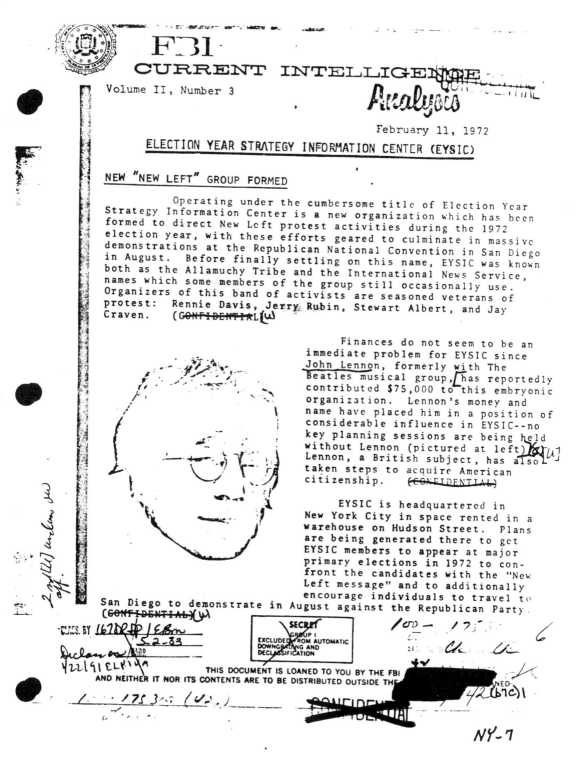

Finances do not seem to be an immediate problem for EYSIC since John Lennon, formerly with The Beatles musical group, has reportedly contributed $75,000 to this embryonic organization. Lennon's money and name have placed him in a position of considerable influence in EYSIC--no key planning sessions are being held without Lennon (pictured at left) (U) Lennon, a British subject, has also taken steps to acquire American citizenship. (CONFIDENTIAL)

EYSIC is headquartered in New York City in space rented in a warehouse on Hudson Street. Plans are being generated there to get EYSIC members to appear at major primary elections in 1972 to confront the candidates with the "New Left message" and to additionally encourage individuals to travel to San Diego to demonstrate in August against the Republican Party. (CONFIDENTIAL) (U)

SECRET
GROUP I
EXCLUDED FROM AUTOMATIC
DOWNGRADING AND
DECLASSIFICATION

THIS DOCUMENT IS LOANED TO YOU BY THE FBI AND NEITHER IT NOR ITS CONTENTS ARE TO BE DISTRIBUTED OUTSIDE THE

NY-7

Figure 31b. NY-7, after court decision.

"ALERT ALL PERTINENT INFORMANTS" Hoover sent instructions to FBI offices in four cities on February 15, 1972, ordering them to "expeditiously alert all pertinent informants" for information about Lennon's Project "Yes" (HQ-5 page 1). Three paragraphs in the two pages have been withheld by the CIA under the national security exemption. The CIA defended this deletion in a ten-page declaration written by the information review officer for the Directorate of Operations and in two other affidavits by CIA officials. These in turn were the focus of a forty-eight-page deposition with a CIA official conducted by the ACLU in 1992. Thus a considerable amount of CIA effort has gone into defending the withholding of three paragraphs in this document.

The CIA "obtained the information contained in the withheld portions . . . from a sensitive CIA source of intelligence," CIA Information Review Officer Louis Dube declared in his affidavit. "The information contained in the withheld portion is of a kind the CIA needs to perform its intelligence functions effectively, and is of a kind that CIA could not reasonably expect to obtain without guaranteeing the confidentiality of those who provide it."

Katherine M. Stricker, information review officer for the Directorate of Operations of the CIA, answered questions under oath about this document in a deposition conducted by Mark Rosenbaum of the ACLU. Stricker told Rosenbaum, "There is no phrase or sentence within that paragraph that could be released without reflecting upon the identity of the source." Rosenbaum asked if she knew how many other people knew the same information in the withheld paragraph. She said she didn't know. What if ten million other people knew the withheld information? Would she still withhold it on the grounds that releasing it would cause damage to the national security? "That is correct," she answered.

Airtel

2-15-72

To: SACs, New York
Los Angeles
San Diego
WFO

1 — Mr. R. L. Shackelford
1 — Mr. D. P. White
1 — Mr. T. J. McNiff
1 — Mr. C. D. Brennan
1 — Mr. R. H. Horner
1 — Mr. R. L. Pence

Classified by SP1 GSK/c/BS
Declassify on: OADR

From: Director, FBI

PROJECT "YES
IS - NEW LEFT

██████████████████████████

Recipients expeditiously alert all pertinent informants
for any information concerning captioned and submit positive
information developed in LHM with airtel cover. Recipients
promptly determine if captioned identical with Election Year

100 - 469910

1 — 100-   (Lennon)
1 — 105-131719   (Rubin)
1 — 100-443916   (Davis)
1 — 100-438281   (Hayden)
1 — 100-   (EYSEC)
1 —

NOT RECORDED
18 FEB 16 1972

APPROPRIATE AGENCIES
AND FIELD OFFICES
ADVISED BY ROUTING
SLIP(S) OF

DATE
SEE NOTE PAGE TWO

ALL INFORMATION CONTAINED
HEREIN IS UNCLASSIFIED EXCEPT
WHERE SHOWN OTHERWISE

FEB 23 1972

DUPLICATE YELLOW

CLASS & EXT. BY
REASON-FCIM III, I-2
DATE OF REVIEW 2/15

HQ-5

"HANDLE BY MATURE, EXPERIENCED AGENTS" Hoover's February 15 instructions to FBI offices (HQ-15 page 2) reminded them that this investigation "must be handled on an expedite basis and by mature, experienced Agents."

The ACLU's deposition of CIA Information Review Officer Stricker focused on the CIA's claim of the national security exemption for the last paragraph on this second page. ACLU attorney Mark Rosenbaum asked Stricker about Project "Yes": "Were meetings of this group public? . . . Do you know if this group publicized its goals, activities, or plans? . . . Do you know if its membership was public? . . . Do you know if anybody could join the organization? . . . Do you know if the CIA or the FBI has a file on this organization? . . . Did you make any effort to find out? . . . Do you know whether John Lennon kept secret his affiliation with this particular group? . . . Do you know whether any member of this group or anyone affiliated with this group was ever prosecuted for any activities with respect to this group? . . . Did you ever make any attempt to find out?" To each question she answered no.

Airtel to New York, et al
RE: [Project "Yes"] (X)(u)

Strategy Information Center (NYSIC), group led by Rennie Davis
allegedly aimed at creating disruptions during Republican
National Convention. (X)(u)

Recipients are reminded that investigative instructions
relating to possible disruptions during Republican National
Convention must be handled on expedite basis and by mature,
experienced Agents. Recipients carefully note dissemination
instructions on above information from C. (X)(u)

NOTE:

(b)(1) CIA

(S)

- 2 -

Figure 33. HQ-5 page 2.

Figure 34a. NY-19 page 1, initial release.

"JOHN WINSTON LENNON: CONFIDENTIAL"   The FBI in its court filings described this document (NY-19 page 1), dated February 22, 1972, as a "Letterhead Memorandum from Legat, London"—the "Legal Attaché" at the American Embassy there. "Legal Attaché" was the cover title the FBI gave its agents working overseas. The text contains "information provided by a foreign government" and "intelligence information gathered by the United States about or from a foreign country, group or individual." Release of the information on this page, according to the FBI, "can reasonably be expected to inter alia: lead to foreign diplomatic, economic and military retaliation against the United States." The withheld information remains the subject of litigation.

UNITED STATES DEPARTMENT OF JUSTICE
FEDERAL BUREAU OF INVESTIGATION
WASHINGTON, D.C. 20535

~~SECRET~~

In Reply, Please Refer to
File No.

February 22, 1972

JOHN WINSTON LENNON

67D

[large redaction block]

b1

X(5)

67D   stated that

[redaction]

b1

X(6)

CLASS. & EXT. BY
REASON FCIM II 7-2/4.2
DATE OF REVIEW
6-15-4

~~SECRET~~

SEARCHED ____ INDEXED ____
SERIALIZED ____ FILED ____
MAR 3 1972
FBI—NEW YORK

100 175319. 18

GROUP
cluded from auto
downgrading and
declassification

"POSSIBLE LOSS OF LIFE"   The continuation of the blacked-out memo dated February 22, 1972, which the FBI in its court filings describes as a "Letterhead Memorandum from Legat, London" has also been mostly withheld (NY-19 page 2).

For this page, the FBI codebook describes "Damage to the National Security Reasonably Expected to Result from Disclosure of This Category of Information: disclosure could reveal the existence of a particular intelligence or counter-intelligence investigation/operation. Disclosure could reveal or indicate the nature, objectives, requirements, priorities, scope or thrust of the intelligence or counter-intelligence investigation/operation. . . . Such disclosure would allow hostile entities' assessment of areas and targets which may have been compromised."

"Disclosure of this category of information can also lead to exposure of intelligence sources. Exposure of an intelligence source can result in termination of the source . . . and possible loss of life, jobs, friends, status, etc., all of which can reasonably be expected to . . . result in damage to the national security."

CONFIDENTIAL

Re: JOHN WINSTON LENNON

(b7D)   related

(b1)

(b7D)   asserted

(b1)

(b7C)
(b7D)

advised on February 15, 1972
that JOHN WINSTON LENNON, born October 9, 1940 in Liverpool,
England, on November 28, 1968, at Marylebone Magistrates
Court, London, pleaded guilty to possessing dangerous drugs
(cannabis). He was fined £150 and ordered to pay £21 costs.

The records of the Visa Section, American Embassy,
London, as of February 15, 1972, revealed that JOHN LENNON
last appeared at this Embassy on August 13, 1971. He was

CONFIDENTIAL

NY-19

2.

Figure 35. NY-19 page 2.

AN "EXTREMIST" AND "KEY ACTIVIST" NY-10 is a handwritten memo dated February 22, 1972, from an unidentified FBI agent to the special agent in charge of the FBI office in New York. The subject heading indicates that Jerry Rubin was classified differently from Lennon. Rubin was listed as an "Extremist" and "Key Activist." According to Ann Mari Buitrago and Leon Immerman's book *Are You Now or Have You Ever Been in the FBI Files?*, the FBI Manual of Instruction defines "extremist" as those whose activities "aimed at overthrowing, destroying, or undermining the Government of the United States . . . by illegal means or denying the rights of individuals under the Constitution." The FBI included among "extremists" the Black Panther Party, the Nation of Islam, the Ku Klux Klan, the American Indian Movement—and Jerry Rubin. The FBI's "Key Activist Program," begun in January 1968, called for "intensive investigation of every facet of the lives of a small number of political activists." Those on the "key activist" index were prime targets for COINTELPRO actions.

Lennon had a lower classification: "SM-NL" ("Security Matter—New Left"). "Security Matter" was the category the FBI had used since 1943 for investigations of individuals considered potentially dangerous to internal security.[*]

Here an FBI agent notes that Lennon and Rubin, both "currently of interest to the Bureau," were scheduled to appear on the *Mike Douglas Show* and requests that "Section 14 record the show." (For the FBI memo on the show, see NY-11, p. 181.)

[*] Ann Mari Buitrago and Leon Andrew Immerman, *Are You Now or Have You Ever Been in the FBI Files?* (New York: Grove Press, 1981), 206.

UNITED STATES GOVERNMENT

Memorandum

TO : SAC New York (100- 157178) P   DATE: 2/22/72

FROM : SA [redacted] (b7c)(1)

SUBJECT: Jerry Rubin.
SM- Youth International Party
(Extremist)
(Key Activist)
OO: NY
(100- 157178)
John Winston Lennon
SM- NL
OO- NY
(100- 175319)

ALL INFORMATION CONTAINED
HEREIN IS UNCLASSIFIED
DATE 6/9/4 7 BY [redacted]
8249/ shs/ alm/ jmg

Captioned subjects will appear on the
Mike Douglas Show, WCBS, New York channel
2 TV on 2/22/72. Show begins at
4:30 pm & runs until 6:00 pm.

In view that both subjects are
currently of interest to the Bureau & that
New York is origin it is requested
that section 14 record the show.

1- 100- 157178 (42)
1- 100- 175 319 (42)
1- Section 14 Supervisor
(3)

100 175319- 9
SEARCHED
SERIALIZED [redacted]
[redacted] YORK
(b7c)(1)

NY-10

Figure 36. NY-10.

Figure 37a. NY-27 page 4, initial release.

"ALEX IS GROWING A FULL BEARD" The New York FBI office sent this confidential informant report, dated February 23, 1972, to its counterpart in Philadelphia (NY-27 page 4). In the original release, all five of the pages of this report were withheld in their entirety. The FBI withheld them on the grounds that they were "investigatory records, compiled for law enforcement purposes, which if released would constitute an unwarranted invasion of the personal privacy of another person" and "investigatory records compiled for law enforcement purposes which if released would disclose the identity of a confidential source who has received an explicit guarantee of confidentiality." Nevertheless the FBI released virtually the complete text as part of the 1997 settlement. This page contains such evidence of criminal activity as "Alex is . . . growing a full beard."

Mike Drobenare went to an unknown address for a meeting today, the address had phone number 431-6624. ✗(u)

There was a Mickey from the Peace Parade Committee (PPC) in the PCPJ office today. He is a white, male, 190 pounds, approximately 25, five feet nine inches, heavy build, shoulder length straight brown hair. ✗(u)

The following were found in Barbara Webster's phone book: Sue Leitner, 175 West 93rd Street, New York, New York, telephone number 865-9193, Steve Schere, PPC, telephone 343-6570; Florida Platform, Post Office Box 17521, Tampa, Florida, 33612. ✗(u)

The Florida Platform appears to be a mailing address for a peace organization. ✗(u)

The following information was also located in Webster's phone book: ✗(u)

As of November 15, 1970 there were 339 Prisoner of War alive in North Vietnam. Twenty have died, of that twenty fifteen died of wounds while parachuting and five died of disease. Nine have been released. ✗(u)

Webster left on February 23, 1972 for Washington D.C. and will be back February 25th. ✗(u)

The 9000 letters being mailed by PCPJ in their fund raising effort will be mailed from the 32nd Street Westside Post Office. ✗(u)

Michael Drobenare is in New York City at the present time. ✗(u)

Alex is still in New York City and is growing a full beard. ✗(u)

During a conversation concerning information received at ███████████████████████████ (name unknown) was attempting to locate ██████████ stated that ████████████ ✗(u)

b7D

- 2 -

"PASSÉ ABOUT UNITED STATES POLITICS"   In the continuation of the February 23 confidential informant report sent by the New York FBI office (NY-27 page 5), the informer makes the significant statement that an unnamed person "had numerous conversations with John Lennon and his wife about becoming active in the New Left movement in the United States and that Lennon and his wife seem uninterested. . . . Lennon and his wife are passé about United States politics." The ACLU argued in court documents that this page provides a classic example of FBI misconduct in monitoring people's political opinions. Despite this report, the FBI continued monitoring Lennon for another nine months, until Nixon was reelected.

has had numerous conversations with John Lennon and his wife about becoming active in the New Left movement in the United States, and that Lennon and his wife seem uninterested. ████████ can't seem to convince them they should become more active. ████ it was his opinion Lennon and his wife are passé about United States politics. ℱ(U)

b7D

- 3 -

THE MIKE DOUGLAS SHOW   Jerry Rubin is the subject of a letterhead memo prepared by the New York FBI for dissemination to other agencies, dated February 25, 1972 (NY-11). It describes Rubin's appearance on the *Mike Douglas Show*, February 22, 1972, during the week in which John Lennon and Yoko Ono were guest hosts. Why would the FBI be interested in the *Mike Douglas Show*? Perhaps because Rubin said, "We're going to support Nixon for President, because by going to China he is furthering communist revolution throughout the world."

The sober-minded author of the FBI memo concluded, "This document contains neither recommendations nor conclusions of the Federal Bureau of Investigation."

The VH-1 cable network replayed the week of Mike Douglas shows hosted by John and Yoko during the summer of 1997, and Rhino released the complete videos in 1998 as a boxed set with extensive annotation.

UNITED STATES DEPARTMENT OF JUSTICE

FEDERAL BUREAU OF INVESTIGATION
New York, New York
February 25, 1972

In Reply, Please Refer to
File No. Bufile (105-131719)
NYfile (100-157178)

Jerry Clyde Rubin

On February 22, 1972, Jerry Rubin appeared on the
Mike Douglas Television Show which was aired on Channel II,
Columbia Broadcasting System, from 4:30 p.m. to 6:00 p.m.
John Lennon, formerly with the Beatles musical group, and his
wife were co-hosts on this show. This program was tape
recorded and pertinent statements made by Rubin are included
in this memorandum.

Mike Douglas introduced Jerry Rubin stating his
feelings were quite negative concerning Rubin but that John
Lennon wanted him on the show.

John Lennon stated that Rubin was not at all like
his image as he and his wife were not like their image.
He stated he found something in Rubin that was artistic.

Mike Douglas asked, "What is Jerry Rubin thinking
about these days?"

Rubin stated, "Glad you asked that! We're going to
support Nixon for President, because by going to China he is
furthering communist revolution throughout the world, and also
encouraging communism at home. Anything to get elected! Even
though it's not appreciated by the right wing, it's appreciated
by the left.-I'm just kidding! What he has really done is
automate the war in Vietnam so that its machines killing people
create a situation where 43 people can be murdered at Attica,
create a situation where four kids can be killed at Kent State
and people are afraid. The atmosphere of the country is one of
his debts. I think the administration did this, and he is the
symbol of it. And so I'm working very hard with people all over
the country to defeat Nixon."

100 175319 10

This document contains neither recommendations nor conclusions
of the Federal Bureau of Investigation (FBI). It is the
property of the FBI and is loaned to your agency; it and its
contents are not to be distributed outside your agency.

SEARCHED
SERIALIZED
INDEXED
FILED

NY-11

Figure 39. NY-11.

A CIA REPORT   On February 23, 1972, the CIA distributed a memo describing "Foreign Support for Activities Planned to Disrupt or Harass the Republican National Convention" (CIA-2). The CIA released the memo in its entirety, according to CIA Information and Privacy Coordinator Larry R. Strawderman.

Lennon looms large in the CIA's report. The first section reports that the "Soviet-Controlled World Assembly for Peace and Independence of the Peoples of Indochina" was not asked to call for international demonstrations. The next point is that John Lennon, "a British subject," has provided financial support to Project "Yes," which paid the travel expenses of "a representative" of Rennie Davis to an antiwar meeting in Paris.

SUBJECT: Foreign Support For Activities Planned to Disrupt
or Harass the Republican National Convention

1. There are only limited indications thus far of
foreign efforts to inspire, support or take advantage of
activities designed to disrupt or harass the National
Convention of the Republican Party in San Diego, 21-23
August 1972.

2. Some American participants at the Soviet-controlled
World Assembly for Peace and Independence of the Peoples of
Indochina, held 11-13 February 1972 in Paris/Versailles,
attempted unsuccessfully to include a call for international
demonstrations to take place at the time of the Republican
National Convention. A representative of the San Diego
Convention Coalition (SDCC), one of the domestic action
groups targetting on the Republican Convention, requested
the American Delegations' Steering Committee at the World
Assembly to include a specific call for international
support of activities against the Republican convention
in their proposal to the Action Commission of the World
Assembly. This request, however, was dropped as too
divisive by the Steering Committee, despite initial indications that the proposal would be taken to the floor of
the Assembly.

3. John LENNON, a British subject, has provided
financial support to Project "YES", which in turn paid
the travel expenses to the World Assembly of a representative of leading antiwar activist Rennie DAVIS. (DAVIS' representative is tentatively planning to assist in preparations
for disruptive actions at the San Diego Convention.)
Project "YES" is an adjunct to another LENNON-supported project, the Election Year Strategy Information Center (EYSIC),
of which Rennie DAVIS is a key leader, which was set up to
direct New Left protest activities at the Republican
National Convention. In Paris Rennie DAVIS' representative
to the World Assembly met at least once with officials of
the Provisional Revolutionary Government of South Vietnam;
it is not known if the Republican National Convention was
discussed.

G

Approved for Release
Date 4 SEP 1984

00552

Figure 40. CIA-2.

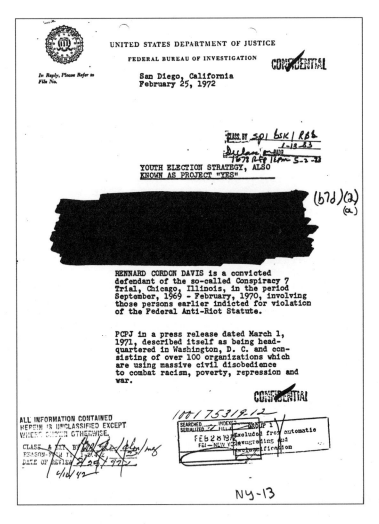

UNITED STATES DEPARTMENT OF JUSTICE

FEDERAL BUREAU OF INVESTIGATION

CONFIDENTIAL

In Reply, Please Refer to
File No.

San Diego, California
February 25, 1972

YOUTH ELECTION STRATEGY, ALSO
KNOWN AS PROJECT "YES"

(b7d)(d)
(a)

RENNARD CORDON DAVIS is a convicted
defendant of the so-called Conspiracy 7
Trial, Chicago, Illinois, in the period
September, 1969 - February, 1970, involving
those persons earlier indicted for violation
of the Federal Anti-Riot Statute.

PCPJ in a press release dated March 1,
1971, described itself as being headquartered in Washington, D. C. and consisting of over 100 organizations which
are using massive civil disobedience
to combat racism, poverty, repression and
war.

CONFIDENTIAL

ALL INFORMATION CONTAINED
HEREIN IS UNCLASSIFIED EXCEPT
WHERE SHOWN OTHERWISE.

CLASS. & EXT. BY
REASON-FCIM II 1-2.4.2
DATE OF REVIEW

SEARCHED _____ INDEX
SERIALIZED _____ FILED
FEB 28 197
FBI — NEW YORK

NY-13

Figure 41a. NY-13 page 1, initial release.

THE RENNIE DAVIS MEMO   The FBI office in San Diego, the city originally scheduled as the site for the 1972 Republican National Convention, distributed a letterhead memo on Project "Yes," dated February 25, 1972 (NY-13 page 1). The first paragraph of the original release was redacted under (b)(7)(D), investigatory records compiled for law enforcement purposes that would disclose the identity of a confidential source who had received an explicit guarantee of confidentiality. After withholding it through fourteen years of litigation, the FBI released it as part of the 1997 settlement.

UNITED STATES DEPARTMENT OF JUSTICE

FEDERAL BUREAU OF INVESTIGATION

CONFIDENTIAL

In Reply, Please Refer to
File No.

San Diego, California
February 25, 1972

CAF 83-1220

DECLASSIFIED BY 9803 RDO/JS
ON 7/2/98

CLASS. BY SP1 bslc/R86
1-13-83
Declan/ADR
1678 R-53 18pm 5-2-23

YOUTH ELECTION STRATEGY, ALSO
KNOWN AS PROJECT "YES"

        On February 3, 1972, a confidential source
advised that a group headed by RENNARD CORDON DAVIS,
also known as Rennie Davis, is in its first phase of
planning for disruption at the Republican National
Convention (RNC) to be held in San Diego, California,
from August 21 - August 23, 1972. According to this,
source, DAVIS and other associates from the People's
Coalition for Peace and Justice (PCPJ) recently moved
from Washington, D. C. to New York City.

        RENNARD CORDON DAVIS is a convicted
defendant of the so-called Conspiracy 7
Trial, Chicago, Illinois, in the period
September, 1969 - February, 1970, involving
those persons earlier indicted for violation
of the Federal Anti-Riot Statute.

        PCPJ in a press release dated March 1,
1971, described itself as being headquartered in Washington, D. C. and consisting of over 100 organizations which
are using massive civil disobedience
to combat racism, poverty, repression and
war.

CONFIDENTIAL

100-175319-12

ALL INFORMATION CONTAINED
HEREIN IS UNCLASSIFIED EXCEPT
WHERE SHOWN OTHERWISE.

CLASS & EXT BY
REASON-FORM II 1, 2, 2
DATE OF REVIEW 2 25 97
4/14/42

SEARCHED_____ INDEXED_____
SERIALIZED_____ FILED_____ GROUP 1
FEB 28 1972 Excluded from automatic
FBI — NEW YORK regrading and
declassification

NY-13

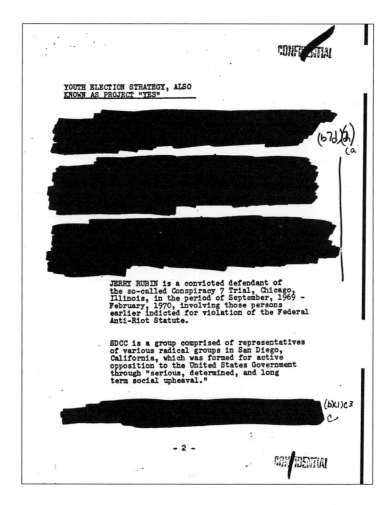

Figure 42a. NY-13 page 2, initial release.

THE "CROWD DRAWERS" MEMO   The second page of the San Diego FBI's memo (NY-13 page 2) also was heavily redacted in the original release on the grounds that it would disclose the identity of a confidential source who had received an explicit guarantee of confidentiality. After withholding it through fourteen years of litigation, the FBI released it as part of the 1997 settlement.

The memo describes "planning for disruption" at the Republican National Convention and reports that "the plans include rock concerts featuring JOHN LENNON . . . as the main crowd drawers." In describing the purposes of Lennon's concert tour, it lists "urge the audience to . . . register to vote" as the first goal, hardly an illegal one.

YOUTH ELECTION STRATEGY, ALSO
KNOWN AS PROJECT "YES"

According to this source, the plans for San Diego
include rock concerts featuring JOHN LENNON, formerly of
the Beatles rock music group, and his wife, YOKO ONO, as
the main crowd drawers backed up by lesser rock group
talents.

It was further related by this source that
dates have been reportedly been arranged in Florida and
New Hampshire and the concerts will include speeches by
JERRY RUBIN and RENNIE DAVIS, along with LENNON who will
urge the audience to (a) register to vote; (b) work for
the legalization of marijuana; and (c) get to San Diego
for the GOP Convention.

This source further stated that conflicting
reports make it difficult to analyze the proposed activities
of JOHN LENNON at this time. While this source indicates
LENNON may be coming to San Diego, other indications are
that he will perform along the East Coast only and contribute
a portion of his proceeds to the San Diego Convention
Coalition.

JERRY RUBIN is a convicted defendant of
the so-called Conspiracy 7 Trial, Chicago,
Illinois, in the period of September, 1969 -
February, 1970, involving those persons
earlier indicted for violation of the Federal
Anti-Riot Statute.

SDCC is a group comprised of representatives
of various radical groups in San Diego,
California, which was formed for active
opposition to the United States Government
through "serious, determined, and long
term social upheaval."

The aforementioned confidential source, along
with other confidential sources familiar with certain
phases of New Left activity in the San Diego area, advised

- 2 -

Figure 42b. NY-13 page 2, after settlement.

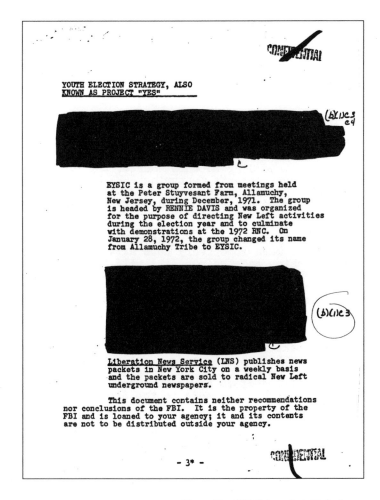

YOUTH ELECTION STRATEGY, ALSO
KNOWN AS PROJECT "YES"

(b)(1)(c.)
e.4

EYSIC is a group formed from meetings held
at the Peter Stuyvesant Farm, Allamuchy,
New Jersey, during December, 1971. The group
is headed by RENNIE DAVIS and was organized
for the purpose of directing New Left activities
during the election year and to culminate
with demonstrations at the 1972 RNC. On
January 28, 1972, the group changed its name
from Allamuchy Tribe to EYSIC.

(b)(1)(c.3)

Liberation News Service (LNS) publishes news
packets in New York City on a weekly basis
and the packets are sold to radical New Left
underground newspapers.

This document contains neither recommendations
nor conclusions of the FBI. It is the property of the
FBI and is loaned to your agency; it and its contents
are not to be distributed outside your agency.

- 3* -

Figure 43a. NY-13 page 3, initial release.

"NO SPECIFIC INFORMATION"   The San Diego FBI memo's third page (NY-13 page 3) contained two paragraphs withheld on a different basis than those in the preceding pages: national security intelligence source information. After withholding it through fourteen years of litigation, the FBI released it as part of the 1997 settlement. The withheld information turned out to be a report that "no specific information has been received regarding any such activities under the name of Election Year Strategy Information Center of Youth Election Strategy, also known as Project 'Yes.'"

YOUTH ELECTION STRATEGY, ALSO KNOWN AS PROJECT "YES"

on February 24, 1972, that information has been received in San Diego regarding proposed activities of a group headed by RENNIE DAVIS and including JOHN LENNON in connection with the RNC but no specific information has been received regarding any such activities under the name of Election Year Strategy Information Center (EYSIC) or Youth Election Strategy, also known as Project "Yes." (X) (U)

> EYSIC is a group formed from meetings held at the Peter Stuyvesant Farm, Allamuchy, New Jersey, during December, 1971. The group is headed by RENNIE DAVIS and was organized for the purpose of directing New Left activities during the election year and to culminate with demonstrations at the 1972 RNC. On January 28, 1972, the group changed its name from Allamuchy Tribe to EYSIC.

> Youth Election Strategy, also known as Project "Yes," is the video-tape arm of EYSIC which will eventually attempt to purchase the Liberation News Service in New York City. This group is controlled by JOHN LENNON, RENNIE DAVIS, and JERRY RUBIN, who are also key figures in EYSIC. They will make the contacts for video tapes, films, special events, and entertainers to raise money for the group to finance demonstrations in opposition to the RNC. X (U)

> Liberation News Service (LNS) publishes news packets in New York City on a weekly basis and the packets are sold to radical New Left underground newspapers.

This document contains neither recommendations nor conclusions of the FBI. It is the property of the FBI and is loaned to your agency; it and its contents are not to be distributed outside your agency.

- 3* -

Figure 43b. NY-13 page 3, after settlement.

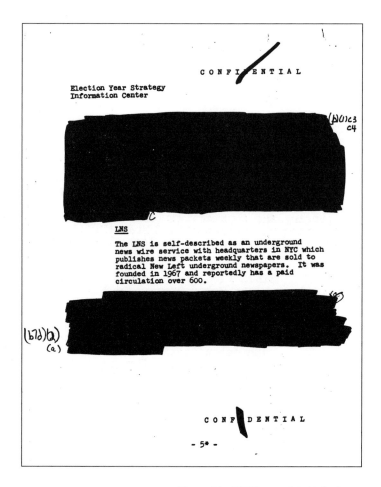

"FORM A MUSICAL BAND"   The New York FBI sent out a letterhead memo
February 28, 1972 (NY-15). The first and last paragraphs were originally redacted
as law enforcement confidential source information provided by an individual
who had received an explicit guarantee of confidentiality. If released, the FBI
argued, it "could reveal the identity of the source." Nevertheless, after withholding these two paragraphs through fourteen years of litigation, the FBI released them as part of the 1997 settlement. They concern office space and the
well-known plan to "form a musical band" that would "travel to several election
primaries."

Election Year Strategy
Information Center

On February 17, 1972, the first source advised
that individuals with EYSIC had formerly planned on using
a warehouse on the corner of West 10th Street and Hudson
Avenue in NYC as their headquarters. However, they had
abandoned the idea due to the warehouse space being in such
dilapidated condition. The source advised that at the present,
Jerry Rubin, Stewart Albert and John Winston Lennon are
working in office space at the Global Village, which is a TV
media type of organization in NYC. They are coordinating
plans to purchase the Liberation News Service (LNS) in NYC and
use its wire services and mailing list to expand the activities
of EYSIC. This group, a segment of EYSIC is calling itself
the Youth Election Strategy (YES), and it has the financial
backing of Lennon.

LNS

The LNS is self-described as an underground
news wire service with headquarters in NYC which
publishes news packets weekly that are sold to
radical New Left underground newspapers. It was
founded in 1967 and reportedly has a paid
circulation over 600.

On February 23, 1972, a fifth source, who has
furnished reliable information in the past, advised that the
Global Village is located at 454 Broome Street, NYC. The
source further advised that several members of EYSIC are
making plans to form a musical band to travel to several
election primaries. They will eventually travel to San Diego,
California to participate in demonstrations at the Republican
National Convention.

Figure 44b. NY-15 page 5, after court decision and settlement.

MILITARY INTELLIGENCE AND THE SECRET SERVICE   The special agent in charge of the FBI in New York sent an airtel to Hoover, dated February 28, 1972 (NY-16), which is significant mainly for the distribution list that appears at the bottom: forty-one copies of this information about Lennon's plans were sent to organizations ranging from military intelligence to the Secret Service to FBI field offices in thirteen cities.

F B I

Date: 2/28/72

CONFIDENTIAL

Transmit the following in _____
(Type in plaintext or code)

Via ___ AIRTEL _____
(Priority)

TO: DIRECTOR, FBI

FROM: SAC, NEW YORK (100-175228) (P)

SUBJECT: ELECTION YEAR STRATEGY INFORMATION CENTER (EYSIC)
           IS-NEW LEFT
           (CALREP)
           (OO:NY)

CLASS. & EXT. BY 92/69/3/ /a/a/ -8
REASON-FCM II 1-8.2   2
DATE OF REVIEW 9/26/92   6/15/82

    ReBuairtel, 1/26/72, Buairtel, 2/15/72, captioned
Project "Yes" IS-NL, and NYairtel, 2/17/72, captioned Youth
Election Strategy, IS-NL, OO:NY, NYfile 100-175438.

    Enclosed for the Bureau are 10 copies of an LHM
captioned and dated as above. Copies are being designated
for those offices having PCPJ, May Day Collective, or National
Political Conventions in their Divisions.

    Copies of the LHM are also being designated to INS,
108 MIG, USA, SDNY, and USSS for information purposes.

```
2 - Bureau (Encls. 10) (RM)
1 - INS, NYC (Encl. 1) (RM)
4 - 108 MIG, NYC (Encl. 1) (RM)
1 - USA, SDNY (Encl. 1) (RM)
1 - USSS, NYC (Encl. 1) (RM)
2 - Albany (Encl. 2) (RM)
2 - Atlanta (Encl. 2) (RM)
3 - Boston (Encl. 3) (RM)
2 - Buffalo (Encl. 2) (RM)
2 - Indianapolis (Encl. 2) (EM)
2 - Los Angeles (Encl. 2) (RM)
2 - Miami (Encl. 4) (RM)
3 - San Diego (Encl. 5) (RM)
2 - San Francisco (Encl. 2) (RM)
Copies Cont'd.
1 - New York
```

CLASS. BY *SP1 bsk/R86.*
1-13-83
Declassify OADR
1678 RFP/Eom 4-2733

100 175319 - 15

SEARCHED ___ INDEXED ___
SERIALIZED ___ FILED ___

trr (b7c)(1)

(b7c)(1)

Approved: _____   Sent _____ M _____ er   CONFIDENTIAL
    Special Agent in Charge   U. S. GOVERNMENT PRINTING OFFICE: 1971—413—135

NY-16

Figure 45. NY-16.

LENNON'S VISA REVOKED   The big news on March 2, 1972, conveyed to Hoover by the special agent in charge of the FBI office in New York, was that the INS had revoked Lennon's visa (NY-17), which meant the Nixon administration was going to try to deport him. The idea of deporting Lennon to silence him as a spokesman for the peace movement had been proposed by Senator Strom Thurmond on February 4. In his memo to Nixon Attorney General John Mitchell and to the White House, Thurmond recommended that Lennon be deported as "a strategy counter-measure" to his plans for an antiwar concert tour (see figures 1–2, pp. 3–4). That was exactly the sort of thing John Dean, the counsel to the president, had suggested in his famous 1971 memo: "We can use the available political machinery to screw our political enemies."

However, the information in this FBI memo is incorrect. Lennon's visa expired February 29. But on March 1, the INS granted Lennon an extension — apparently by mistake, since it was revoked five days later. March 6 is thus the day Lennon's visa was officially revoked.

FBI

Date: 3/2/72

~~CONFIDENTIAL~~

Transmit the following in ____________ (Type in plaintext or code)

Via AIRTEL ____________ (Priority)

TO: DIRECTOR, FBI

FROM: SAC, NEW YORK (100-175228) (P)

SUBJECT: ELECTION YEAR STRATEGY
INFORMATION CENTER
IS - NEW LEFT
(CALREP)
(OO:NY)

Re NY airtel and LHM dated 2/28/72; and San Diego airtel and LHM dated 2/25/72 captioned "YOUTH ELECTION STRATEGY IS - NL".

(b7c)(4)

On 3/2/72, [redacted] Immigration Officer, Immigration and Naturalization Service, 20 West Broadway, NYC, advised that on 3/1/72 INS served notice to JOHN WINSTON LENNON and his wife YOKO ONO LENNON to be out of the United States by 3/15/72, that their visas had been recalled.

LEAD:

NEW YORK

AT NEW YORK, NEW YORK. Will keep Bureau advised

4-Bureau (RM)
2-Miami (RM)
2-San Diego (RM)
0-New York (100-175319) (LENNON)
1-New York (100-175433) (YES) #4
1-New York

[redacted] ems
(12) (b7c)(1)

ALL INFORMATION CONTAINED HEREIN IS UNCLASSIFIED DATE 6/23/82 BY

100-175319-16

SEARCHED ____ INDEXED
SERIALIZED Ck FILED Ck
1972

CLASS. & EXT. BY
REASON-FCIM II, 1-2.4.2, 2
DATE OF REVIEW 3/2/92

Approved: ____________ Sent ____________ M

Special Agent in Charge

6.15.82 ALL INFORMATION CONTAINED HEREIN IS UNCLASSIFIED EXCEPT WHERE SHOWN OTHERWISE.

~~CONFIDENTIAL~~

(b7c)(1)

NY-17

Figure 46. NY-17.

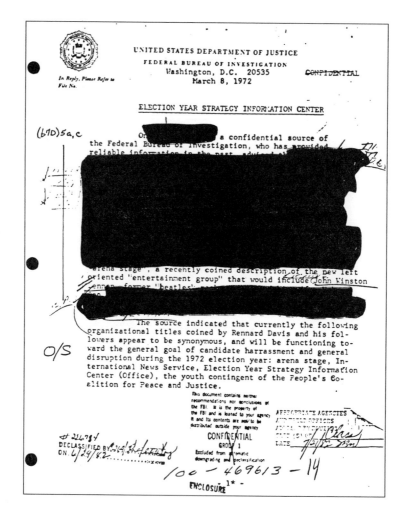

Figure 47a. INS-1, initial release.

"TO ENCOURAGE YOUTHS"   On March 8, 1972, FBI headquarters sent a letterhead memorandum to the INS, reporting on FBI information that Tom Hayden met with Rennie Davis and discussed, among other things, "arena stage," "the new left oriented 'entertainment group'" that would include Lennon and Ono "and function as a stimulus to encourage youths to be in the vicinity of election candidates when they are on tour" (INS-1)—not exactly a crime.

The entire document was withheld originally under the confidential source exemption, then released with extensive deletions, and finally released in its entirety.

UNITED STATES DEPARTMENT OF JUSTICE

FEDERAL BUREAU OF INVESTIGATION

Washington, D.C. 20535 ~~CONFIDENTIAL~~

March 8, 1972

ELECTION YEAR STRATEGY INFORMATION CENTER

On March 1, 1972, a confidential source of
the Federal Bureau of Investigation who has provided
reliable information in the past, advised that Thomas Hayden,
a convicted Chicago Seven conspiracy trial defendant, flew
to the Washington, D.C. area on February 26, 1972, and met
with Rennard Cordon Davis, another convicted Chicago Seven
conspiracy trial defendant. These two individuals discussed the possibility of forming a group calling itself
the "anti-war union". This was described as a coalition
of individuals who, in the past, had shown leadership in
various new left oriented organizations. The projected
purpose of the anti-war union would be to formulate tactics
in regard to movement actions during the 1972 election year
primary elections. including confrontations with candidates
during their speaking tours, and as a support base for the
"arena stage" a recently coined description of the new left
oriented "entertainment group" that would include John Winston
Lennon. former "beatles" rock singer, and his wife, Yoko
Ono. and function as a stimulus to encourage youths to be
in the vicinity of election candidates when they are on tour.

The source indicated that currently the following
organizational titles coined by Rennard Davis and his fol-
lowers appear to be synonymous, and will be functioning toward the general goal of candidate harrassment and general
disruption during the 1972 election year: arena stage, International News Service, Election Year Strategy Information
Center (Office), the youth contingent of the People's Coalition for Peace and Justice.

100 - 469613 - 14

ENCLOSURE 1* -

INS-1

Figure 47b. INS-1, after settlement.

IRISH REPUBLICAN CLUB MEETING   Lennon joined protests in New York against British troops who fired on civil rights demonstrators in Northern Ireland in January 1972. Thirteen demonstrators were killed on what became known as "Bloody Sunday." The Irish Republican Club of New York held a meeting on February 6 to plan a protest, and an FBI informer reported on the proceedings (NY-22 page 1). This document appears in the Lennon file only because his name was mentioned at this meeting. The cover sheet suggests the FBI was slow in its paperwork: the meeting was held on February 6, the informer's report was received eight days later, but the cover sheet was not prepared for more than a month after the meeting was held.

Cover Sheet for Informant Report or Material
FD-306 (Rev. 5-20-69)

Date prepared: 3/8/72

Date received: 2/14/72

Received from (name or symbol number): [redacted] b2 b7D

Received by: SA [redacted] b7C

Method of delivery (check appropriate blocks)

[X] in person [ ] by telephone [ ] by mail [ ] orally [ ] recording device [X] written by Informant

If orally furnished and reduced to writing by Agent:

Date

Dictated ________ to ________

Transcribed ________

Authenticated by Informant ________

Date of Report: 2/6/72

Date(s) of activity: 2/6/72

Brief description of activity or material

Irish Republican Club meeting, NYC 2/6/72.

File where original is located if not attached: [redacted] b2 b7D

INDIVIDUALS DESIGNATED BY AN ASTERISK (*) ONLY ATTENDED A MEETING AND DID NOT ACTIVELY PARTICIPATE. VIOLENCE OR REVOLUTIONARY ACTIVITIES WERE NOT DISCUSSED.

[ ] Information recorded on a card index by ________ on date ________.

Remarks:

All necessary action taken.

1-[redacted] b2 b7D
1-105-113426 (
1-105-109381 (31)
1-105-113425 (31)
1-105-115623 (31)
1-100-4013 (45)
1-100-175319 (42)
1-105-110758 (31)
1-100-164962 (45)
1-105-117501 (31)
1-105-103115 (31)
1-105-115849

[redacted] b7C
(12)

42

Block Stamp

100-175319-20

SEARCHED ____ INDEXED ____
SERIALIZED CK FILED CK
MAR 8 1972
FBI — NEW YORK
[redacted] b7C

NY-22

ALL INFORMATION CONTAINED HEREIN IS UNCLASSIFIED DATE 6/9/97 BY

Figure 48. NY-22 page 1.

NY 105-115849

- 2 -

Figure 49a. NY-22 page 2, initial release.

"IRISH" SURVEILLANCE The informant report describing the meeting planning a New York protest against "Bloody Sunday" was titled "Irish" (NY-22 page
2). It was withheld in its entirety through fourteen years of litigation until the
1997 settlement. Lennon is not mentioned on this page, which describes a meeting of the Committee against Internment in Northern Ireland and reports that
a proposal to send money for guns to the IRA "wasn't even accepted by the chair."

NY 105-115849

February 6, 1972

Irish

A meeting of the committee against internment in
Northern Ireland took place at the Irish Institute at 326
West 48th St., at 4:05 PM.

An amendment to the purpose of the group was made, so
that the body was now not just against internment, but also
for the immediate withdrawel of British troops from Northern
Ireland.

A speaker from the floor asked that the purpose of the
body be amended to include support for the Irish Republican
Army in money and even in guns. This motion wasn't even
accepted by the chair, and the gentleman declared he would
leave the meeting.

A steering committee was set up after much discussion
and argumentation. The original committee contained two
representatives from the following clubs: Irish Republican
Clubs, Northern Aid Committee, National Association for
Irish Freedom, and the American Committee for Ulster Justice.

Members of the Socialist Workers Party were present,
and they came into the meeting as a unit and argued the
following points: "with four organizations it's packed (the
steering committee)...the steering committee must be broad,
the four organizations have shown that they can't cooperate
freely...it is important that the steering committee be
representative of all tendencies and individuals...those people
who want to take responsibility will be able to do so (in the
broad steering committee). There are talented people who want
to do work".

The broad steering committee motion was passed.

- 2 -

Figure 49b. NY-22 page 2, after settlement.

NY 105-115849

It was announced that JOHN LENNON had offered entertainment.

- 3 -

Figure 50a. NY-22 page 3, initial release.

"LENNON HAD OFFERED ENTERTAINMENT"   The informer's report on the meeting of the Committee against Internment in Northern Ireland mentions Lennon on its third page (NY-22 page 3). He is said to have offered "entertainment" as part of a demonstration calling for immediate withdrawal of British troops from Northern Ireland. Lennon did join a demonstration on February 6 and sang a new song he had written for the occasion, "Luck of the Irish." The news appeared on page one of the *London Times* the next day.

A March 1 or 4th action date was proposed. The SWP people called for a mass demonstration.

It was announced that JOHN LENNON had offered entertainment. One route proposed was a march from Columbus Circle to Bryant Park, or Central Park.

Someone suggested that all British people, and all British organizations be harrassed, as the Jewish Defense League does with the Soviets.

A boycott of British goods was proposed.

It was suggested that the Irish ask the Chinese in the Hotel Roosevelt (Red Chinese) to talk to NIXON when he is in Peking. This idea was strongly put down.

Three members of the SWP (if not more) were named to the steering committee: RAY "MARKY" (1930-local of the New York Public Library System), GENE "BERTINE" of Local 1199, and NAT LONDON, formerly of the Peace Action Coalition. In all 28 names were accepted for the committee.

The Irish Republican Clubs are aware of the presence of SWP people, and they are watching them. MARY COTTER was a spokesman for the Irish group, and she's a SWP person (this occurred at a BOAC demonstration previous to this meeting), and as such served the interests of the Irish group rather than the SWP.

Figure 50b. NY-22 page 3, after settlement.

"INS WILL RECONSIDER THEIR ATTEMPTS TO DEPORT LENNON" Ten days after Lennon's visa was revoked, the New York FBI sent a coded teletype to Hoover marked "urgent" (HQ-6, dated March 16, 1972). This memo reports that Lennon had won a delay in his deportation, that he would "fight a narcotics conviction in England," and that "if Lennon wins overthrow of British narcotic conviction, INS will reconsider their attempts to deport Lennon." That was bad news for those in the Nixon administration hoping that deportation would put an end to plans for a national concert tour that would combine rock music with anti-Nixon political organizing.

The routing stamp in upper right hand corner indicates it was seen by Clyde Tolson, Mark Felt, E. S. Miller; signed by R. L. Shackelford, and stamped at the bottom "Mr. Rosen for the Director." Felt and Miller were later convicted of authorizing unlawful break-ins as part of FBI surveillance of other left-wing groups in the same period; Shackelford was an unindicted co-conspirator in that case.

This is the first mention in the FBI file of Vincent Schiano, the INS chief trial attorney who had been put in charge of deporting Lennon. Schiano had been in charge of the biggest deportation cases: mob boss Carlo Gambino, happy hooker Xavieria Hollander, former Nazi Hermine Braunsteiner Ryan, and IRA revolutionary Joe Cahill. After the Lennon case, Schiano left the INS, protesting that he was given carte blanche in the Lennon case but was given no power to go after former Nazis.*

* Joe Treen, "Justice for a Beatle," *Rolling Stone*, December 5, 1974.

FEDERAL BUREAU OF INVESTIGATION
COMMUNICATIONS SECTION

MAR 16 1972

TELETYPE

ALL [illegible] CONTAINED
HERE[illegible]IED
DATE 2/9/81 BY SP4/SKM/MG

Mr. Tolson
Mr. Felt
Mr. Rosen
Mr. Mohr
Mr. Bishop
Mr. Miller, E.S.
Mr. Callahan
Mr. Casper
Mr. Conrad
Mr. Dalbey
Mr. Cleveland
Mr. Ponder
Mr. Bates
Mr. Walkart
Mr. Walters
Mr. Soyars
Tele. Room
Miss Holmes
Miss Gandy

NR 028 NY CODE

440 PM URGENT 3-16-72 BGW

TO DIRECTOR

ATTN: DID

FROM NEW YORK (100-175319) 2P

Security Matter

JOHN WINSTON LENNON; SM-NEW LEFT OO:NY

ON MARCH SIXTEENTH INSTANT MR. VINCENT SCHIANO, CHIEF TRIAL ATTORNEY, INS, NYC, [Immigration and Naturalization Service, New York City] ADVISE THAT JOHN LENNON AND HIS WIFE YOKO ONO [Lennon — Mrs John Winston Lennon] APPEARED AT INS, NYC THIS DATE FOR DEPORTATION PROCEEDINGS. BOTH INDIVIDUALS THRU THEIR ATTORNEY WON DELAY OF HEARINGS. LENNON REQUESTED DELAY WHILE HE ATTEMPTED TO FIGHT A NARCOTOCS CONVICTION IN ENGLAND. YOKO ONO REQUESTED DELAY ON BASIS OF CHILD CUSTODY CASE IN WHICH SHE IS INVOLVED.

100-469910-2

ST-111 REC-36 MCT-1

16 MAR 20 1972

MR. SCHIANO ADVISED THAT NEW HEARINGS WOULD BE HELD ON APRIL EIGHTEEN NEXT. IF LENNON WINS OVERTHROW OF BRITISH NARCOTIC CONVICTION, INS WILL RECONSIDER THEIR ATTEMPTS

END PAGE ONE

MAY 18 1972

MR. ROSEN FOR THE DIRECTOR

HQ-6

Figure 51. HQ-6.

TWELVE COPIES OF "JOHN WINSTON LENNON" MEMO   HQ-7 page 2 is an airtel from the New York FBI to Hoover dated March 16, 1972. It was released with no redactions. It is the cover page for the five-page letterhead memo which follows. The cover page indicates that twelve copies were prepared by the New York FBI office for distribution and that another copy has been given to the INS office in New York. The special agent in charge of the New York FBI asks Hoover to give a copy to "Legat London"—the FBI official at the American embassy there.

The large number of stamps and markings on this page mostly concern declassifying it in 1981–83. One of the signatures is "Shackelford," who the ACLU team subsequently subpoenaed for a deposition in which they planned to ask him whether the FBI engaged in any illegal acts during its surveillance of Lennon. The Justice Department got a District of Columbia federal judge to quash that subpoena (see pp. 65–67).

FD-36

CA#83-1720

Transmit the following in _____
(Type in plaintext or code)

Via   AIRTEL
_____
(Priority)

APPROPRIATE AGENCIES
AND FIELD OFFICES
ADVISED BY ROUTING
SLIP(S) OF
TO: Class
DATE

TO: DIRECTOR, FBI

FROM: SAC, NEW YORK (100-175319) (P)

SUBJECT: JOHN WINSTON LENNON
         SM-NEW LEFT
         (OO:NY)

Classified by SP65XR00
Declassify on: OADR

ReNYairtel and LHM captioned "ELECTION YEAR
STRATEGY INFORMATION CENTER, IS-NL", dated 2/28/72 and Legat
London airtel and LHM, dated 2/22/72.

     Enclosed for the Bureau are 12 copies of an LHM
dated and captioned as above.

     A copy of this LHM has been disseminated locally
at INS, NYC.

     It is requested that Legat London be furnished
appropriate copies of this LHM.

     WFO is being furnished a copy of this LHM due to
their previous interest.

APPROPRIATE AGENCIES
AND FIELD OFFICES
ADVISED BY ROUTING
SLIP(S) OF

3 - Bureau (Encls. 12) (RM)
2 - Washington Field Office (Encls. 2) (RM)
1 - New York (100-175228)
1 - New York

ENCLOSURE

REC-88

DATE 3-12

100-469910-3

CJL:lh
(10)

AGENCY. ARMY, ONI, OSI, SLC. SER., STATE, CIA

2 cc's   INS/narotic   RAO (ISD,

DATE FORW. 3/21/72
HOW FORW.

MAR 18 1972

5 5 APR 10 1972

CLASS.& EXT. BY SP
EDASO on ECIM 11,
DATE OF REVIEW 3-16-

Special Agent in Charge

HQ-

OVERNMENT PRINTING OFFICE: 1971-413-135

Figure 52. HQ-7 page 2.

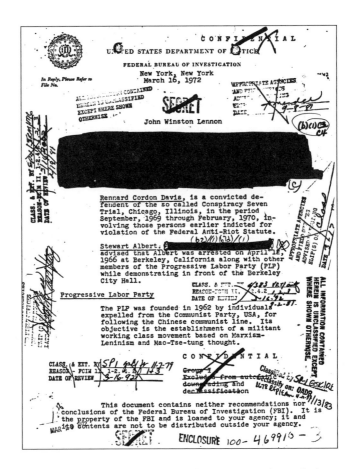

Figure 53a. HQ-7 page 4, initial release.

"FOLLOWING THE CHINESE COMMUNIST LINE" The New York FBI prepared for distribution to other agencies a letterhead memorandum, dated March 16, 1972, describing Lennon's political plans (HQ-7 page 4). The first paragraph was originally withheld as national security intelligence source information. It turned out to be a report that Lennon was part of a group planning "to coordinate New Left movement activities during this election year."

The paragraph on Stewart Albert identifies him incorrectly as associated with the Progressive Labor Party (PLP). The implication was clear: Lennon was associating with Communists. Although the First Amendment protected that kind of association, Albert in fact was not associated with the PLP—a rigid, doctrinaire organization opposed to the counterculture and to the New Left. Albert later described his arrest at that PLP demonstration as "a youthful indiscretion."

208

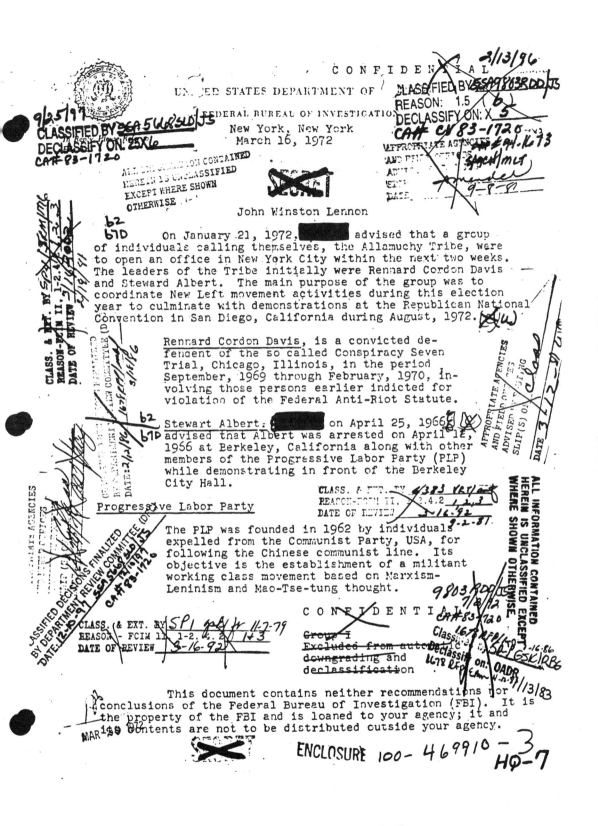

C O N F I D E N T I A L

UNITED STATES DEPARTMENT OF ~~JUSTICE~~
FEDERAL BUREAU OF INVESTIGATION
New York, New York
March 16, 1972

~~SECRET~~

ALL INFORMATION CONTAINED
HEREIN IS UNCLASSIFIED
EXCEPT WHERE SHOWN
OTHERWISE

John Winston Lennon

On January 21, 1972, ███ advised that a group
of individuals calling themselves, the Allamuchy Tribe, were
to open an office in New York City within the next two weeks.
The leaders of the Tribe initially were Rennard Cordon Davis
and Steward Albert. The main purpose of the group was to
coordinate New Left movement activities during this election
year to culminate with demonstrations at the Republican National
Convention in San Diego, California during August, 1972.

Rennard Cordon Davis, is a convicted defendent of the so called Conspiracy Seven
Trial, Chicago, Illinois, in the period
September, 1969 through February, 1970, involving those persons earlier indicted for
violation of the Federal Anti-Riot Statute.

Stewart Albert. ███ on April 25, 1966
advised that Albert was arrested on April 12,
1966 at Berkeley, California along with other
members of the Progressive Labor Party (PLP)
while demonstrating in front of the Berkeley
City Hall.

Progressive Labor Party

The PLP was founded in 1962 by individuals
expelled from the Communist Party, USA, for
following the Chinese communist line. Its
objective is the establishment of a militant
working class movement based on Marxism-
Leninism and Mao-Tse-tung thought.

C O N F I D E N T I A L

~~Group I
Excluded from automatic
downgrading and
declassification~~

This document contains neither recommendations nor
conclusions of the Federal Bureau of Investigation (FBI). It is
the property of the FBI and is loaned to your agency; it and
its contents are not to be distributed outside your agency.

~~SECRET~~

ENCLOSURE 100- 469910 - 3
HQ-7

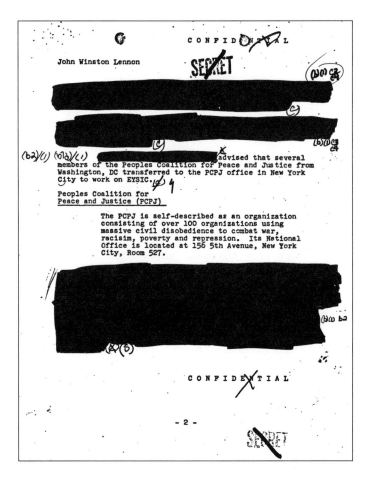

John Winston Lennon

advised that several members of the Peoples Coalition for Peace and Justice from Washington, DC transferred to the PCPJ office in New York City to work on EYSIC.

Peoples Coalition for
Peace and Justice (PCPJ)

The PCPJ is self-described as an organization consisting of over 100 organizations using massive civil disobedience to combat war, racism, poverty and repression. Its National Office is located at 156 5th Avenue, New York City, Room 527.

- 2 -

Figure 54a. HQ-7 page 5, initial release.

"FOREIGN MILITARY RETALIATION" The continuation of the New York FBI's March 16 memo "John Winston Lennon" (HQ-7 page 5) includes one blacked-out portion at the bottom of the page; the FBI continues to maintain that releasing it would endanger the national security. That claim remains in litigation. The FBI has identified the withheld portion as "information provided by a foreign government with the expectation, expressed or implied, that the information is to be kept in confidence." The release of this information, the FBI has stated, could "allow hostile entities' assessment of areas and targets which may have been compromised" and lead to "termination of the source . . . and possible loss of life" and to "foreign military retaliation" by the country that provided the information.

John Winston Lennon

~~SECRET~~

On January 24, 1972, [redacted] advised that John Winston Lennon, who was formerly associated with the Beatles Music Group, donated seventy-five thousand dollars to the Allamuchy Tribe, to further their cause of New-Left activities. (S)u

On January 28, 1972, [redacted] advised that the Allamuchy Tribe had changed its name to the Election Year Strategy Information Center (EYSIC), so as to be more effectively known to the general public. (S)u

b2
b7D

On February 2, 1972, [redacted] advised that several members of the Peoples Coalition for Peace and Justice from Washington, DC transferred to the PCPJ office in New York City to work on EYSIC. (S) u

Peoples Coalition for
Peace and Justice (PCPJ)

The PCPJ is self-described as an organization consisting of over 100 organizations using massive civil disobedience to combat war, racisim, poverty and repression. Its National Office is located at 156 5th Avenue, New York City, Room 527.

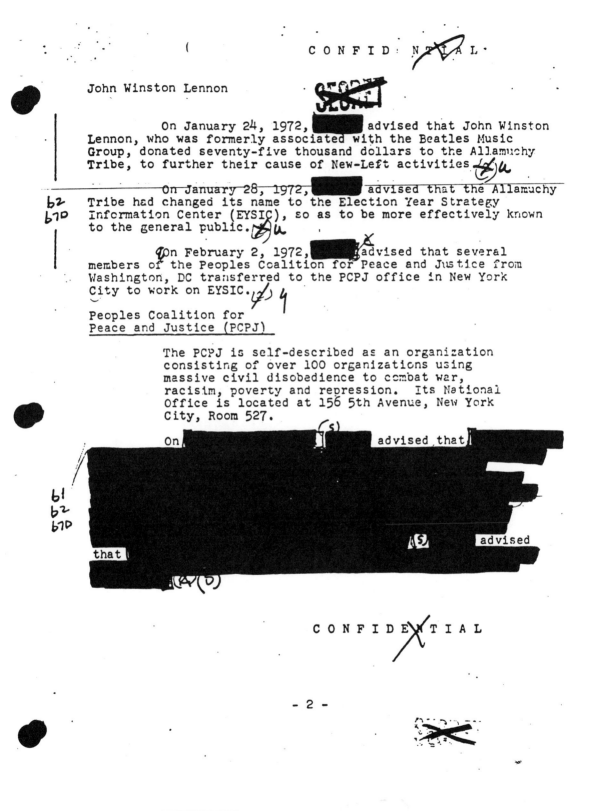

On [redacted] (S) [redacted] advised that [redacted]

b1
b2
b7D

[redacted] (S) advised

that [redacted]

(S)(5)

Figure 54b. HQ-7 page 5, after settlement.

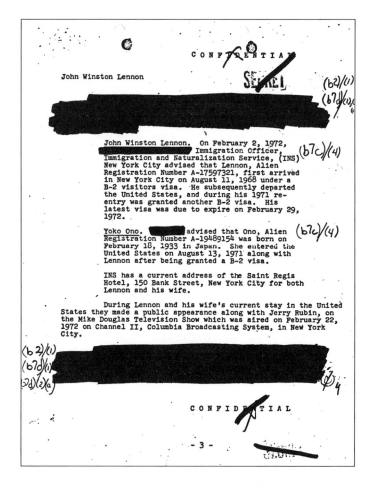

Figure 55a. HQ-7 page 6, initial release.

LENNON PLED GUILTY   Initially the FBI withheld the top paragraph as "investigatory records compiled for law enforcement purposes which would disclose the identity of a confidential source." The information provided by the confidential source turned out to be a report that Lennon had pled guilty to charges of possession of drugs in England in 1969, a fact known worldwide.

The FBI here continues to list the wrong address for Lennon—see HQ-7 p. 151.

John Winston Lennon

b2
b7D

On February 15, 1972, ███████ advised that John
Lennon on November 28, 1969, pled guilty in Marylebone
Magistrates Court, London, England to possession of dangerous
drugs (Cannabis). He was fined L150 and ordered to pay L21
in court cost. ██

b7C

John Winston Lennon. On February 2, 1972,
███████████████████ Immigration Officer,
Immigration and Naturalization Service, (INS)
New York City advised that Lennon, Alien
Registration Number A-17597321, first arrived
in New York City on August 11, 1968 under a
B-2 visitors visa. He subsequently departed
the United States, and during his 1971 re-
entry was granted another B-2 visa. His
latest visa was due to expire on February 29,
1972.

b7C

Yoko Ono. ████████ advised that Ono, Alien
Registration Number A-19489154 was born on
February 18, 1933 in Japan. She entered the
United States on August 13, 1971 along with
Lennon after being granted a B-2 visa.

INS has a current address of the Saint Regis
Hotel, 150 Bank Street, New York City for both
Lennon and his wife.

During Lennon and his wife's current stay in the United
States they made a public appearance along with Jerry Rubin, on
the Mike Douglas Television Show which was aired on February 22,
1972 on Channel II, Columbia Broadcasting System, in New York
City.

b2
b7D

During February, 1972, ████████ advised that Rennard
Davis, Stewart Albert, Jerry Rubin and John Lennon are heavy
users of narcotics. Source advised that Rubin and Davis are
apparently at odds with Lennon due to his excessive use of
drugs, which are referred to in the Vernacular as "Downers".

C O N F I D E N T I A L

- 3 -

Figure 55b. HQ-7 page 6, after settlement.

"NOT A TRUE REVOLUTIONIST"   The last page of the March 16 memo headed "John Winston Lennon" reports on Lennon's politics: "Source advised that Lennon appears to be radically orientated, however he does not give the impression he is a true revolutionist" (HQ-7 page 7). The ACLU cited this passage in court arguments as evidence that the FBI lacked a legitimate law enforcement purpose in investigating Lennon. The bureau here was monitoring his political views, the expression of which is protected by the First Amendment.

CONFIDENTIAL

John Winston Lennon

Source advised that Lennon appears to be radically orientated, however he does not give the impression he is a true revolutionist since he is constantly under the influence of narcotics.

Jerry Rubin, is a convicted defendent of the so called Conspiracy Seven Trial, Chicago, Illinois, in the period September, 1969 through February, 1970, involving those persons earlier indicted for violation of the Federal Anti-Riot Statute.

On March 14, 1972, Mr. Vincent Schiano, Chief Trial Attorney, INS, New York City, advised that Lennon and his wife Yoko Ono on March 6, 1972 were served with an INS order to show cause as to why they should not be deported from the United States as over-stayed visitors. Mr. Schiano advised that Lennon and his wife are scheduled to appear at INS, New York City on March 16, 1972 to answer the show cause order.

CONFIDENTIAL

Figure 56. HQ-7 page 7.

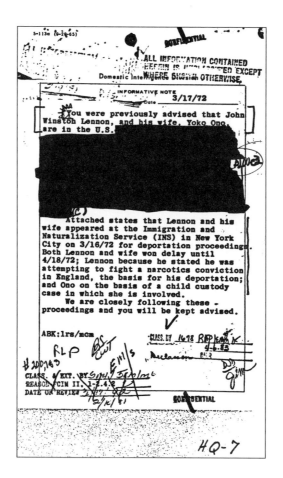

Figure 57a. HQ-7 page 1, initial release.

"DYING ON THE VINE" Lennon's FBI file also contains "Informative Notes." This one (HQ-7 page 1), dated March 17, 1972, reports that "EYSIC has been 'dying on the vine' recently due to Lennon's imminent deportation and recent dissatisfaction with Rennie Davis." A portion was originally withheld as "detailed information pertaining to or provided by an intelligence source."

The FBI declared in court that this could consist of "details obtained from a one-on-one conversation between a source and another individual . . . and thus reveal a style of reporting peculiar to that source along with other clues as to authorship, such as handwritten or typewritten reports of the information . . . [D]isclosure of this information would enable a hostile analyst to unravel the cloak of secrecy that protects the intelligence source's identity." The passage nevertheless was eventually released.

5-113a (9-29-65)

Domestic Intelligence Division

INFORMATIVE NOTE

Date **3/17/72**

You were previously advised that John Winston Lennon, and his wife, Yoko Ono, are in the U.S. and that Lennon is the major financial contributor to Election Year Strategy Information Center (EYSIC) which was organized to conduct disruptive demonstrations during the Republican National Convention. EYSIC has been "dying on the vine" recently due to Lennon's imminent deportation and recent dissatisfaction with Rennie Davis, militant revolutionary, who is the head of EYSIC.

Attached states that Lennon and his wife appeared at the Immigration and Naturalization Service (INS) in New York City on 3/16/72 for deportation proceedings. Both Lennon and wife won delay until 4/18/72; Lennon because he stated he was attempting to fight a narcotics conviction in England, the basis for his deportation; and Ono on the basis of a child custody case in which she is involved.

We are closely following these proceedings and you will be kept advised.

ABK:lrs/mcm

CLASS. BY

CLASS. & EXT. BY
REASON FCIM II. 1-2.4.2
DATE OF REVIEW

HQ-7

"INTENSIFY DISCREET INVESTIGATION OF SUBJECT"   An informer in Alexandria, Virginia, provided information about Lennon that Hoover sent to the FBI in New York on April 10, 1972 (HQ-8 page 1). Here Hoover worries that Lennon will succeed in "lengthy delaying tactics" in his deportation case and thus "might engage in activities in U.S. leading toward disruption of Republican National Convention." Hoover orders New York to "promptly initiate discreet efforts to locate subject and remain aware of his activities and movements" but warns that inquiries should be "only through established sources and discreet pretext inquiries."

This is one of two documents that had previously been withheld and that the Ninth Circuit Court of Appeals described in detail in its decision, providing an example of how the FBI ought to describe documents it was withholding. Instead of providing abbreviations in the margins that referred to boilerplate passages in the FBI codebook, the Ninth Circuit declared, the FBI Vaughn index "could have stated" that this document "recites information provided by a third party to an FBI informant detailing the third party's knowledge of several activists and protest activities planned at the 1972 Republican National Convention, discussing the possibility that John Lennon would organize a series of concerts to raise money to finance the activity, and describing rivalries and jealousies within activist organizations."

Airtel

4/10/72

To: SAC, New York (100-175319) (Enclosures - 2)

From: Director, FBI (100-469910)

JOHN WINSTON LENNON
SM - NEW LEFT

1 - Mr. Horner
1 - Mr. Preusse
1 - Mr. Shackelford
1 - Mr. Pence

ReNYtel 3/16/72.

Enclosed for information of New York are two copies of
Alexandria airtel dated 3/31/72 captioned "White Panther Party,
IS - WPP; CALREP; MIDEM," which contains information from Alexandria
source relating to current activities of subject.

It appears from referenced New York teletype that subject
and wife might be preparing for lengthy delaying tactics to avert
their deportation in the near future. In the interim, very real
possibility exists that subject, as indicated in enclosed airtel,
might engage in activities in U.S. leading toward disruption of
Republican National Convention (RNC), San Diego, 8/72. For this
reason New York promptly initiate discreet efforts to locate subject
and remain aware of his activities and movements. Handle inquiries
only through established sources and discreet pretext inquiries.
Careful attention should be given to reports that subject is heavy
narcotics user and any information developed in this regard should be
furnished to narcotics authorities and immediately furnished to
Bureau in form suitable for dissemination.

1 - Alexandria
1 - San Diego

RLP:mcm (9)

CLASS. & EXT. BY
REASON-FCIM II, 1-2 4.2
DATE OF REVIEW

EX-105   REC-33

100-469910-4

MAILED 21
APR 7 - 1972

SEE NOTE PAGE TWO   APR 10 1972

ALL INFORMATION CONTAINED
HEREIN IS UNCLASSIFIED
DATE 3/9/81 BY

Tolson
Felt
Campbell
Rosen
Mohr
Bishop
Miller, E.S.
Callahan
Casper
Conrad
Dalbey
Cleveland
Ponder
Bates
Waikart
Walters
Soyars
Tele. Room
Holmes
Gandy

51 APR 12 1972

MAIL ROOM   TELETYPE UNIT

CONFIDENTIAL

ALL INFORMATION CONTAINED
HEREIN IS UNCLASSIFIED EXCEPT
WHERE SHOWN OTHERWISE

HQ-8

Figure 58. HQ-8 page 1.

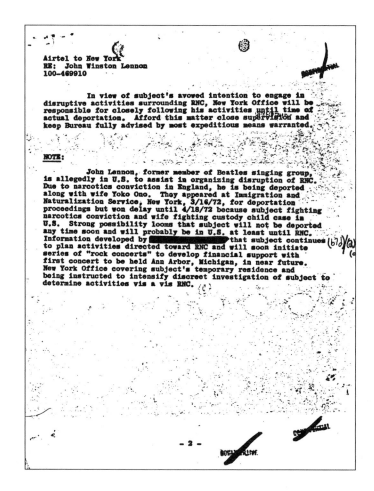

Airtel to New York
RE: John Winston Lennon
100-469910

In view of subject's avowed intention to engage in
disruptive activities surrounding RNC, New York Office will be
responsible for closely following his activities until time of
actual deportation. Afford this matter close supervision and
keep Bureau fully advised by most expeditious means warranted.

NOTE:

John Lennon, former member of Beatles singing group,
is allegedly in U.S. to assist in organizing disruption of RNC.
Due to narcotics conviction in England, he is being deported
along with wife Yoko Ono. They appeared at Immigration and
Naturalization Service, New York, 3/16/72, for deportation
proceedings but won delay until 4/18/72 because subject fighting
narcotics conviction and wife fighting custody child case in
U.S. Strong possibility looms that subject will not be deported
any time soon and will probably be in U.S. at least until RNC.
Information developed by ████████████that subject continues
to plan activities directed toward RNC and will soon initiate
series of "rock concerts" to develop financial support with
first concert to be held Ann Arbor, Michigan, in near future.
New York Office covering subject's temporary residence and
being instructed to intensify discreet investigation of subject to
determine activities vis a vis RNC.

- 2 -

Figure 59a. HQ-8 page 2, initial release.

"ASSIST IN ORGANIZING DISRUPTION"   In the continuation of Hoover's air-tel dated April 10 (HQ-8 page 2), he refers to "subject's avowed intention to engage in disruptive activities surrounding RNC." But Lennon had expressed no such intention. An FBI confidential informant would report ten days later that Lennon said he would participate in demonstrations at the Republican National Convention only "if they are peaceful."

Hoover here is confused here about Lennon's plans: "subject . . . will soon initiate series of 'rock concerts' to develop financial support," he writes, "with first concert to be held in Ann Arbor, Michigan, in near future." That concert had been held four months earlier, and the FBI had been there (see DE-4, p. 110).

Airtel to New York
RE: John Winston Lennon
100-469910

In view of subject's avowed intention to engage in
disruptive activities surrounding RNC, New York Office will be
responsible for closely following his activities until time of
actual deportation. Afford this matter close supervision and
keep Bureau fully advised by most expeditious means warranted.

NOTE:

John Lennon, former member of Beatles singing group,
is allegedly in U.S. to assist in organizing disruption of RNC.
Due to narcotics conviction in England, he is being deported
along with wife Yoko Ono. They appeared at Immigration and
Naturalization Service, New York, 3/16/72, for deportation
proceedings but won delay until 4/18/72 because subject fighting
narcotics conviction and wife fighting custody child case in
U.S. Strong possibility looms that subject will not be deported
any time soon and will probably be in U.S. at least until RNC.
Information developed by Alexandria source that subject continues
to plan activities directed toward RNC and will soon initiate
series of "rock concerts" to develop financial support with
first concert to be held Ann Arbor, Michigan, in near future.
New York Office covering subject's temporary residence and
being instructed to intensify discreet investigation of subject to
determine activities vis a vis RNC.

- 2 -

Figure 59b. HQ-8 page 2, after settlement.

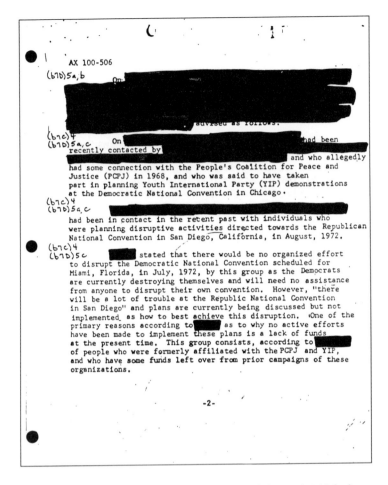

Figure 60a. HQ-8 page 4, initial release.

"THERE WILL BE A LOT OF TROUBLE"　　Information provided by the confidential informant in Alexandria, Virginia, continues here (HQ-8 page 4). According to another page, the FBI informer received the information from "a third party who stated he did not want to contact the FBI himself, and the third party did not wish to discuss the matter with anyone other than" the FBI informer. Originally this page was withheld in its entirety under the claim that the information was provided by an individual who had received an express assurance of confidentiality. "Given the specific nature of the information," the FBI declared, "disclosure would actually identify the third party and also lead to the identification of the FBI source." These two pages were withheld through fourteen years of litigation and then released as part of the 1997 settlement.

AX 100-506

      On 3/31/72, Alexandria source mentioned in referenced
letter who has furnished reliable information in the past
concerning the WPP and who has been characterized by the Detroit
Office on the basis of information furnished as "a competent
observer and an efficient interviewer who obtained very factual
and significant information" advised as follows:

      On 3/26/72, ████████████ told source that he had been
recently contacted by one ████████ who is allegedly ████████████
██ and who allegedly
had some connection with the People's Coalition for Peace and
Justice (PCPJ) in 1968, and who was said to have taken
part in planning Youth International Party (YIP) demonstrations
at the Democratic National Convention in Chicago.

      ████████ told source that ████ related to him that he
had been in contact in the recent past with individuals who
were planning disruptive activities directed towards the Republican
National Convention in San Diego, California, in August, 1972.

      ████ stated that there would be no organized effort
to disrupt the Democratic National Convention scheduled for
Miami, Florida, in July, 1972, by this group as the Democrats
are currently destroying themselves and will need no assistance
from anyone to disrupt their own convention. However, "there
will be a lot of trouble at the Republic National Convention
in San Diego" and plans are currently being discussed but not
implemented as how to best achieve this disruption. One of the
primary reasons according to ████ as to why no active efforts
have been made to implement these plans is a lack of funds
at the present time. This group consists, according to ████
of people who were formerly affiliated with the PCPJ and YIP,
and who have some funds left over from prior campaigns of these
organizations.

-2-

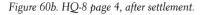

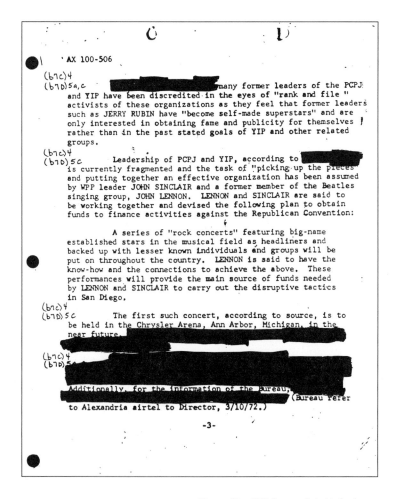

AX 100-506

(b7c)4
(b7D)5a,c ▮▮▮▮▮▮▮▮▮many former leaders of the PCPJ and YIP have been discredited in the eyes of "rank and file " activists of these organizations as they feel that former leaders such as JERRY RUBIN have "become self-made superstars" and are only interested in obtaining fame and publicity for themselves rather than in the past stated goals of YIP and other related groups.

(b7c)4
(b7D)5c   Leadership of PCPJ and YIP, according to ▮▮▮▮▮▮ is currently fragmented and the task of "picking up the pieces" and putting together an effective organization has been assumed by WPP leader JOHN SINCLAIR and a former member of the Beatles singing group, JOHN LENNON. LENNON and SINCLAIR are said to be working together and devised the following plan to obtain funds to finance activities against the Republican Convention:

A series of "rock concerts" featuring big-name established stars in the musical field as headliners and backed up with lesser known individuals and groups will be put on throughout the country. LENNON is said to have the know-how and the connections to achieve the above. These performances will provide the main source of funds needed by LENNON and SINCLAIR to carry out the disruptive tactics in San Diego.

(b7c)4
(b7D)5c   The first such concert, according to source, is to be held in the Chrysler Arena, Ann Arbor, Michigan, in the near future. ▮▮▮▮▮▮▮▮▮▮▮▮▮▮▮▮▮

(b7c)4
(b7D)5 ▮▮▮▮▮▮▮▮▮▮▮▮▮▮▮▮▮▮▮▮▮▮▮

Additionally, for the information of the Bureau, ▮▮▮▮ (Bureau refer to Alexandria airtel to Director, 3/10/72.)

-3-

Figure 61a. HQ-8 page 5, initial release.

"THE OPENING GUN"   This page of information provided by the Alexandria, Virginia, source (HQ-8 page 5) was withheld in its entirety as confidential source information through fourteen years of litigation and then released as part of the 1997 settlement.

It contains some high-level gossip about criticism of Jerry Rubin for being "interested in obtaining fame and publicity," which has meant "the task of 'picking up the pieces'" has fallen to Lennon, who has "the know-how and the connections." The informer reports that Lennon soon will perform at a concert in Ann Arbor, Michigan, which will be "the opening gun of the campaign." In fact Lennon had held that concert four months earlier, as other FBI informers had reported (see DE-4, p. 110).

b7C
b7D

████ told ████ that many former leaders of the PCPJ
and YIP have been discredited in the eyes of "rank and file "
activists of these organizations as they feel that former leaders
such as JERRY RUBIN have "become self-made superstars" and are
only interested in obtaining fame and publicity for themselves
rather than in the past stated goals of YIP and other related
groups.

Leadership of PCPJ and YIP, according to ████
is currently fragmented and the task of "picking up the pieces"
and putting together an effective organization has been assumed
by WPP leader JOHN SINCLAIR and a former member of the Beatles
singing group, JOHN LENNON. LENNON and SINCLAIR are said to
be working together and devised the following plan to obtain
funds to finance activities against the Republican Convention:

A series of "rock concerts" featuring big-name
established stars in the musical field as headliners and
backed up with lesser known individuals and groups will be
put on throughout the country. LENNON is said to have the
know-how and the connections to achieve the above. These
performances will provide the main source of funds needed
by LENNON and SINCLAIR to carry out the disruptive tactics
in San Diego.

The first such concert, according to source, is to
be held in the Chrysler Arena, Ann Arbor, Michigan, in the
b7C near future. This will be, according to ████ "the opening
b7D gun of the campaign."

Alexandria source again advised that ████ reminde
him that he desired no direct contact with the Federal Bureau
of Investigation but would furnish information only to him.
Additionally, for the information of the Bureau, Alexandria
source still desires an interview with ████ (Bureau refer
to Alexandria airtel to Director, 3/10/72.)

-3-

Figure 61b. HQ-8 page 5, after settlement.

"OUTSPOKEN REMARKS CONCERNING U.S. POLICY"   Events at Lennon's deportation hearing are the subject of this urgent coded teletype from the New York FBI to Hoover dated April 18, 1972 (HQ-9 page 1). Hoover is informed here that, at a well-attended press conference, Lennon's attorney "commented that his client felt he was being deported due to his outspoken remarks concerning US policy in S.E. Asia."

The ACLU cited this passage in court arguments as evidence that the FBI lacked a legitimate law enforcement purpose in investigating Lennon. Lennon did not commit a crime when he criticized the Nixon administration's attempt to deport him. Nor did this have anything to do with plans to disrupt the Republican National Convention.

The report here that Lennon's immigration attorney Leon Wildes "read into court record where subject had been appointed onto the Presidents Council for Drug Abuse" set off a flurry of FBI activity, which appears in the files for the next week, including transmittal of this claim to H. R. Haldeman, Nixon's chief of staff. In fact it was the president of the ABA, not the USA, who appointed Lennon, and the appointment was to the Committee on Drug Abuse of the Young Lawyers' Section of the American Bar Association. Nixon's commission had a different name: the National Commission on Marijuana and Drug Abuse. Wildes had never mentioned that commission; he had referred to "a national anti-drug media effort." All of this would become clear at the May 12 INS hearing.*

* Jon Wiener, *Come Together* (New York: Random House, 1984), 236; INS Deportation Hearings, transcript of hearings, May 12, 1972, in author's possession.

Mr. Tolson
Mr. Felt
Mr. Campbell
Mr. Rosen
Mr. Mohr
Mr. Bishop
Mr. Miller, E.S.
Callahan
Casper
Conrad
Mr. Dalbey
Mr. Cleveland
Mr. Ponder
Mr. Bates
Mr. Walkart
Mr. Walters
Mr. Soyars
Tele. Room
Miss Holmes
Miss Gandy

FEDERAL BUREAU OF INVESTIGATION
COMMUNICATIONS SECTION

APR 18 1972

TELETYPE

ALL INFORMATION CONTAINED
HEREIN IS UNCLASSIFIED
DATE 3/10/81

NR41 NY CODE

926 PM URGENT 4-18-72 FPH

TO DIRECTOR

ATT DID

FROM NEW YORK (100-175319) 2P

JOHN WINSTON LENNON SM-NEW LEFT OONY

ON APRIL EIGHTEEN INSTANT A REPRESENTATIVE OF IMMIGRATION AND NATURALIZATION SERVICE (INS) TWENTY WEST BROADWAY NYC ADVISED THAT SUBJECT AND WIFE YOKO ONO LENNON APPEARED BEFORE SPECIAL INQUIRY OFFICER IRA FIELDSTEEL THIS DATE FOR PURPOSE OF DEPORTATION HEARINGS. THE LENNONS WERE REPRESENTED BY THEIR ATTORNEY LEON WILDES OF NYC.

MR. WILDES, MADE COMMENTS CONCERNING THE LENNONS CHILD CUSTODY CASE IN HOUSTON, TEXAS, IN WHICH HE INDICATED THE CHILD HAD BEEN ABDUCTED BY HIS NATURAL FATHER, AND THAT THE LENNONS WERE ATTEMPTING TO LOCATE CHILD. THE ATTORNEY COMMENTED THAT HIS CLIENT FELT HE WAS BEING DEPORTED DUE TO HIS OUTSPOKEN REMARKS CONCERNING U S POLICY IN S. E. ASIA. THE ATTORNEY REQUESTED DELAY SO AS SECURE CHARACTER WITNESSES TO TESTIFY ON BEHALF OF SUBJECT. WILDES READ INTO COURT RECORD WHERE SUBJECT HAD BEEN APPOINTED ONTO THE PRESIDENTS COUNCIL FOR DRUG ABUSE AND AS WELL ONTO FACULTY OF NY UNIVERSITY IN NYC.

EX-114 REC 51 100-469910-5

8 APR 25 1972

END PG ONE

HQ-9

Figure 62. HQ-9 page 1.

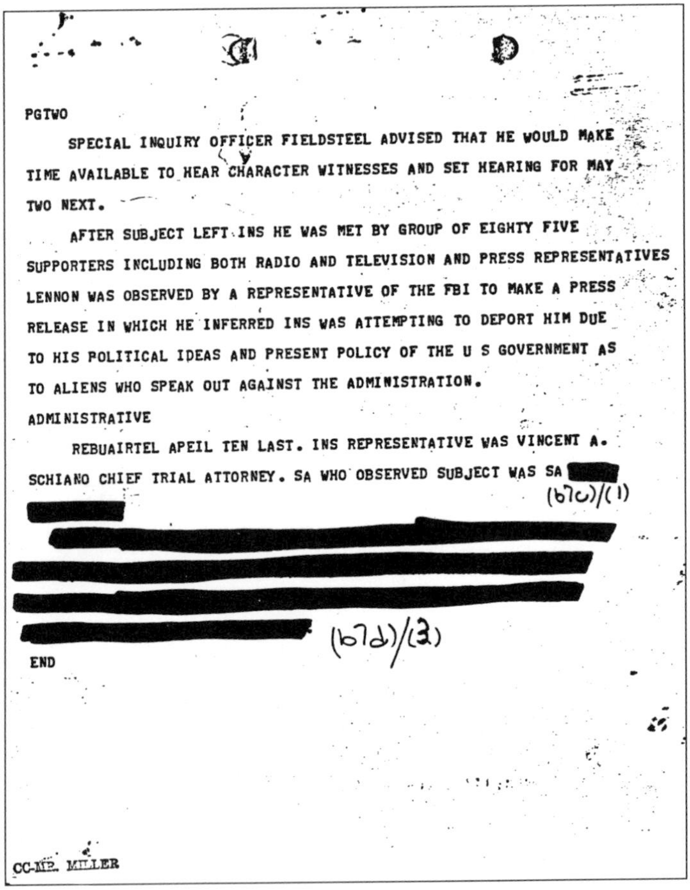

PGTWO

SPECIAL INQUIRY OFFICER FIELDSTEEL ADVISED THAT HE WOULD MAKE
TIME AVAILABLE TO HEAR CHARACTER WITNESSES AND SET HEARING FOR MAY
TWO NEXT.

AFTER SUBJECT LEFT INS HE WAS MET BY GROUP OF EIGHTY FIVE
SUPPORTERS INCLUDING BOTH RADIO AND TELEVISION AND PRESS REPRESENTATIVES
LENNON WAS OBSERVED BY A REPRESENTATIVE OF THE FBI TO MAKE A PRESS
RELEASE IN WHICH HE INFERRED INS WAS ATTEMPTING TO DEPORT HIM DUE
TO HIS POLITICAL IDEAS AND PRESENT POLICY OF THE U S GOVERNMENT AS
TO ALIENS WHO SPEAK OUT AGAINST THE ADMINISTRATION.

ADMINISTRATIVE

REBUAIRTEL APEIL TEN LAST. INS REPRESENTATIVE WAS VINCENT A.
SCHIANO CHIEF TRIAL ATTORNEY. SA WHO OBSERVED SUBJECT WAS SA ▮▮▮▮

(b7c)/(1)

(b7d)/(2)

END

CC-MR. MILLER

Figure 63a. HQ-9 page 2, initial release.

"ARREST BOTH SUBJECT AND WIFE"　For fourteen years the FBI withheld four lines of this page (HQ-9 page 2), the continuation of an urgent coded teletype from the New York FBI to Hoover, reporting on events at the deportation hearing held that day. The withheld lines were released in the 1997 settlement. They reported that the New York City Police Department was "attempting to obtain enough info to arrest both subject and wife" on narcotics charges.

PGTWO

SPECIAL INQUIRY OFFICER FIELDSTEEL ADVISED THAT HE WOULD MAKE
TIME AVAILABLE TO HEAR CHARACTER WITNESSES AND SET HEARING FOR MAY
TWO NEXT.

AFTER SUBJECT LEFT INS HE WAS MET BY GROUP OF EIGHTY FIVE
SUPPORTERS INCLUDING BOTH RADIO AND TELEVISION AND PRESS REPRESENTATIVES
LENNON WAS OBSERVED BY A REPRESENTATIVE OF THE FBI TO MAKE A PRESS
RELEASE IN WHICH HE INFERRED INS WAS ATTEMPTING TO DEPORT HIM DUE
TO HIS POLITICAL IDEAS AND PRESENT POLICY OF THE U S GOVERNMENT AS
TO ALIENS WHO SPEAK OUT AGAINST THE ADMINISTRATION.

ADMINISTRATIVE

REBUAIRTEL APEIL TEN LAST. INS REPRESENTATIVE WAS VINCENT A.
SCHIANO CHIEF TRIAL ATTORNEY. SA WHO OBSERVED SUBJECT WAS SA ████ b7c
████

FOR INFO OF BUREAU , NYCPD, NARCOTICS DIVISION IS AWARE OF
SUBJECTS RECENT USE OF NARCOTICS AND ARE ATTEMPTING TO OBTAIN
ENOUGH INFO TO ARREST BOTH SUBJECT AND WIFE YOKO BASED ON PD
INVESTIGATION. NYO FOLLOWING. P.

END

CC-LR. MILLER

Figure 63b. HQ-9 page 2, after settlement.

A JOB AT NEW YORK UNIVERSITY?   Hoover sent a coded urgent teletype (HQ-10) dated April 20, 1972, to the special agents in charge of the FBI field offices in New York and Washington, ordering the New York office to find out whether Lennon had a job at NYU and to "advise extent live informant coverage concerning subject and insure any information developed regarding subject's use of narcotics while in U.S. immediately disseminated to pertinent local and federal narcotics officials." The "Note" declares that Lennon is "in U.S. to assist organizing disruption of Republican National Convention," a false statement, as is the statement "subject illegally in U.S."

1 - Mr. R. L. Shackelford
1 - Mr. T. J. Smith (Horner)
1 - Mr. R. L. Pence

CODE TELETYPE NITEL

4-20-72

TO SACS NEW YORK (100-175319)
WFO (100-55429)

EX-114

FROM DIRECTOR FBI (100-469910) -5

COMMUNICATIONS SECTION
APR 20 1972
9:53PM
TELETYPE

JOHN WINSTON LENNON, SM - NEW LEFT.

RENYTEL APRIL EIGHTEEN LAST (COPY FURNISHED WFO UNDER SEPARATE COVER).

REGARDING INFORMATION FURNISHED BY SUBJECT'S ATTORNEY TO IMMIGRATION AND NATURALIZATION SERVICE (INS) THAT SUBJECT HAD BEEN APPOINTED TO PRESIDENT'S COUNCIL FOR DRUG ABUSE AND TO FACULTY OF NEW YORK UNIVERSITY, NEW YORK EXPEDITIOUSLY CONDUCT DISCREET INQUIRIES IN ATTEMPT TO CORROBORATE THIS INFORMATION. WFO CONDUCT INQUIRY ATTEMPT CORROBORATE SUBJECT'S ALLEGED APPOINTMENT PRESIDENT'S COUNCIL FOR DRUG ABUSE, CORRECTLY KNOWN AS NATIONAL COMMISSION ON MARIJUANA AND DRUG ABUSE. RECIPIENTS SUTEL.

NEW YORK ADVISE EXTENT LIVE INFORMANT COVERAGE CONCERNING SUBJECT AND INSURE ANY INFORMATION DEVELOPED REGARDING SUBJECT'S USE OF NARCOTICS WHILE IN U.S. IMMEDIATELY DISSEMINATED TO PERTINENT LOCAL AND FEDERAL NARCOTICS OFFICIALS.

RLP:plm
(5)

NOTE: Subject, former member of Beatles singing group, allegedly in U.S. to assist organizing disruption of Republican National Convention. He is under deportation proceedings and is attempting to delay deportation mainly due to argument that wife, Yoko Ono, should have custody of child currently in U.S. At deportation hearing in New York City 4-18-72 before INS, subject's attorney made statement subject appointed to President's Council for Drug Abuse and to faculty of New York University. Subject illegally in U.S. and New York and WFO should determine immediately whether statements made by subject's attorney are true.

Tolson
Felt
Campbell
Rosen
Mohr
Bishop
Miller, E.S.
Callahan
Casper
Conrad
Dalbey
Cleveland
Ponder
Bates
Waikart
Walters
Soyers
Tele. Room
Holmes
Gandy

HQ-10

ALL INFORMATION CONTAINED
HEREIN IS UNCLASSIFIED
DATE 3/9/81

MAY 1 1972
MAIL ROOM
TELETYPE UNIT

Figure 64. HQ-10.

LENNON'S "TEACHING POSITION WITH NEW YORK UNIVERSITY" Hoover received this coded urgent teletype (HQ-13), dated June 21, 1972, from the head
of the New York FBI, reporting that Lennon "has been offered a teaching position with New York University over the summer" and that "officials presume
that subject will accept." That would indeed be urgent news, especially for
Lennon fans in New York City.

WR 47 NY CODE

915 PM URGENT 04-21-72 KEH

FEDERAL BUREAU OF INVESTIGATION
COMMUNICATIONS SECTION
APR 21 1972
TELETYPE

TO   DIRECTOR (100-469910)

ATTENTION DOMESTIC INTELLIGENCE DIVISION

WASHINGTON FIELD (100-55429)

FROM   NEW YORK (100-175319)

JOHN WINSTON LENNON, SM - NEW LEFT.

ON APRIL TWENTY ONE, INSTANT, A SOURCE WHO IS IN A

POSITION TO FURNISH RELIABLE INFORMATION ADVISED THAT SUBJECT

HAS BEEN OFFERED A TEACHING POSITION WITH NEW YORK UNIVERSITY

(NYU) DURING THE SUMMER. NYU HAS APPARENTLY SENT SUBJECT A

LETTER REQUESTING HIS AFFIRMATIVE ANSWER REGARDING THE POSITION

AND SCHOOL OFFICIALS PRESUME THAT SUBJECT WILL ACCEPT.

ADMINISTRATIVE-----

b7c/(5) REFERENCE BUREAU TELETYPE DATED APRIL TWENTY, LAST.

b7D/(3)

NYO HAS SEVERAL SOURCES IN A POSITION TO FURNISH INFOR-

MATION ON SUBJECT'S ACTIVITIES BUT SOURCES DO NOT HAVE

PERSONAL CONTACT WITH THE SUBJECT.   EX-116

REC-36   100-469910-81

NYO CONTINUING INVESTIGATION ON SUBJECT. LHM FOLLOWS. ET APR 27 1972

END

JDJ FBI WASH DC

MSG 029 027 028 030 039 07/// 041 040 047

CLR

AGENCY: ARMY, ONI, OSI, SEC. SER., STATE, OIA

INS

DATE FORW: 4/24/72

HOW FORW: E/S

BY: RLP/WJE

70 MAY 2 1972

HQ-13

Figure 65. HQ-13.

NO APPOINTMENT TO THE NATIONAL COMMISSION ON MARIJUANA AND DRUG ABUSE Hoover received an urgent coded teletype (HQ-14) from the FBI's Washington field office, dated April 21, 1972, reporting that Lennon had not been named to the National Commission on Marijuana and Drug Abuse. The teletype was signed or initialed by numerous top FBI officials, indicating its importance.

FEDERAL BUREAU OF INVESTIGATION
COMMUNICATIONS SECTION

APR 21 1972

TELETYPE

NR003 WF CODED

947AM URGENT 4-21-72 SKA

TO DIRECTOR(100-469910)

NEW YORK (100-175319)

FROM WASHINGTON FIELD (100-55429)

JOHN WINSTON LENNON, SM-NEW LEFT.

RE BUREAU TELETYPE APRIL TWENTY INSTANT.

NO NAME INQUIRY THIS DATE AT NATIONAL COMMISSION ON

MARIJUANA AND DRUG ABUSE(NCMDA), EIGHT ZERO ONE NINETEENTH

STREET, NORTHWEST, WASHINGTON, D.C. OF ███████████ (b7c)(5)

████████████████ NCMDA, DEVELOPED NO INFORMATION

INDICATING LENNON HAS BEEN APPOINTED TO THE NCMDA.

END

KJB FBI WA DC CLR

EX-109

20 MAY 2 1972

RBC-18 100-469910-9

ALL INFORMATION CONTAINED
HEREIN IS UNCLASSIFIED
DATE 2/12/91 BY SP9/SRM/mg

70 MAY 3 1972

AGENCY: ARMY, ONI, OSI, SEC. SER., STATE, CIA
INS
DATE FORW: 4/24/72
HOW FORW:
BY: RLP/umz

HQ-14

Figure 66. HQ-14.

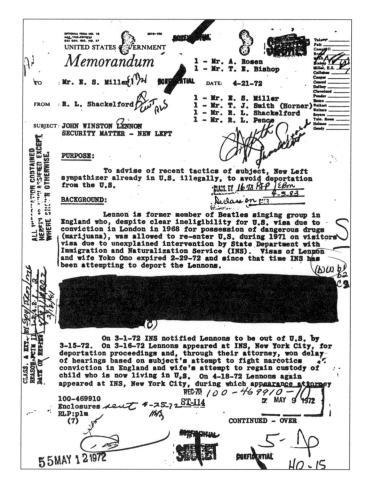

Figure 67a. HQ-15 page 1, initial release.

FROM R. L. SHACKELFORD TO E. S. MILLER E. S. Miller served as head of the FBI's Domestic Intelligence Division beginning in 1971. A key, trusted loyalist to Director Hoover, Miller was convicted in 1980, along with Mark Felt, of conspiring to violate individuals' civil rights by authorizing break-ins and searches of the homes of five people suspected of having ties to fugitives who belonged to the Weather Underground. Miller and Felt were at that point the only FBI agents ever to have been convicted of crimes committed while on duty. Shackelford was an unindicted co-conspirator. Prior to sentencing, Miller and Felt received "full and unconditional" pardons from President Reagan. The ACLU sought to ask the FBI whether Miller or others engaged in illegal activities in the Lennon investigation. The FBI settled the case rather than answering.

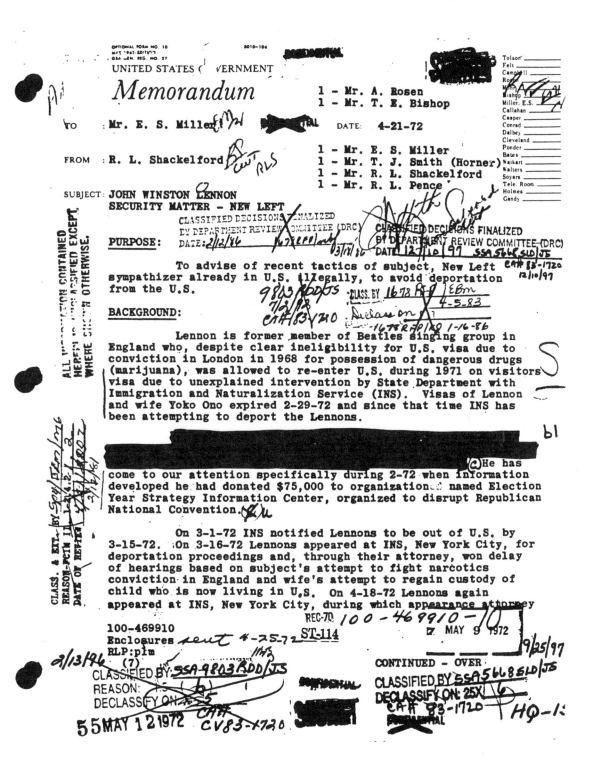

OPTIONAL FORM NO. 10
MAY 1962 EDITION
GSA GEN. REG. NO. 27

UNITED STATES GOVERNMENT

Memorandum

TO : Mr. E. S. Miller   DATE: 4-21-72

FROM : R. L. Shackelford

SUBJECT: JOHN WINSTON LENNON
SECURITY MATTER - NEW LEFT

1 - Mr. A. Rosen
1 - Mr. T. E. Bishop

1 - Mr. E. S. Miller
1 - Mr. T. J. Smith (Horner)
1 - Mr. R. L. Shackelford
1 - Mr. R. L. Pence

Tolson
Felt
Campbell
Rosen
Mohr
Bishop
Miller, E.S.
Callahan
Casper
Conrad
Dalbey
Cleveland
Ponder
Bates
Waikart
Walters
Soyars
Tele. Room
Holmes
Gandy

PURPOSE:

To advise of recent tactics of subject, New Left sympathizer already in U.S. illegally, to avoid deportation from the U.S.

BACKGROUND:

Lennon is former member of Beatles singing group in England who, despite clear ineligibility for U.S. visa due to conviction in London in 1968 for possession of dangerous drugs (marijuana), was allowed to re-enter U.S. during 1971 on visitors visa due to unexplained intervention by State Department with Immigration and Naturalization Service (INS). Visas of Lennon and wife Yoko Ono expired 2-29-72 and since that time INS has been attempting to deport the Lennons.

He has come to our attention specifically during 2-72 when information developed he had donated $75,000 to organizations named Election Year Strategy Information Center, organized to disrupt Republican National Convention.

On 3-1-72 INS notified Lennons to be out of U.S. by 3-15-72. On 3-16-72 Lennons appeared at INS, New York City, for deportation proceedings and, through their attorney, won delay of hearings based on subject's attempt to fight narcotics conviction in England and wife's attempt to regain custody of child who is now living in U.S. On 4-18-72 Lennons again appeared at INS, New York City, during which appearance attorney

100-469910
Enclosures   sent 4-25-72   ST-114
RLP:plm
(7)

REC-70   100 - 469910 - 10
          MAY 9 1972

CONTINUED - OVER

Figure 67b. HQ-15 page 1, after settlement.

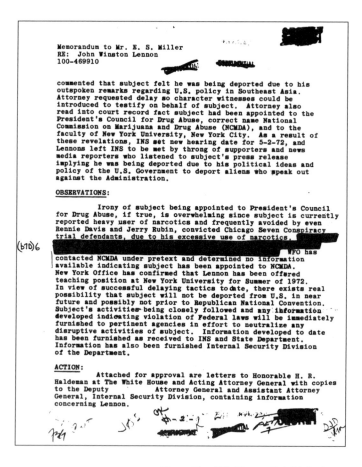

Memorandum to Mr. E. S. Miller
RE: John Winston Lennon
100-469910

commented that subject felt he was being deported due to his
outspoken remarks regarding U.S. policy in Southeast Asia.
Attorney requested delay so character witnesses could be
introduced to testify on behalf of subject. Attorney also
read into court record fact subject had been appointed to the
President's Council for Drug Abuse, correct name National
Commission on Marijuana and Drug Abuse (NCMDA), and to the
faculty of New York University, New York City. As a result of
these revelations, INS set new hearing date for 5-2-72, and
Lennons left INS to be met by throng of supporters and news
media reporters who listened to subject's press release
implying he was being deported due to his political ideas and
policy of the U.S. Government to deport aliens who speak out
against the Administration.

OBSERVATIONS:

        Irony of subject being appointed to President's Council
for Drug Abuse, if true, is overwhelming since subject is currently
reported heavy user of narcotics and frequently avoided by even
Rennie Davis and Jerry Rubin, convicted Chicago Seven Conspiracy
trial defendants, due to his excessive use of narcotics.

                                                WFO has
contacted NCMDA under pretext and determined no information
available indicating subject has been appointed to NCMDA.
New York Office has confirmed that Lennon has been offered
teaching position at New York University for Summer of 1972.
In view of successful delaying tactics to date, there exists real
possibility that subject will not be deported from U.S. in near
future and possibly not prior to Republican National Convention.
Subject's activities being closely followed and any information
developed indicating violation of Federal laws will be immediately
furnished to pertinent agencies in effort to neutralize any
disruptive activities of subject. Information developed to date
has been furnished as received to INS and State Department.
Information has also been furnished Internal Security Division
of the Department.

ACTION:

        Attached for approval are letters to Honorable H. R.
Haldeman at The White House and Acting Attorney General with copies
to the Deputy   Attorney General and Assistant Attorney
General, Internal Security Division, containing information
concerning Lennon.

Figure 68a. HQ-15 page 2, initial release.

THE "NEUTRALIZE" MEMO   Under "Observations" on this second page of HQ-15, the bureau pledges to "neutralize any disruptive activities of subject."

At the bottom to the left of the page number, the initials "OK H" appear. This is the signature of J. Edgar Hoover, indicating he approves the recommendation that the attached letter be sent to H. R. Haldeman (see HQ-12, p. 240).

The memo comments, "In view of successful delaying tactics to date, there exists real possibility that subject will not be deported from U.S. in near future and possibly not prior to Republican National Convention." It also reports that Lennon stated he "felt he was being deported due to his outspoken remarks regarding U.S. policy in Southeast Asia." The ACLU cited these passages as evidence that the FBI lacked a legitimate law enforcement purpose in investigating Lennon.

Memorandum to Mr. E. S. Miller
RE: John Winston Lennon
100-469910

commented that subject felt he was being deported due to his
outspoken remarks regarding U.S. policy in Southeast Asia.
Attorney requested delay so character witnesses could be
introduced to testify on behalf of subject. Attorney also
read into court record fact subject had been appointed to the
President's Council for Drug Abuse, correct name National
Commission on Marijuana and Drug Abuse (NCMDA), and to the
faculty of New York University, New York City. As a result of
these revelations, INS set new hearing date for 5-2-72, and
Lennons left INS to be met by throng of supporters and news
media reporters who listened to subject's press release
implying he was being deported due to his political ideas and
policy of the U.S. Government to deport aliens who speak out
against the Administration.

OBSERVATIONS:

        Irony of subject being appointed to President's Council
for Drug Abuse, if true, is overwhelming since subject is currently
reported heavy user of narcotics and frequently avoided by even
Rennie Davis and Jerry Rubin, convicted Chicago Seven Conspiracy
trial defendants, due to his excessive use of narcotics. New York
City Police Department currently attempting to develop enough
information to arrest both Lennons for narcotics use. WFO has
contacted NCMDA under pretext and determined no information
available indicating subject has been appointed to NCMDA.
New York Office has confirmed that Lennon has been offered
teaching position at New York University for Summer of 1972.
In view of successful delaying tactics to date, there exists real
possibility that subject will not be deported from U.S. in near
future and possibly not prior to Republican National Convention.
Subject's activities being closely followed and any information
developed indicating violation of Federal laws will be immediately
furnished to pertinent agencies in effort to neutralize any
disruptive activities of subject. Information developed to date
has been furnished as received to INS and State Department.
Information has also been furnished Internal Security Division
of the Department.

ACTION:
        Attached for approval are letters to Honorable H. R.
Haldeman at The White House and Acting Attorney General with copies
to the Deputy   Attorney General and Assistant Attorney
General, Internal Security Division, containing information
concerning Lennon.

Figure 68b. HQ-15 page 2, after settlement.

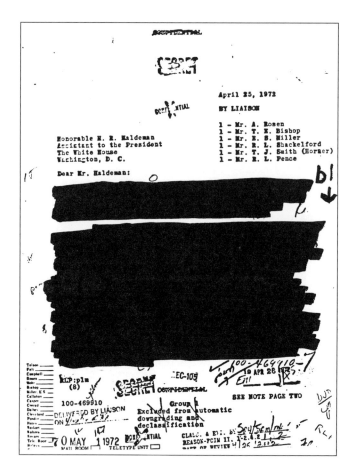

Figure 69a. HQ-12 page 1, initial release.

THE HALDEMAN LETTER J. Edgar Hoover's letter (HQ-12) to H. R. Haldeman, the president's chief of staff, dated April 25, 1972, provides crucial evidence that the Lennon investigation was a political one, of significance at the highest levels of the Nixon White House. In the original release, virtually the entire text was withheld on national security grounds. The FBI describes the portion still withheld as "intelligence information provided by a foreign government." The FBI has stated that releasing it could lead to "foreign military retaliation." In 1992 the FBI reported that "the foreign government was recently contacted" and that it "continues to insist that the information remain confidential." The withheld portion remains in litigation. The ACLU cited this document as evidence that the FBI lacked a legitimate law enforcement purpose in investigating Lennon.

9-25-97
CLASSIFIED BY SSA5668 SLD/JS
DECLASSIFY ON: 25X 6
CA# 83-1720

CLASSIFIED DECISIONS FINALIZED
BY DEPARTMENT REVIEW COMMITTEE (DRC)
DATE 2/13/96

SECRET

CONFIDENTIAL

2/13/96

CLASSIFIED BY SSA9803 ROD/J
REASON: 1.5 (b) (4)
DECLASSIFY ON: X 5
CA# CV 83-1720
94-1673
SPA CH/MLT

April 25, 1972

BY LIAISON

1 - Mr. A. Rosen
1 - Mr. T. E. Bishop
1 - Mr. E. S. Miller
1 - Mr. R. L. Shackelford
1 - Mr. T. J. Smith (Horner)
1 - Mr. R. L. Pence

Honorable H. R. Haldeman
Assistant to the President
The White House
Washington, D. C.

CLASSIFIED DECISIONS FINALIZED
BY DEPARTMENT REVIEW COMMITTEE (DRC)
DATE: 12/10/97   SSA5668 SLD/JS 12/10/97
CA# 83-1720

Dear Mr. Haldeman:

John Winston Lennon is a British citizen and former
member of the Beatles singing group.

(C)

Despite his apparent ineligibility for a United States
visa due to a conviction in London in 1968 for possession of
dangerous drugs, Lennon obtained a visa and entered the United
States in 1971. During February, 1972, a confidential source,
who has furnished reliable information in the past, advised that
Lennon had contributed $75,000 to a newly organized New Left
group formed to disrupt the Republican National Convention.
The visas of Lennon and his wife, Yoko Ono, expired on
February 29, 1972, and since that time Immigration and
Naturalization Service (INS) has been attempting to deport
them. During the Lennons' most recent deportation hearing at
INS, New York, New York, on April 18, 1972, their attorney
stated that Lennon felt he was being deported due to his
outspoken remarks concerning United States policy in Southeast
Asia. The attorney requested a delay in order that character
witnesses could testify for Lennon, and he then read into the
court record that Lennon had been appointed to the President's
Council for Drug Abuse (National Commission on Marijuana and
Drug Abuse) and to the faculty of New York University,
New York, New York.

RLP:plm
(8)

EC-105

SECRET CONFIDENTIAL

100-469910-7
19 APR 26 1972

SEE NOTE PAGE TWO

Tolson
Felt
Campbell
Rosen
Mohr
Bishop
Miller, E.S.
Callahan
Casper
Conrad
Dalbey
Cleveland
Ponder
Bates
Gaikart
Walters
Soyars
Tele. Room
Holmes
Gandy

100-469910
DELIVERED BY LIAISON
ON 4/6/

70 MAY 1 1972
MAIL ROOM ☐   TELETYPE UNIT ☐

CONFIDENTIAL

Group 1
Excluded from automatic
downgrading and
declassification

CLASS. & EXT. BY SP4/Sem/mb
REASON-FCIM II.
DATE OF REVIEW

HQ-1

Figure 69b. HQ-12 page 1, after settlement.

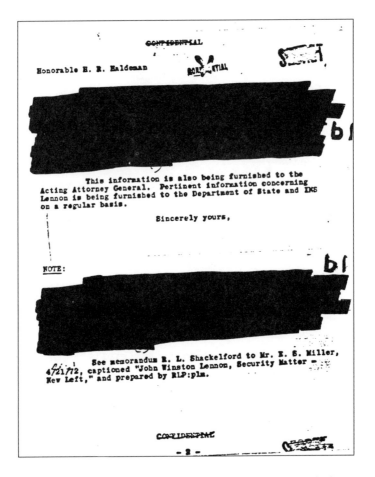

Honorable H. R. Haldeman

This information is also being furnished to the Acting Attorney General. Pertinent information concerning Lennon is being furnished to the Department of State and INS on a regular basis.

Sincerely yours,

NOTE:

See memorandum R. L. Shackelford to Mr. E. S. Miller, 4/21/72, captioned "John Winston Lennon, Security Matter - New Left," and prepared by RLP:plm.

CONFIDENTIAL

- 2 -

Figure 70a. HQ-12 page 2, initial release.

THE HALDEMAN LETTER, CONTINUED On the second page of the letter to Haldeman, Hoover reports on perfectly legal activities: whether Lennon had been appointed to a commission on drug abuse and to a teaching position at NYU.

Originally two paragraphs were withheld under the national security exemption, and part of the "note" at the bottom continues to be withheld as foreign government information. Robert F. Peterson, an FBI agent with "original Top Secret classification authority," wrote in his 1983 declaration that release of this information could lead to "political or economic instability, or to civil disorder or unrest" in the foreign country or to "military retaliation against the United States."

Honorable H. R. Haldeman

A second confidential source, who has furnished reliable information in the past, advised that Lennon continues to be a heavy user of narcotics. On April 21, 1972, a third confidential source in a position to furnish reliable information advised that there was no information available indicating that Lennon has been appointed to the National Commission on Marijuana and Drug Abuse. A fourth confidential source in a position to furnish reliable information advised that Lennon has been offered a teaching position at New York University for the Summer of 1972.

This information is also being furnished to the Acting Attorney General. Pertinent information concerning Lennon is being furnished to the Department of State and INS on a regular basis.

Sincerely yours,

NOTE:

Classified "Confidential" since information is contained from ███████████ first confidential source is ███████ second confidential source is ███████ third confidential source is ███████ pretext inquiry by WFO with ███████ National Commission on Marijuana and Drug Abuse, Washington, D. C.; and fourth confidential source is ███████ , New York University, New York, New York.

See memorandum R. L. Shackelford to Mr. E. S. Miller, 4/21/72, captioned "John Winston Lennon, Security Matter - New Left," and prepared by RLP:plm.

b1
b2
b7c
b7d

- 2 -

HQ-12

Figure 70b. HQ-12 page 2, after settlement.

CLASSIFIED BY: [redacted]
DECLASSIFY ON: 25X6

1 - Mr. A. Rosen
1 - Mr. T. E. Bishop

The Acting Attorney General   April 25, 1972

Director, FBI

1 - Mr. E. S. Miller
1 - Mr. R. L. Shackelford
1 - Mr. T. J. Smith (Horner)
1 - Mr. R. L. Pence

JOHN WINSTON LENNON
SECURITY MATTER - NEW LEFT

      John Winston Lennon is a British citizen and former
member of the Beatles singing group. [redacted]

      Despite his apparent ineligibility for a United States
visa due to a conviction in London in 1968 for possession of
dangerous drugs, Lennon obtained a visa and entered the United
States in 1971. During February, 1972, a confidential source,
who has furnished reliable information in the past, advised that
Lennon had contributed $75,000 to a newly organized New Left
group formed to disrupt the Republican National Convention.
The visas of Lennon and his wife, Yoko Ono, expired on
February 29, 1972, and since that time Immigration and
Naturalization Service (INS) has been attempting to deport
them. During the Lennons' most recent deportation hearing at
INS, New York, New York, on April 18, 1972, their attorney
stated that Lennon felt he was being deported due to his
outspoken remarks concerning United States policy in Southeast
Asia. The attorney requested a delay in order that character
witnesses could testify for Lennon, and he then read into the
court record that Lennon had been appointed to the President's
Council for Drug Abuse (National Commission on Marijuana and
Drug Abuse) and to the faculty of New York University,
New York, New York.   REC 27 100-469910-6
                                                         5 APR 26 1972
      A second confidential source, who has furnished
reliable information in the past, advised that Lennon continues
to be a heavy user of narcotics. On April 21, 1972, a third
confidential source in a position to furnish reliable information
advised that there was no information available indicating that

MAILED 2
APR 26 1972

Tolson ___
Felt ___
Campbell ___
Rosen ___
Mohr ___
Bishop ___
Miller, E.S. ___
Callahan ___
Casper ___
Conrad ___
Dalbey ___
Cleveland ___
Ponder ___
Bates ___
Walters ___
Gandy ___

100-469910
RLP:plm

CONFIDENTIAL
Group 1
Excluded from automatic
downgrading and
declassification

SEE NOTE PAGE TWO

ALL INFORMATION CONTAINED
HEREIN IS UNCLASSIFIED EXCEPT
WHERE SHOWN OTHERWISE.

HQ-11

Figure 71. HQ-11 page 1.

The Acting Attorney General

Lennon has been appointed to the National Commission on
Marijuana and Drug Abuse. A fourth confidential source in a
position to furnish reliable information advised that Lennon
has been offered a teaching position at New York University
for the Summer of 1972. (u)

This information is also being furnished to the
Honorable H. R. Haldeman, Assistant to the President, at The
White House. Pertinent information concerning Lennon is being
furnished to the Department of State and INS on a regular
basis.

1 - The Deputy Attorney General

1 - Assistant Attorney General
    Internal Security Division

NOTE:

Classified "Confidential" since information is
contained from   first confidential source is   second
confidential source is   third confidential source is
pretext inquiry by WFO with
          , National Commission on Marijuana and Drug Abuse,
Washington, D. C.; and fourth confidential source is
                              , New York University, New York,
New York. (u)

See memorandum R. L. Shackelford to Mr. E. S. Miller,
4/21/72, captioned as above, prepared by RLP:plm.

HQ-11

Figure 72. HQ-11 page 2.

AN INFORMER'S TRIP TO NEW YORK   On March 2, an FBI informer in Madison traveled to New York with two local activists to meet with movement leaders there. The documentation on her trip begins with a cover page from the special agent in charge of the Milwaukee FBI office to Hoover, dated April 26, 1972, headed "Youth International Party" (NY-88 page 1).

The confidential informant who wrote this report, Julie Maynard, contacted Jon Wiener after reading about the Lennon FOIA lawsuit and declared she no longer wanted her identity to be secret. She joined the ACLU's lawsuit with a declaration to that effect. Her story appears in chapters 2 and 4 of this volume.

246

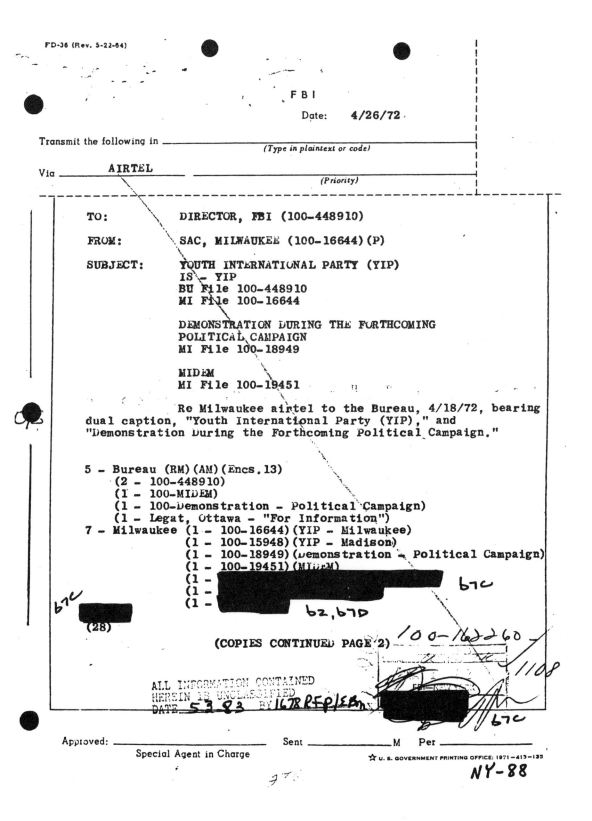

FD-36 (Rev. 5-22-64)

F B I

Date: **4/26/72**

Transmit the following in _____
(Type in plaintext or code)

Via _____ **AIRTEL** _____
(Priority)

TO: DIRECTOR, FBI (100-448910)

FROM: SAC, MILWAUKEE (100-16644)(P)

SUBJECT: YOUTH INTERNATIONAL PARTY (YIP)
           IS - YIP
           BU File 100-448910
           MI File 100-16644

           DEMONSTRATION DURING THE FORTHCOMING
           POLITICAL CAMPAIGN
           MI File 100-18949

           MIDEM
           MI File 100-19451

           Re Milwaukee airtel to the Bureau, 4/18/72, bearing
dual caption, "Youth International Party (YIP)," and
"Demonstration During the Forthcoming Political Campaign."

5 - Bureau (RM)(AM)(Encs.13)
     (2 - 100-448910)
     (1 - 100-MIDEM)
     (1 - 100-Demonstration - Political Campaign)
     (1 - Legat, Ottawa - "For Information")
7 - Milwaukee (1 - 100-16644)(YIP - Milwaukee)
               (1 - 100-15948)(YIP - Madison)
               (1 - 100-18949)(Demonstration - Political Campaign)
               (1 - 100-19451)(MIDEM)
               (1 -
               (1 -
               (1 -

(28)

(COPIES CONTINUED PAGE 2)

ALL INFORMATION CONTAINED
HEREIN IS UNCLASSIFIED
DATE 5-3-83 BY 1678 RFP/SB

Approved: _____   Sent _____ M   Per _____
           Special Agent in Charge
                                      ☆ U. S. GOVERNMENT PRINTING OFFICE: 1971-413-135

NY-88

Figure 74a. NY-88 page 4, initial release.

INFORMING ON THE YIPPIES   The first page of Julie Maynard's confidential informant report describes the trip she took from Madison to New York City in March 1972 to attend meetings about Yippie plans for demonstrations at the Republican convention (NY-88 page 4). It was withheld in its entirety for fourteen years as confidential source information and then released as part of the 1997 settlement. It reports various comings and goings at a conference at Stony Brook, none of which involved any reports of plans for criminal activity.

This entire report had been published in an underground newspaper in Madison in 1977 (see p. 89).

YOUTH INTERNATIONAL PARTY (YIP)

DEMONSTRATIONS DURING THE DEMOCRATIC
NATIONAL CONVENTION, JULY, 1972 -
MIAMI, FLORIDA

Source, who has furnished reliable information
in the past, advised on April 17, 1972, that Shirley Jane
Hopper traveled to New York City, from Madison, Wisconsin,
on March 2, 1972, until March 6, 1972, to meet with Yippie
and Zippie representatives.

The following is an account of that trip furnished by
source:

Thursday - March 2, 1972

Jane Hopper took a bus to Chicago and stayed with the
Halsted people. She got up early and went down to Continental
Driveaway Company and made arrangements for cars to New York
and back. She went to the bus station and picked up John
Mattes who came down on the bus that morning.

Friday - March 3, 1972

After picking John up she went and picked up the car which
turned out to be a used squad car that was being sent to Brooklyn
for resale.

Saturday - March 4, 1972

They arrived in New York at 3:00 AM and went to A. J.
Heberman's house at 6 Bleeker Street. After getting some sleep,
A. J. went over to Tom Forcade's house to get him up. He came
back with Frank Rose, who lives with Tom. They decided to make a
Zippie presence at the Stonybrook Conference. Jane drove out
there with John, Pat Small, and Kathy Morales, (who are living
with A. J.) and Frank Rose. Pat Small made a plea for the people
there to join Zippie and announced that there would be a separate
caucus for Zip in another room. The Zips drew off maybe a third
of the people there. Most people were stopped by the campus police
either coming or going. Hopper was stopped and I.D.'d while
waiting to pick her friends up after the thing broke up.

2

Figure 74b. NY-88 page 4, after settlement.

Figure 75a. NY-88 page 5, initial release.

THE PARROT STORY   The informer's report written by Julie Maynard about her trip from Madison to New York in March 1972 continues with a story about "a girl there name Linda" who has a parrot that "interjects 'Right On' whenever the conversation gets rousing" (NY-88 page 5). That story was featured in news reports on the settlement as an example of the trivial information the FBI had been collecting in 1972, information to which the FBI devoted substantial resources to keep secret through ensuing decades. This page includes a variety of other movement gossip and information, none of which describes plans for criminal activity. This page was withheld in its entirety for fourteen years as confidential source information and then released as part of the 1997 settlement.

YOUTH INTERNATIONAL PARTY (YIP)

DEMONSTRATIONS DURING THE DEMOCRATIC
NATIONAL CONVENTION, JULY, 1972 -
MIAMI, FLORIDA

Sunday, March 5, 1972
      Hopper went over to the New York Switchboard and made
arrangements for Zip announcements to appear in a newsletter they
are planning to set up for all the underground switchboards in
the next month. She went over to Rex Weiner's house. He is
the editor of the 'New York Ace' which is an up and coming underground
paper. He seems to be an old political hand. He was very glad
to see us and proposed a party that night to welcome us to New
York, at his newspaper office. The party started at about 9:00 PM
so Hopper had time to go eat at Tom Forcade's house. He lives in
a real dump at 209 East 5th Street. His office is at 204 West
10th Street (basement). He has no legitimate phone. To call
out he taps into a Hungarian person's phone. There is a girl
there name Linda who acts as a servent for Tom and Frank.
Linda's parrot interjects "Right On" whenever the conversation gets
rousing. Tom is trying to train it to say "eat shit" whenever
he argues with anyone but the bird now says it to him whenever
he sees him. The cage is surrounded by small objects that Tom
has thrown in response. From there Hopper went to the party.
She was introduced to the elite of the radical left. Jerry
Rubin rushed up to Jane and begged her to let him be a Zippie.
She said we would have to iron out a few differences first and
she agreed to meet with him the next day. Jane left with Forcade
for a while so John, A. J., and his girl Ann mingled for a while.
Frank was acting as a chauffeur dressed up in a fancy uniform.
Jane got quite drunk and Jerry began to give her trouble about it.

Monday - March 6, 1972
      This was Hopper's and John's last day in New York so it
was packed with business meetings. Hopper had to take care of
delivering the car to Brooklyn. When Hopper got back to A. J.'s,
Tom was there and they were finalizing plans for the smoke-ins.
They are apparently going to take place in twenty states and five
foreign countries including England, Netherlands, France, Germany,
and New Zealand. Debi from the Toronto Guerilla arrived to get a
ride back with us as far as Erie, Pennsylvania. They left A. J.'s
and went over to Jerry Rubin's house at 156 Prince Street. Stev
Albert was there. Jerry told us that the bad press we were giving
him had hurt him badly politically. He said he would be finished
in politics unless we patched things up. They replied that they
thought he was an asshole. He said that Abby was coming back next

Figure 75b. NY-88 page 5, after settlement.

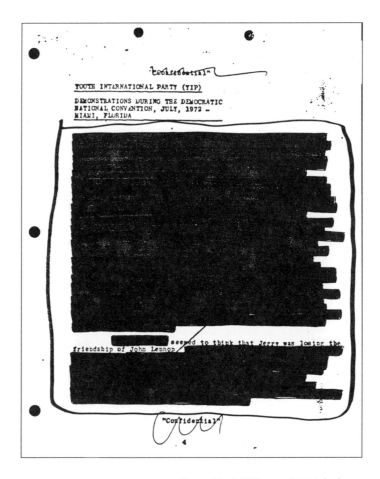

YOUTH INTERNATIONAL PARTY (YIP)

DEMONSTRATIONS DURING THE DEMOCRATIC
NATIONAL CONVENTION, JULY, 1972 –
MIAMI, FLORIDA

seemed to think that Jerry was losing the
friendship of John Lennon.

"Confidential"

Figure 76a. NY-88 page 6, initial release.

"IF THEY ARE PEACEFUL"   The informer's report written by Julie Maynard about her trip to New York in March, 1972 concludes with one crucial piece of information: Lennon sent a "message" that he would come to the demonstrations at the Republican National Convention in Miami "if they are peaceful."

The FBI told the courts and the public they had been conducting a legitimate criminal investigation of Lennon because they had information that he intended to participate in violent, disruptive demonstrations in Miami. The FBI went all the way to the Supreme Court to prevent this document from being released to the public. It undermines the entire pretext of the FBI's investigation of Lennon.

252

YOUTH INTERNATIONAL PARTY (YIP)

DEMONSTRATIONS DURING THE DEMOCRATIC NATIONAL CONVENTION, JULY, 1972 - MIAMI, FLORIDA

month and that he wouldn't let us kick him around. They told him that they would meet Abby at the airport and throw him out of the party also. He layed down on the floor close to tears. Stew said they were being too rough on him so they chewed him up in like fashion. Jerry asked us to negotiate with him and we agreed to it. We listed our bitches with him, 1. His superstar ego which enables him to appear to lead us while he does none of the work yet gets the credit; 2. Financial deals that have netted him money in the past that he made in the name of Yippie but then used for himself; 3. His b.o. and other bad habits; 4. His feud with Tom and other Zip people. He said that he would do anything and we should just tell him what we wanted. They told him they wanted money and they told him that they wanted him to get signatures for the Armstrong petition. They also told him that we would stop bad-rapping his in accordance with how well he performs his assignments. We will make no interferences in his affairs political or otherwise as long as he didn't claim leadership in Zip or Yip. He will have no decision making powers. If he or Abby want responsibilities in the new party they will have to earn them like everyone else. The fact that they are superstars and can get coverage of events does not impress us at all. They are a liability within the movement. They have turned too many people off. John and Hopper left for Madison. The only trouble they had on the way home was an incident in Pennsylvania. Their car was identified as having been involved in a burglarly. They were stopped for about an hour and then released. They were somewhere around Sharon and Mercer, Pennsylvania.

Jane and John seemed to think that Jerry was losing the friendship of John Lennon. John had thought that he was the cent of radical politics and by throwing him out we let the thought enter Lennon's head that perhaps Jerry was washed up. Lennon had a message delivered to us at Stonybrook that he would do an Armstrong benefit if we didn't let it out that he was coming. In other words, it had to be happening on its own steam before he would come. He will also come to the conventions if they are peaceful, under the same terms.

4

Figure 76b. NY-88 page 6, after settlement.

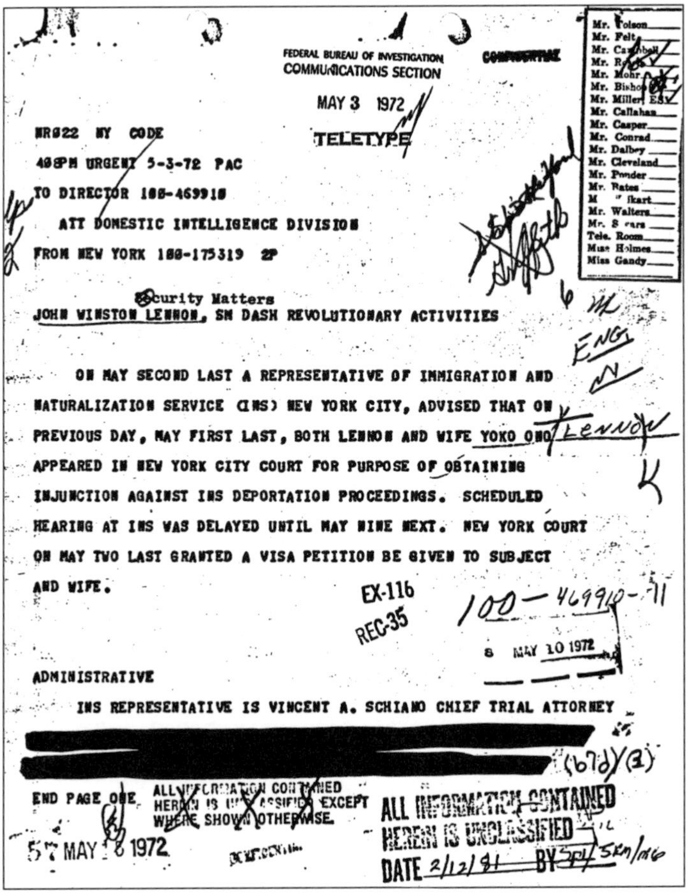

Figure 77a. HQ-16 page 2, initial release.

"REVOLUTIONARY ACTIVITIES"   Hoover received an urgent coded teletype (HQ-16 page 2) from the New York FBI office, dated May 3, 1972. The full text was released only after fourteen years of litigation, in the 1997 settlement. Here, Lennon's classification has been upgraded from "Security Matter—New Left" (see "From Shackelford to Miller," HQ-15 page 1, p. 237) to "Security Matter— Revolutionary Activities." No reason is given for the change, and nothing Lennon did in the period before May 3 would explain why the FBI made this change. The withheld information declared that "British authorities . . . advised that Lennon's narcotics conviction in England is not likely to be overturned."

FEDERAL BUREAU OF INVESTIGATION
COMMUNICATIONS SECTION

MAY 3 1972

TELETYPE

NR22 NY CODE

448PM URGENT 5-3-72 PAC

TO DIRECTOR 100-469910

ATT DOMESTIC INTELLIGENCE DIVISION

FROM NEW YORK 100-175319 2P

Security Matters
JOHN WINSTON LENNON, SM DASH REVOLUTIONARY ACTIVITIES

ON MAY SECOND LAST A REPRESENTATIVE OF IMMIGRATION AND

NATURALIZATION SERVICE (INS) NEW YORK CITY, ADVISED THAT ON

PREVIOUS DAY, MAY FIRST LAST, BOTH LENNON AND WIFE YOKO ONO

APPEARED IN NEW YORK CITY COURT FOR PURPOSE OF OBTAINING

INJUNCTION AGAINST INS DEPORTATION PROCEEDINGS. SCHEDULED

HEARING AT INS WAS DELAYED UNTIL MAY NINE NEXT. NEW YORK COURT

ON MAY TWO LAST GRANTED A VISA PETITION BE GIVEN TO SUBJECT

AND WIFE.

EX-116
REC-35

100—469910—11

8 MAY 10 1972

ADMINISTRATIVE

INS REPRESENTATIVE IS VINCENT A. SCHIANO CHIEF TRIAL ATTORNEY

WHO FURTHER ADVISED THAT BRITISH AUTHORITIES HAVE ADVISED THAT

LENNON'S NARCOTICS CONVICTION IN ENGLAND IS NOT LIKELY TO

END PAGE ONE. ALL INFORMATION CONTAINED
HEREIN IS UNCLASSIFIED EXCEPT
WHERE SHOWN OTHERWISE.

5 MAY 18 1972

ALL INFORMATION CONTAINED
HEREIN IS UNCLASSIFIED
DATE 2/12/81 BY SPL/SKM/m16

Figure 77b. HQ-16 page 2, after settlement.

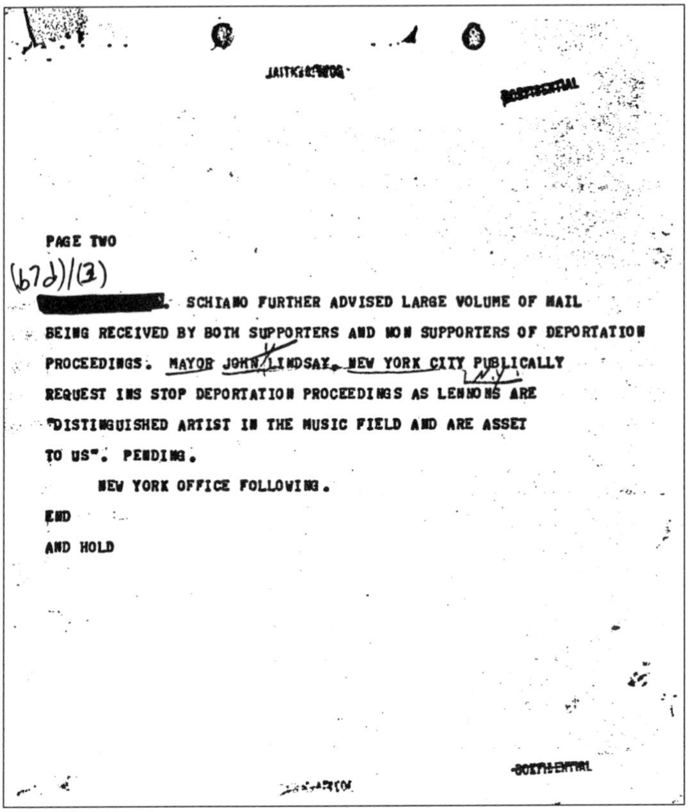

PAGE TWO

(b7d)/(3)

██████████ SCHIANO FURTHER ADVISED LARGE VOLUME OF MAIL
BEING RECEIVED BY BOTH SUPPORTERS AND NON SUPPORTERS OF DEPORTATION
PROCEEDINGS. MAYOR JOHN LINDSAY, NEW YORK CITY PUBLICALLY
REQUEST INS STOP DEPORTATION PROCEEDINGS AS LENNONS ARE
"DISTINGUISHED ARTIST IN THE MUSIC FIELD AND ARE ASSET
TO US". PENDING.
    NEW YORK OFFICE FOLLOWING.
END
AND HOLD

Figure 78a. HQ-16 page 3, initial release.

"NON SUPPORTERS OF DEPORTATION"   The urgent coded teletype Hoover received on May 3 from the New York FBI office continues by informing the Director about the "large volume of mail being received by both supporters and non supporters of deportation proceedings" and reports that New York Mayor John Lindsay did "publically request INS stop deportation proceedings" (HQ-16 page 3). The ACLU cited this page in court arguments as evidence that the FBI lacked a legitimate law enforcement purpose in investigation of Lennon but rather was monitoring constitutionally protected political expression.

CONFIDENTIAL

PAGE TWO

BE OVERTURNED. SCHIANO FURTHER ADVISED LARGE VOLUME OF MAIL BEING RECEIVED BY BOTH SUPPORTERS AND NON SUPPORTERS OF DEPORTATION PROCEEDINGS. MAYOR ~~JOHN LINDSAY,~~ NEW YORK CITY N.Y. PUBLICALLY REQUEST INS STOP DEPORTATION PROCEEDINGS AS LENNONS ARE "DISTINGUISHED ARTIST IN THE MUSIC FIELD AND ARE ASSET TO US". PENDING.

NEW YORK OFFICE FOLLOWING.

END

AND HOLD

CONFIDENTIAL

Figure 78b. HQ-16 page 3, after settlement.

Figure 79a. NY-47 page 1, initial release.

"BENIFIT [SIC] FOR JOHN LENNON"   This FBI informant report dated May 13 gives as its subject "Report on Benifit for John Lennon" (NY-47 page 1). However, the report concerns a benefit for the Attica Defense Committee, which, it states, Lennon plugged on the *Dick Cavett Show*. The ACLU cited this passage in court arguments as evidence that the FBI lacked a legitimate law enforcement purpose in investigating Lennon. It was not a crime to "plug" a benefit concert; it's a constitutionally protected activity.

Both of these pages were originally withheld in their entirety under the national security exemption as intelligence source information. Releasing the information, the FBI claimed, could lead to "possible loss of life, jobs, friends, status, etc., all of which can reasonably be expected to . . . result in damage to the national security."

Cover Sheet for Informant Report or Ma'
FD-306 (Rev. 9-3-69)

Date prepared
6/6/72

Date received	Received from (name or symbol number)	Received by
5/23/72	(Protect) b2 b7D	SA b7C

Method of delivery (check appropriate blocks)

☐ in person ☐ by telephone ☒ by mail ☐ orally ☐ recording device ☐ written by Informant

If orally furnished and reduced to writing by Agent:
Date

Dictated _____ to _____

Transcribed _____ DECLASSIFIED BY 5/2/83
ON 1678 RFP/2Bm

Authenticated
by Informant _____

Date of Report
5/13/72

Date(s) of activity
5/13/72

Brief description of activity or material

Report on Benifit for JOHN LENNON and
structure of NYRU.

File where original is located if not attached
b2 b7D

* INDIVIDUALS DESIGNATED BY AN ASTERISK (*) ONLY ATTENDED A MEETING AND DID NOT ACTIVELY PARTICIPATE.
OLENCE OR REVOLUTIONARY ACTIVITIES WERE NOT DISCUSSED.

☐ Information recorded on a card index by _____ on date _____

Remarks:

All necessary action taken

22- New York
1- b2, b7D.
1- 100- (JOHN LENNON)
1- 100-174832 (ATTICA DEFENSE COMMITTEE)
1- 100-156088 (ASIAN INFO OFFICE)
1-
1-
1-
1-
b7C 1-
1-
1-
1-
1-
1- 100-174986 (NYRC)

Copies Continued.

CLASS. BY 1678 RFP/6Bm
5.2 83
Declass OADR

ALL INFORMATION CONTAINED
HEREIN IS UNCLASSIFIED EXCEPT
WHERE SHOWN OTHERWISE.

Block Stamp
100 - 175319 - 45

b7C (22) CLASS. & EXT. BY
REASON FCIM II,
DATE OF REVIEW
6/22/82

NY-47

Figure 79b. NY-47 page 1, after settlement.

Figure 80a. NY-47 page 3, initial release.

THE DICK CAVETT SHOW   On the same *Dick Cavett Show* reported on in the FBI confidential informant report dated May 13, Lennon declared he would not participate in antiwar activities at the Republican National Convention (NY-47 page 3). "They think we're going to San Diego, or Miami, or wherever it is," he said. "We've never said we're going, there'll be no big jam with Dylan, because there's too much going on."* This information does not appear in the Lennon FBI file, though the pretext the FBI claimed for investigating Lennon was that he planned to participate in violent, disruptive, illegal demonstrations at the Republican National Convention.

* Wiener, *Come Together*, 239.

Saturday May 13, 1972](X)(u)

        After JOHN LENNON p;ugged it on the Dick Cavett Show,
the benefit concert for the Attica Defense Committee turned a
larger crowd than expected. Among the people who came were
CTTO PREMINGER č a party of 5 people. Security was tight.
The AIO core group included RONALD ROSEN, JOSEPHINE PIZZINO
(both new members of AIO), JAMES DUFFY, MAURICE WADE, and was
led by WALTER TEAGUE. Also on security were WALTER APONTI
(recently purged from AIO) LAWRENCE REMER, DIANE DANHAN, and
STEPHEN POMEPANTE. The benefit was held at the Wash. Sq. Meth
Ch, began at about 20:00, was ended about 1:30 Sunday morning
by a bomb threat, and neted $2,000 for the Defense Comm and $200
for the WSM Ch, (X)(u)

        At 15:00 the NYRC had a meeting on re-organization
at its hq (98 B third Ave). The meeting was fruitless. The
two factions are basically these: LAWRENCE LEVY and HENRY
PLATSKY want to form a more, intellectually oriented group which
functions as a study group, at least at the outset. ROBERT HENES,
EUGENIE S. JOSEPH, SUSAN LNU, WILLIAM SMITH, LESTER BAUM, and
some unidentified members of the Prison Collective (on arm of
NYRC concerned č prisoner liason) wish the group to become more
action oriented feeling that any form of movement toward the
study group idea is a cowardly retreat. X(u)

Other facts: (X)(u)

b7C
b7D

(X)(u)

Figure 80b. NY-47 page 3, after settlement.

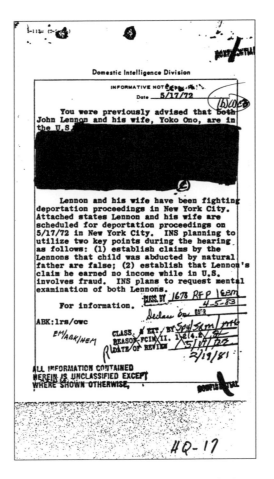

Figure 81a. HQ-17 page 1, initial release.

"PERJURY CHARGES"　An "Informative Note" accompanied an urgent coded teletype from the New York FBI to Acting FBI director L. Patrick Gray, who was appointed on Hoover's death on May 2 (HQ-17 page 1). It reports on the Nixon administration's strategy in upcoming deportation hearings by the INS Chief Trial Attorney Vincent Schiano, opening the door to "perjury charges against the Lennons."

The report that EYSIC was "'dying on the vine' due to Lennon's possible deportation" was originally withheld as national security intelligence source information. Releasing that information, the FBI declared in court, "would enable a hostile analyst to unravel the cloak of secrecy that protects the intelligence source's identity." Nevertheless the information was eventually released.

Domestic Intelligence Division

INFORMATIVE NOTE

Date __5/17/72__

You were previously advised that both John Lennon and his wife, Yoko Ono, are in the U.S. and that Lennon is the major financial contributor to the Election Year Strategy Information Center (EYSIC) which was organized to conduct disruptive demonstrations during the Republican National Convention. EYSIC has been "dying on the vine" due to Lennon's possible deportation which he is fighting in court.

Lennon and his wife have been fighting deportation proceedings in New York City. Attached states Lennon and his wife are scheduled for deportation proceedings on 5/17/72 in New York City. INS planning to utilize two key points during the hearing as follows: (1) establish claims by the Lennons that child was abducted by natural father are false; (2) establish that Lennon's claim he earned no income while in U.S. involves fraud. INS plans to request mental examination of both Lennons.

For information.

ABK:lrs/owc

CLASS. BY 1678 RFP IEBM
4-5-83

CLASS. & EXT. BY SPH/SLM/MHG
REASON FCIM XII. 1, 2, 4. 2, 81
DATE OF REVIEW 5/17/22
2/19/81

Figure 81b. HQ-17 page 1, after court decision.

HQ-17

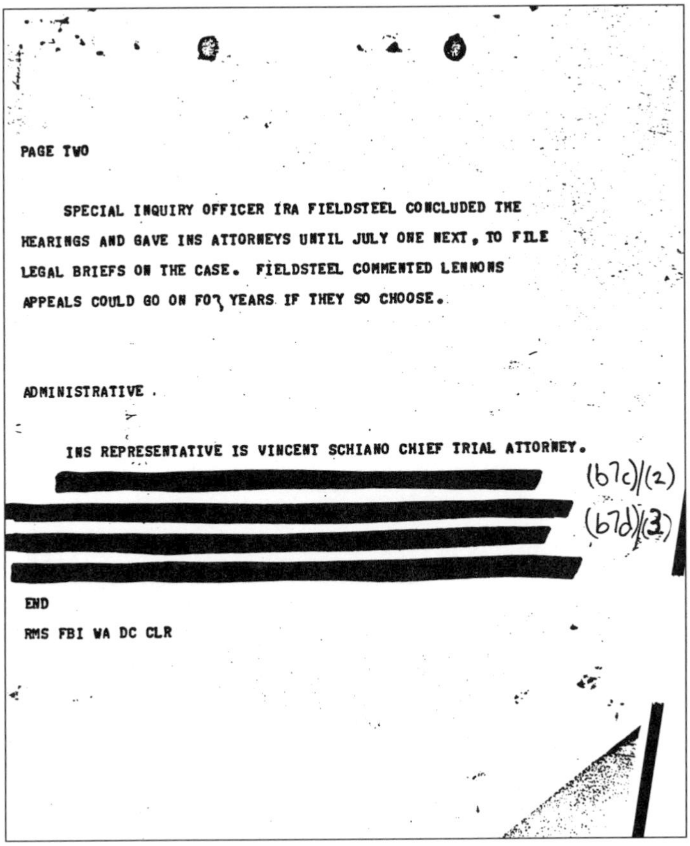

Figure 82a. HQ-18 page 2, initial release.

"UNABLE TO MAKE A NARCOTICS CASE" The urgent coded teletype sent to Acting Director Gray on May 18 by the New York FBI continues with a report on the previous day's immigration hearings (HQ-18 page 2). Exactly why this would be sent in code is a mystery—the same information had been reported widely in the day's newspapers and TV news shows.

The last four lines were withheld for fourteen years as confidential source information and released only in the 1997 settlement: they report that "New York police department . . . has been unable to make a narcotics case on the Lennons." This came after the FBI had been trying to orchestrate a drug bust to expedite Lennon's deportation at a time when, as this page reports, "appeals go could on for years."

PAGE TWO

SPECIAL INQUIRY OFFICER IRA FIELDSTEEL CONCLUDED THE
HEARINGS AND GAVE INS ATTORNEYS UNTIL JULY ONE NEXT, TO FILE
LEGAL BRIEFS ON THE CASE. FIELDSTEEL COMMENTED LENNONS
APPEALS COULD GO ON FOR YEARS IF THEY SO CHOOSE.

ADMINISTRATIVE

INS REPRESENTATIVE IS VINCENT SCHIANO CHIEF TRIAL ATTORNEY.
ON MAY SIXTEEN, LAST, ███████████████████, THIRD   b7c
NARCOTICS DEISTRICT, NEW YORK POLICE DEPARTMENT ADVISED THAT   b7D
HIS DEPARTMENT HAS BEEN UNABLE TO MAKE A NARCOTICS CASE ON
THE LENNONS. NYPD CONTINUING. NYO FOLLOWING. NO LHM FOLLOWS.
END
RMS FBI WA DC CLR

Figure 82b. HQ-18 page 2, after settlement.

ANTIWAR NEWS   The FBI Lennon file included a clip from the *New York Post* for May 19 (NY-85). The FBI documents Lennon's continuing engagement with the antiwar movement, despite pressure from the INS. The article reports that the demonstrations, sponsored by the National Peace Action Council, would be held outside more than thirty military bases, and that as a result the annual Armed Forces Day parade in New York had been canceled. Clearly Lennon was one small part of an immense movement.

FBI agents also collected leaflets from demonstrators: NY-86 is a memo from an FBI agent to the special agent in charge of the FBI in New York, conveying a leaflet the agent collected at the demonstrations on May 20. Lennon's name is included among the sponsors, an impressive list that ranges from Anais Nin to William Styron to Kurt Vonnegut. The underlining of endorsers' names suggests that each has an FBI file containing a copy of this document.

Of course the FBI had no legitimate law enforcement purpose in monitoring or collecting information about Lennon's endorsement of an antiwar candle-light vigil.

John and Yoko Joining Vigil Here

By MILTON ADAMS

A weekend of massive demonstrations has been scheduled to take place here and across the country by several peace groups demanding complete withdrawal of U. S. forces from Indochina.

A candlelight vigil and "procession for peace" tomorrow night in Duffy Square, at Broadway between 46th and 47th Sts., from 8 to 11 p.m., will highlight local activities.

Sponsored by the National Peace Action Coalition, the vigil is expected to attract a number of prominent members of the city's art community, and rally support for a massive demonstration scheduled for Washington on Sunday.

The two demonstrations were announced by NPAC National Coordinator Katherine Sojourner yesterday.

Supporters of the Sunday march in Washington include about 25 members of Congress, a number of local politicians, and trade union leaders from across the country.

John and Yoko

Members of the art community endorsing the Washington march and expected to attend tomorrow's vigil include John Lennon and Yoko Ono; satirist Jules Feif-

fer; producer Joseph Papp; writers Arthur Miller and William Styron and others.

"This Sunday in Washington, thousands of Americans will express their opposition to Nixon's latest and most dangerous escalations," said novelist Kurt Vonnegut, Jr., reading a statement signed by about 50 prominent artists.

"At this critical time, we believe it important to share some time and feeling for peace," the statement said.

On Monday, Washington demonstrators plan what they call a "blockade" of the Pentagon by blocking entrances to the building.

Plans were also announced today by the U. S. Servicemen's Fund, for a series of antiwar demonstrations at Fort Dix and more than 30 other military bases and installations across the country tomorrow.

Similar Armed Forces Day demonstrations organized by active-duty military personnel last year have forced the Pentagon to cancel official parades and ceremonies at these bases.

Such fears by officials of the Military Order of the World Wars resulted in the cancellation of New York's 23rd annual Armed Forces Day parade this week.

New York Post
5/19/72
P 5

Date:
Edition:
Author:
Editor:
Title:

Character:
or
Classification:
Submitting Office:
☐ Being Investigated

100-170471-1347

SEARCHED _____ INDEXED _____
SERIALIZED _____ FILED _____
MAY 19 1972
FBI—NEW YORK

NY-85

DO NOT DESTROY — PENDING LITIGATION

Figure 83. NY-85.

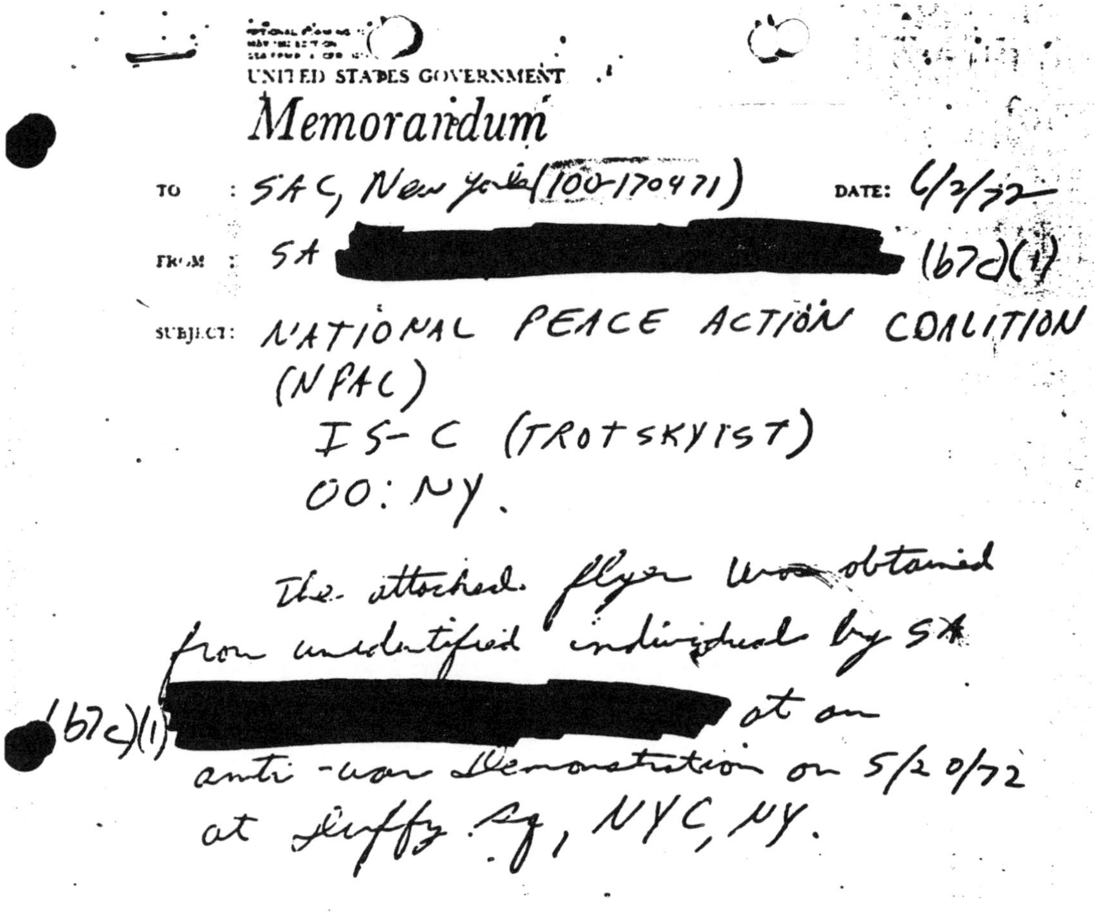

OPTIONAL FORM NO. 10
MAY 1962 EDITION
GSA FPMR (41 CFR) 101-11.6

UNITED STATES GOVERNMENT

Memorandum

TO : SAC, New York (100-170471)   DATE: 6/2/72

FROM : SA ███████████████████████ (67c)(1)

SUBJECT: NATIONAL PEACE ACTION COALITION
(NPAC)
IS-C (TROTSKYIST)
OO: NY.

The attached flyer was obtained
from unidentified individual by SA
(67c)(1) ████████████████████████ at an
anti-war demonstration on 5/20/72
at Duffy Sq, NYC, NY.

Figure 37a. NY-27 page 4, initial release

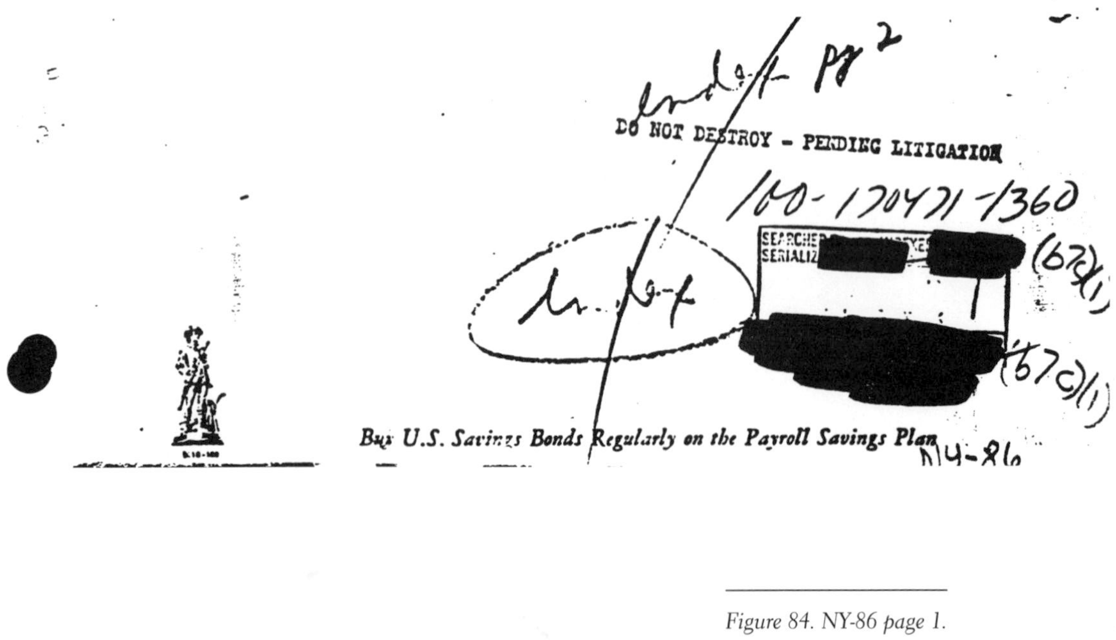

cont d /t pg 2

DO NOT DESTROY – PENDING LITIGATION

100-170471-1360
(67c)(1)

m. d-t

SEARCHED_____INDEXED_____
SERIALIZED_____

(67c)(1)

Buy U.S. Savings Bonds Regularly on the Payroll Savings Plan

NY-86

Figure 84. NY-86 page 1.

Join us Saturday night, May 20, 1972 — 8 to 11 p.m. in Duffy Square, Broadway between 46th & 47th Sts

for a

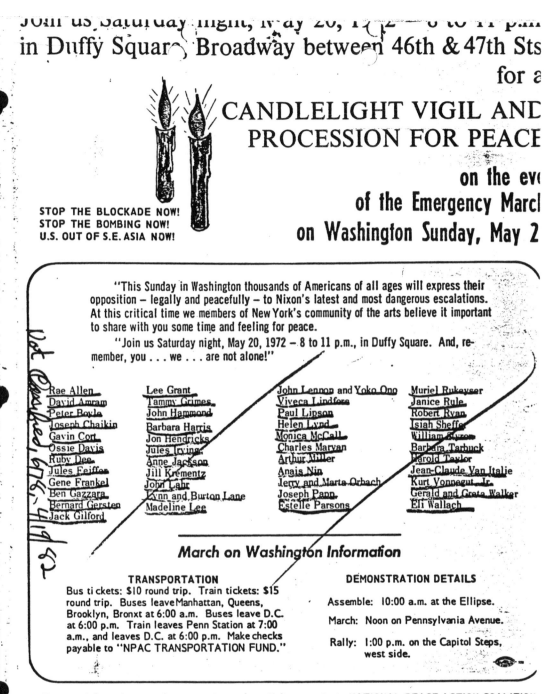

CANDLELIGHT VIGIL AND
PROCESSION FOR PEACE

on the eve
of the Emergency March
on Washington Sunday, May 21

STOP THE BLOCKADE NOW!
STOP THE BOMBING NOW!
U.S. OUT OF S.E. ASIA NOW!

"This Sunday in Washington thousands of Americans of all ages will express their opposition — legally and peacefully — to Nixon's latest and most dangerous escalations. At this critical time we members of New York's community of the arts believe it important to share with you some time and feeling for peace.

"Join us Saturday night, May 20, 1972 — 8 to 11 p.m., in Duffy Square. And, remember, you . . . we . . . are not alone!"

Rae Allen
David Amram
Peter Boyle
Joseph Chaikin
Gavin Cort
Ossie Davis
Ruby Dee
Jules Feiffer
Gene Frankel
Ben Gazzara
Bernard Gersten
Jack Gilford

Lee Grant
Tammy Grimes
John Hammond
Barbara Harris
Jon Hendricks
Jules Irving
Anne Jackson
Jill Krementz
John Lahr
Lynn and Burton Lane
Madeline Lee

John Lennon and Yoko Ono
Viveca Lindfors
Paul Lipson
Helen Lynd
Monica McCall
Charles Marvan
Arthur Miller
Anais Nin
Jerry and Marta Orbach
Joseph Papp
Estelle Parsons

Muriel Rukeyser
Janice Rule
Robert Ryan
Isiah Sheffer
William Styron
Barbara Tarbuck
Harold Taylor
Jean-Claude Van Italie
Kurt Vonnegut, Jr.
Gerald and Greta Walker
Eli Wallach

March on Washington Information

TRANSPORTATION
Bus tickets: $10 round trip. Train tickets: $15 round trip. Buses leave Manhattan, Queens, Brooklyn, Bronxt at 6:00 a.m. Buses leave D.C. at 6:00 p.m. Train leaves Penn Station at 7:00 a.m., and leaves D.C. at 6:00 p.m. Make checks payable to "NPAC TRANSPORTATION FUND."

DEMONSTRATION DETAILS

Assemble: 10:00 a.m. at the Ellipse.

March: Noon on Pennsylvania Avenue.

Rally: 1:00 p.m. on the Capitol Steps, west side.

For more information, to volunteer, or to purchase tickets, contact: NATIONAL PEACE ACTION COALITION 150 Fifth Avenue, New York, N.Y. 10011. (212) 741-2018. Urgent — we need money now to help pay for May 21

Figure 85. NY-86 page 2.

SEARCHING FOR KYOKO   Acting Director Gray sent an urgent coded teletype on May 23 to the FBI offices in Houston and New York, ordering them to search for Kyoko Cox, Yoko's daughter from her first marriage (HQ-19 page 1). This episode provides a strange and particularly mean-spirited chapter in the Lennon deportation fight. Kyoko's father, Anthony Cox, had agreed to joint custody, but Cox was violating the custody agreement and keeping Kyoko, who was eight years old at the time, hidden. In the deportation hearings, Lennon said one reason why he wanted to stay in the U.S. was that he wanted to help Yoko search for Kyoko. The FBI was investigating whether Lennon and Ono were participating in keeping Kyoko hidden to avoid deportation. They weren't.

The teletype states that "subject and wife Yoko Ono involved in antiwar activities," as if that were a crime.

| Mr. Tolson |
| Mr. Felt |
| Mr. Campbell |
| Mr. Rosen |
| Mr. Mohr |
| Mr. Bishop |
| Mr. Miller, E. |
| Mr. Callahan |
| Mr. Casper |
| Mr. Conrad |
| Mr. Dalbey |
| Mr. Cleveland |
| Mr. Ponder |
| Mr. Bates |
| Mr. Walkert |
| Mr. Walters |
| Mr. S |
| Tele. Room |
| Miss Ho |
| Miss Gandy |

NR 039 NY CODE

1716 PM URGENT 5-23-72 BGW

TO ACTING DIRECTOR (100-469910)

    ATTN: DID

    HOUSTON

FROM NEW YORK

JOHN WINSTON LENNON, SM-REVOLUTIONARY ACTIVITES (ORIGIN:
NEW YORK)

    RE NEW YORK TEL TO BUREAU MAY ONE EIGHT LAST. HOUSTON
NOT IN RECEIPT OF REFERENCED TEL.

    FOR INFORMATION OF HOUSTON, SUBJECT AND WIFE YOKO ONO
INVOLVED IN ANTI-WAR ACTIVITES AND PLAN TO TRAVEL TO
REPUBLICAN AND DEMOCRATIC CONVENTION THIS YEAR. INS ATTEMPTING
TO DEPORT BOTH LENNONS ON GROUNDS OF SUBJECT'S ONE NINE SIX
EIGHT NARCOTIC CONVICTION IN ENGLAND. box 442 KOUNTZE TEXAS

    LENNONS USING DELAY TACTICS IN DEPORTATION OF ATTEMPTING
TO LOCATE YOKO ONO'S CHILD KYOKO COX WHO WAS REPORTED ABDUCTED
BY NATURAL FATHER ANTHONY DAVID COX. HOUSTON COURT HAS
AWARDED CUSTODY OF CHILD TO LENNONS. NO PROCESS OUT ON COX

    END PAGE ONE

TEXAS REC 31 100-469910-14

EZ MAY 25 1972

Figure 86. HQ-19 page 1.

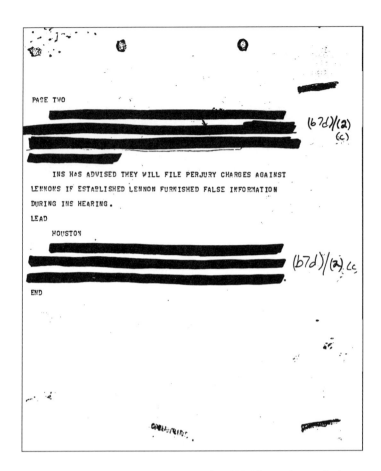

PAGE TWO

(b7d)/(2)
(c)

INS HAS ADVISED THEY WILL FILE PERJURY CHARGES AGAINST
LENNONS IF ESTABLISHED LENNON FURNISHED FALSE INFORMATION
DURING INS HEARING.
LEAD
    HOUSTON

(b7d)/(2) cc

END

Figure 87a. HQ-19 page 2, initial release.

"HIDDEN CHILD"   The urgent coded teletype from Acting Director Gray ordering a search for Yoko's daughter Kyoko continues here (HQ-19 page 2). In the initial release two-thirds of the page was withheld as law enforcement confidential source information. Here Gray informs the New York FBI that "INS will file perjury charges against Lennons" if they were lying about not knowing where Kyoko was.

PAGE TWO

NYO IN RECEIPT OF INFORMATION THIS DATE THAT LENNONS

HAVE HIDDEN CHILD AT RESIDENCE OF ▓▓▓▓▓▓▓▓▓▓▓▓ b7c

▓▓▓▓▓▓▓▓▓▓▓▓▓▓▓▓▓▓▓▓▓▓▓▓▓▓▓▓▓▓ IN ATTEMTPS

TO DELAY DEPORATION.

INS HAS ADVISED THEY WILL FILE PERJURY CHARGES AGAINST

LENNONS IF ESTABLISHED LENNON FURNISHED FALSE INFORMATION

DURING INS HEARING.

LEAD

HOUSTON

AT ▓▓▓▓▓▓▓▓ CONDUCT APPROPRIATE INVESTIGATION

b7c

TO DETERMINE IF KYOKO COX IS AT ABOVE ADDRESS, AND ATTEMPT

TO ESTABLISH IF ▓▓▓▓ IN CONTACT WITH LENNONS IN NYC. SUTEL.

END

Figure 87b. HQ-19 page 2, after court decision.

"DISREGARD LEAD"   Acting FBI Director Gray sent an urgent coded teletype (HQ-20) to FBI offices in New York and Houston on May 24 ordering Houston to "disregard lead set [sent] by New York" concerning the whereabouts of Yoko's daughter Kyoko Cox. In telegraphic style, Gray declared that "aspects investigation relating to subject's appearance at hearings and possible perjury involved in false statements made by subject strictly responsibility of INS."

The FBI continues to claim that releasing the three blacked-out lines at the bottom of the page would endanger the national security; this deletion remains the subject of litigation. The FBI has withheld this information as foreign government confidential information. In court papers the FBI identified the "Logical Nexus Between Disclosure of This Information and Damage to the National Security": disclosure could lead to "military retaliation" by the government that provided the information.

2/13/96
CLASSIFIED BY: CODE 9803R DD/JS   TELETYPE   IMMEDIATE
REASON: 1.5 (b)   CA# CV83-1720
DECLASSIFY ON: X 5

CLASSIFIED DECISIONS FINALIZED
BY DEPARTMENT REVIEW COMMITTEE (DRC)
DATE: 12/16/99   SSA SLD/JS 12/16/99

5/24/72

TO   SACS NEW YORK (100-175319)   1 - Mr. C.W. Bates
         HOUSTON   (C.A. Nuzum)

FROM   ACTING DIRECTOR FBI (100-469910) _14   1 - Mr. R.L. Shackelford
                                                 1 - Mr. R.L. Pence

JOHN WINSTON LENNON, SM - REVOLUTIONARY ACTIVITIES.

RENYTEL MAY TWENTY-THREE LAST.   CLASSIFIED DECISIONS FINALIZED
                                        BY DEPARTMENT REVIEW COMMITTEE (DRC)
                                        DATE: 2/12/96

HOUSTON DISREGARD LEAD SET BY NEW YORK IN REFERENCED TELETYPE

EXCEPT FOR CONTACT WITH ESTABLISHED SOURCES ONLY.

     BUREAU FULLY AWARE PROGRESS OF NEW YORK OFFICE IN DEVELOPING

EXCELLENT COVERAGE SUBJECT'S ACTIVITIES, HOWEVER, ASPECTS INVESTI-

GATION RELATING TO SUBJECT'S APPEARANCE AT INS HEARINGS AND POSSIBLE

PERJURY INVOLVED IN FALSE STATEMENTS MADE BY SUBJECT STRICTLY

RESPONSIBILITY OF INS. INFORMATION DEVELOPED BY NEW YORK SHOULD BE

IMMEDIATELY, IF NOT ALREADY, FURNISHED TO INS. ALL SUBSEQUENT

INFORMATION DEVELOPED REGARDING SUBJECT'S VIOLATIONS OF FEDERAL AND

LOCAL LAWS INCLUDING NARCOTICS OR PERJURY, SHOULD LIKEWISE BE

DISSEMINATED WITHOUT DELAY TO PERTINENT AGENCIES.

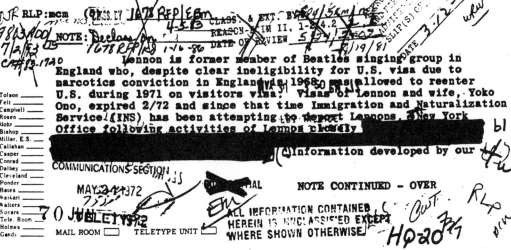

TJR RLP:mcm   CLASS. BY 1678 REP/EBm   CLASS & EXT BY
9803 ADD   NOTE: Declass/on   4-5-83   REASON: CIM II, 1-2.4.2
7/2/83   1678 REP/28 1-16-86   DATE OF REVIEW
CA#83-1720
         Lennon is former member of Beatles singing group in
     England who, despite clear ineligibility for U.S. visa due to
     narcotics conviction in England in 1968, was allowed to reenter
     U.S. during 1971 on visitors visa. Visas of Lennon and wife, Yoko
     Ono, expired 2/72 and since that time Immigration and Naturalization
     Service (INS) has been attempting to deport Lennons. New York
     Office following activities of Lennon closely

Tolson ___
Felt ___
Campbell ___
Rosen ___
Mohr ___
Bishop ___
Miller, E.S. ___
Callahan ___
Casper ___
Conrad ___
Dalbey ___
Cleveland ___
Ponder ___
Bates ___
Waikart ___
Walters ___
Soyars ___
Tele. Room ___
Holmes ___
Gandy ___

                                             Information developed by our

COMMUNICATIONS SECTION

MAY 24 1972   CONFIDENTIAL   NOTE CONTINUED - OVER

70 JUN 6 1972
MAIL ROOM ☐   TELETYPE UNIT ☐   ALL INFORMATION CONTAINED
                                 HEREIN IS UNCLASSIFIED EXCEPT
                                 WHERE SHOWN OTHERWISE   HQ-20

Figure 88. HQ-20 page 1.

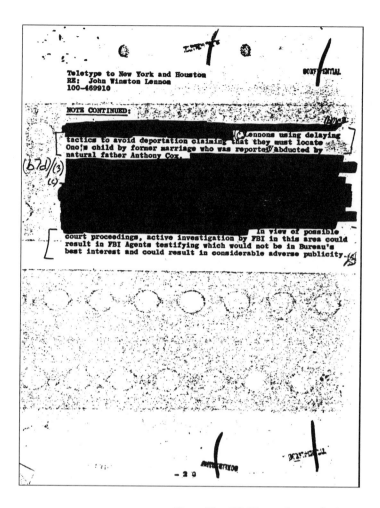

Teletype to New York and Houston
RE: John Winston Lennon
100-469910

NOTE CONTINUED:

(U) Lennons using delaying tactics to avoid deportation claiming that they must locate Ono's child by former marriage who was reported abducted by natural father Anthony Cox.

In view of possible court proceedings, active investigation by FBI in this area could result in FBI Agents testifying which would not be in Bureau's best interest and could result in considerable adverse publicity.

- 2 9

Figure 89a. HQ-20 page 2, initial release.

"ADVERSE PUBLICITY"   The urgent coded teletype from Acting Director Gray ordering the Houston FBI to "disregard lead" continues here (HQ-20 page 2). The reason: "In view of possible court proceedings, active investigation by FBI in this area could result in FBI Agents testifying which would not be in Bureau's best interest and could result in considerable adverse publicity."

The ACLU cited this passage in court arguments as evidence that the FBI lacked a legitimate law enforcement purpose in investigating Lennon; instead, concerns about "adverse publicity" governed the FBI's actions.

CONFIDENTIAL

Teletype to New York and Houston
RE: John Winston Lennon
100-469910

NOTE CONTINUED:

sources that Lennon donated $75,000 to organization formed to disrupt Republican National Convention. Lennons using delaying tactics to avoid deportation claiming that they must locate Ono's child by former marriage who was reportedly abducted by natural father Anthony Cox. New York developed information that Lennons actually have child hidden at certain residence in Houston Division for purpose of delaying deportation. INS considering filing perjury charges against Lennons if information can be established they furnished false information during hearing. New York has set urgent lead for Houston Division to attempt to locate Ono's child and attempt to establish if person keeping child is in contact with Lennons. Actual location of Ono's child and subsequent prosecution for perjury in this instance is responsibility of INS and Houston being instructed to disregard lead except for contact with established sources only. In view of possible court proceedings, active investigation by FBI in this area could result in FBI Agents testifying which would not be in Bureau's best interest and could result in considerable adverse publicity.

CONFIDENTIAL

Figure 89b. HQ-20 page 2, after court decision.

SEARCHING FOR KYOKO, AGAIN   The New York FBI office reported to Acting Director Gray on May 25 that INS chief trial attorney Vincent Schiano had more information about Yoko's missing daughter, Kyoko Cox (HQ-21). Ten days later FBI agents reported that the writer "turned out to be a 'flower child' who says she had a 'vision' that Kyoko was being held someplace 7/? miles from Monterey."

FD-36 (Rev. 5-22-64)

F B I

Date: 5/25/72

Transmit the following in _____
                        (Type in plaintext or code)

Via _____ AIRTEL _____
                        (Priority)

TO: ACTING DIRECTOR, FBI (100-469910)

FROM: SAC, NEW YORK (100-175319) (P)

SUBJECT: JOHN WINSTON LENNON
         SM-REVOLUTIONARY ACTIVITIES
         (OO:NY)

ReButel and Houston teletype both dated 5/24/72.

On 5/25/72, Mr. VINCENT SCHIANO, Chief Trial
Attorney, INS, NYC, advised that his agency is in receipt
of a letter from ▓▓▓▓▓▓▓▓▓▓▓▓▓▓▓▓▓▓▓▓▓▓ dated
5/19/72, which states the following: (b7d)/(2)(a)(b)

        "I can no longer remain silent, I know the where-
abouts of KYOKO COX, and I wish to be of assistance. I am
willing to help..."

        The letter was signed ▓▓▓▓▓▓▓▓▓▓▓ (b7d)/(2)(a)

        SCHIANO advised that he will contact his headquarters
in Washington this date and advise the appropriate official,
Mr. CARL BURROWS, who is in charge of INS Investigation of
the above information. He will request INS officials in
Texas to contact ▓▓▓▓▓▓▓ concerning her letter.

                              (b7d)/(2)(a)

②- Bureau (RM)
1 - Houston (INFO) (RM)
3 - Miami (RM)
    (1 - MIDEM)
    (1 - MIREP)
1 - New York
CJL:slb
  (8)

100-469910- 15

REC-110

ALL INFORMATION CONTAINED
HEREIN IS UNCLASSIFIED
DATE 2/12/81 BY SP4/Smm/mc

■ MAY 27 1972

51 JUN 1 1972

Approved: _____   Sent _____ M   Per _____
          Special Agent in Charge

HQ-21

"ROCK CONCERT TO BE HELD IN FRONT OF THE CONVENTION HALL" In an airtel (HQ-23) dated June 5, Acting Director Gray conveyed to the Miami FBI office information the New York FBI obtained from the INS ten days earlier, that the Lennons "are planning a large rock concert" to be held "in front of the convention hall." This was erroneous. Back in December, six months earlier, Lennon's friends had been talking about a concert, but those plans were canceled on the insistence of Lennon's immigration attorney, Leon Wildes. The file listings at the bottom indicate that a new file is to be opened in Miami for Lennon.

FD-36 (Rev. 5-22-64)

FBI

Date: 6/5/72

Transmit the following in ______________ (Type in plaintext or code)

ALL INFORMATION CONTAINED HEREIN IS UNCLASSIFIED DATE 2/12/81 BY SP4/3cm

Via AIRTEL (Priority)

TO: ACTING DIRECTOR, FBI (100-469910)
(100-469601)

FROM: SAC, MIAMI (100-NEW) (P)
(80-1353) (P)

SUBJECT: JOHN WINSTON LENNON
SM - REVOLUTIONARY ACTIVITIES
(OO: NEW YORK)

MIDEM

Re New York airtel to the Bureau dated 5/25/72, under first caption above.

New York airtel indicated information was received from VINCENT SCHIANO, Chief Trial Attorney, INS, New York City, on 5/25/72, to the effect that he had received information that subject LENNON and his wife, YOKO ONO, are planning a large rock concert in Miami during the conventions and that the rock concert was to be held in front of the convention hall.

LEAD

NEW YORK

4 - Bureau (RM)
(2 - 100-469910)
(2 - 100-469601)
2 - New York (RM) (100-175319)
3 - Miami
(2 - 100-NEW)
(1 - 80-1353)
JCB:mly
(9)

REC-112

100-469910-17

JUN 8 1972

UNRECORDED COPY FILED IN

HQ-23

Approved: ______ Sent ______ M Per ______

Figure 91. HQ-23.

MONITORING THE NEWS   The FBI file includes a UPI wire story dated June 17 (HQ-30) reporting that Lennon filed suit against Attorney General Mitchell for "selective prosecution." Lennon's immigration attorney Leon Wildes had learned of the Thurmond memo. The routing stamp in the corner indicates that Acting Director Gray, two deputy directors, and several assistant directors saw the clip. The released portions of the FBI file contained nothing about this law-suit except for this UPI wire report. Subsequent news clips included a June 28 photo (WFO-13) of John and Yoko in coolie hats at a demonstration at the South Vietnamese embassy in Washington.

The ACLU cited these documents in court arguments as evidence that the FBI lacked a legitimate law enforcement purpose in investigating Lennon. It was not a crime for Lennon to file a lawsuit, to demonstrate in Washington, or to await the decision in the immigration case. These news clips provide evidence that the FBI was closely monitoring Lennon's public statements and activities critical of the Nixon administration, which were constitutionally protected. Moreover, nothing in these clips has any bearing on plans for demonstrations at the Republican National Convention, which the FBI claimed provided its justification for gathering information about Lennon.

And the FBI file contains HQ-39, a *New York Times* clip from July 18 about the deportation case. Notable is the large inscription, "Falsely Claiming Citizenship." Nothing in the article indicates Lennon was claiming to be a U.S. citizen; indeed he never made such a claim.

0-20 (Rev. 8-5-74)

Assoc. Dir. ___
Dep. AD Adm. ___
Dep. AD Inv. ___
Asst. Dir.:
Admin. ___
Comp. Syst. ___
Ext. Affairs ___
Files & Com. ___
Gen. Inv. ___
Ident. ___
Inspection ___
Intell. ___
Laboratory ___
Legal Coun. ___
Plan. & Eval. ___
Spec. Inv. ___
Training ___
Telephone Rm. ___
Director Sec'y ___

A054
D A
LENNON 6-17
DAY LD
NEW YORK (UPI) -- FORMER BEATLE JOHN LENNON, FIGHTING A 1972
DEPORTATION ORDER, HAS FILED SUIT AGAINST THE JUSTICE DEPARTMENT,
FORMER ATTORNEY GENERAL JOHN N. MITCHELL AND OTHER OFFICIALS,
CHARGING THEY SINGLED HIM OUT FOR "IMPROPER SELECTIVE PROSECUTION."
LEON WILDES, LENNON'S ATTORNEY, SAID MONDAY HE HAS DOCUMENTS
SHOWING LENNON'S DEPORTATION WAS ORDERED FROM WASHINGTON BECAUSE OF A
SENATE INTERNAL SECURITY COMMITTEE REPORT WHICH SOUGHT TO LINK LENNON
WITH PLANS TO DISRUPT THE 1972 REPUBLICAN NATIONAL CONVENTION.
IN 1973, NEW YORK IMMIGRATION DIRECTOR SOL MARKS SAID AT A NEWS
CONFERENCE HE MADE THE DECISION TO PROCEED AGAINST LENNON HIMSELF.
WILDES SAID MARKS SAID IN A DEPOSITION LAST WEEK HE ACTED AS A
"CONDUIT" FOR INSTRUCTIONS FROM WASHINGTON, WHICH HE UNDERSTOOD TO
MEAN THAT "WE WERE NOT TO GIVE THIS MAN A BREAK."
MARKS ALSO ADMITTED HE HAD MISINFORMED THE PRESS AT HIS 1973 NEWS
CONFERENCE, WILDES SAID.
PROCEEDINGS AGAINST LENNON, BEGUN IN MARCH 1972 WHEN HE WAS
CHARGED WITH OVERSTAYING HIS VISA, ARE STILL PENDING. PROSECUTORS
CITED A 1968 BRITISH CONVICTION FOR MARIJUANA POSSESSION AS THE BASIS
FOR DENYING HIM PERMANENT RESIDENCE.
WILDES SAID SEN. STROM THURMOND, R-S.C. SENT A LETTER TO MITCHELL
IN FEBRUARY 1972, ENCLOSING THE COMMITTEE MEMORANDUM.
"THIS APPEARS TO ME TO BE AN IMPORTANT MATTER, AND I THINK IT
WOULD BE WELL TO TO BE CONSIDERED AT THE HIGHEST LEVEL ... AS I CAN
SEE MANY HEADACHES MIGHT BE AVOIDED IF IF APPROPRIATE ACTION BE
TAKEN IN TIME," WILDES QUOTED THURMOND'S LETTER AS SAYING.
WILDES SAID OTHER DOCUMENTS SHOW KLEINDIENST SENT THE MEMO TO
IMMIGRATION COMMISSIONER RAYMOND FARRELL AND THAT FARRELL'S DEPUTY
INSTRUCTED SUBORDINATES IN NEW YORK TO SEEK DEPORTATION OF LENNON AND
HIS WIFE, YOKO ONO.
WILDES SAID THE SUIT NAMES THE JUSTICE DEPARTMENT, MITCHELL,
RICHARD KLEINDIENST, DEPUTY ATTORNEY GENERAL AT THE TIME AND
MITCHELL'S SUCCESSOR, AND "VARIOUS IMMIGRATION OFFICERS."
UPI 06-17 05:39 AED

100-46 9910-A

NOT RECORDED
7 SEP 2 1975

58 SEP 5 1975

WASHINGTON CAPITAL NEWS SERVICE

file
5.cm
HQ-30

Figure 92. HQ-30.

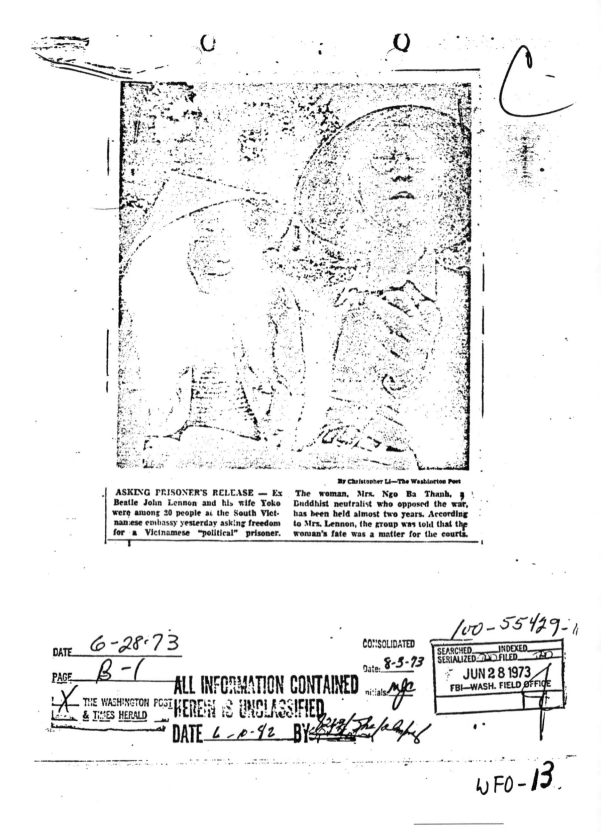

By Christopher Li—The Washington Post

ASKING PRISONER'S RELEASE — Ex Beatle John Lennon and his wife Yoko were among 20 people at the South Vietnamese embassy yesterday asking freedom for a Vietnamese "political" prisoner. The woman, Mrs. Ngo Ba Thanh, a Buddhist neutralist who opposed the war, has been held almost two years. According to Mrs. Lennon, the group was told that the woman's fate was a matter for the courts.

Figure 93. WFO-13.

John & Yoko Wait & Wait

A decision in the deportation proceedings against former Beatle John Lennon and his Japanese-born wife, Yoko Ono may not be reached until September, the U.S. Immigration and Naturalization Service said yesterday.

The government and the defense were to have submitted briefs by July 1, but they are still waiting for a transcript of the May 17 hearing.

Special inquiry officer Ira Fieldsteel, who is hearing the case, will be away in August, and so a decision is not expected until September.

The government wants to deny Lennon permanent residence here because of a 1968 marijuana conviction in England.

PacTel Appeals Refund

Pacific Telephone & Telegraph asked the U.S. Supreme Court yesterday to stop a $145 million refund to its customers which was ordered by the California Supreme Court Tuesday. The California court denied Pacific Tel's $143 million rate increase.

P. BL 30
7/14/72
DAILy NEws
NEW YORK, N.Y.

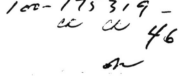

NY-48

Figure 94. NY-48.

Lennon Decision Delayed

NEW YORK (AP)—A decision in the deportation proceedings against former Beatle John Lennon and his wife, Yoko Ono, may not be reached until September, the United States Immigration and Naturalization Service reported today.

The government was awaiting a transcript of a May 17 hearing in the case before submitting its brief. Special Inquiry Officer Ira Fieldsteel, in charge of the case, had set July 1 as the final date for both sides to submit briefs supporting their cases.

Fieldsteel will be away for the month of August, immigration officials reported, saying they do not expect a decision until September.

The Lennons are seeking permanent residence in the U.S., but the government has balked over granting residence to Lennon, on grounds of a 1968 narcotics conviction in England.

DATE 7-14-72
PAGE B-2

X THE WASHINGTON POST & TIMES HERALD

_____ THE EVENING STAR

_____ THE SUNDAY STAR

_____ THE WASHINGTON DAILY NEWS

_____ WASHINGTON AFRO AMERICAN

100 - 55429 - 10

SEARCHED _____ INDEXED _____
SERIALIZED _____ FILED _____
JUL 14 1972
FBI — WASH. FIELD OFFICE

(b7c)(1)

WFO-12

Figure 95. WFO-12.

Assoc. Dir. _____
Asst. Dir.: _____
Admin. _____
Comp. Syst. _____
Ext. Affairs _____
Files & Com. _____
Gen. Inv. _____
Ident. _____
Inspection _____
Intell. _____
Laboratory _____
Plan. & Eval. _____
Spec. Inv. _____
Training _____
Legal Coun. _____
Telephone Rm. _____
Director Sec'y _____

Lennon Is Given 60 Days to Leave

The Justice Department announced yesterday that John Lennon, the former Beatle, had been given 60 days to leave the country or be forcibly deported. The order is based on a decision reached by the Board of Immigration Appeals on July 10, and Mr. Lennon's departure deadline is retroactive to that date.

Mr. Lennon, who has been living in New York and other American cities since 1971, has fought lengthy and costly legal battles, through the Immigration and Naturalization Service and the Federal courts, to have his visa extended.

Extensions have been denied because he pleaded guilty in Britain, in 1968, to a charge of possession of marijuana. In his appeals of earlier denials of extensions Mr. Lennon contended the marijuana had been planted in his home and he had pleaded guilty to the possession charge only to spare his former wife, then pregnant, the ordeal of a court appearance.

A spokesman for Mr. Lennon's lawyer said that "various avenues for appealing the order are being explored."

England

(Falsely Claiming Citizenship)

ALL INFORMATION CONTAINED
HEREIN IS UNCLASSIFIED
DATE 4-8-83 BY 1678 RFP/Lcm

BO___ICK (LAST)

The Washington Post
    Times Herald _____
The Evening Star (Washington) _____
The Sunday Star (Washington) _____
Daily News (New York) _____
Sunday News (New York) _____
New York Post _____
The New York Times _29_
The Daily World _____
The New Leader _____
The Wall Street Journal _____
The National Observer _____
People's World _____

Date _7-18-74_

EX-117   REC-25 39-0-A-

NOT RECORDED
25 JUL 23 1974

56 JUL 31 1974

HQ-39

Figure 96. HQ-39.

"ARREST IF AT ALL POSSIBLE"   Acting FBI Director Gray received an airtel (HQ-24) from the New York FBI office, dated July 27, suggesting that it be "emphasized" to "local Law Enforcement Agencies" in Miami that Lennon should be "arrested if at all possible on possession of narcotics charge." The New York office provided a helpful explanation: "Local INS has very loose case in NY for deporting subject. . . . if LENNON were to be arrested . . . he would become more likely to be immediately deportable." This memo sounds like a proposal to set Lennon up for a drug bust. The ACLU cited this passage as evidence that the FBI was engaged in an "abuse of its authority in order to neutralize dissent."

FD- (564)

F B I

Date: 7/27/72

Transmit the following in _____
                            (Type in plaintext or code)

Via ___ AIRTEL ___

CLASSIFIED ON 4-27-84
BY

TO: ACTING DIRECTOR, FBI)(100-469910)

FROM: SAC, NEW YORK (100-175319) (P)

SUBJECT: JOHN WINSTON LENNON
           SM - REVACT
           (OO: NY)   CLASS. BY 1673 RFP / EBm

           MIREP   Declass on 4-5-83

ReNYairtel, dated 5/25/72, and Miami airtel,
dated 6/5/72,

        Attached are 5 copies for the Bureau, and seven
copies for Miami, of an LHM dated and captioned as above.

        Miami should note that LENNON is reportedly a
"heavy user of narcotics" known as "downers". This information should be emphasized to local Law Enforcement
Agencies covering MIREP, with regards to subject being
arrested if at all possible on possession of narcotics
charge.

        Local INS has very loose case in NY for de-
porting subject on narcotics charge involving 1968 arrest
in England.

        INS has stressed to Bureau that if LENNON were
to be arrested in US for possession of narcotics he would
become more likely to be immediately deportable.

2 - Bureau (Encls. 5) (RM)
2 - Miami (Encls. 7) (RM)   ST-111
1 - New York .   REC5 100 - 469910 - 18

                    SS, RAO-ISD (2), 'D
                    8/7/72
                    d/S
CJL;rbj   RFP/42
(6)

                                   25 JUL 29 1972

REC.D
cc 10:

                        XEROX

Approved: _____ Special Agent in Charge

61 AUG 2 1972

ALL INFORMATION CONTAINED
HEREIN IS UNCLASSIFIED EXCEPT
WHERE SHOWN OTHERWISE

SEE REVERSE SIDE FOR
ADD. DISSEMINATION
HQ-24

UNRECORDED COPY FILED IN 100-469910 - NEW YORK

Figure 98. Apple Records publicity.

THE "WANTED" POSTER   The FBI prepared a "wanted"-style flyer for distribution to local law enforcement agencies in Miami to facilitate the arrest of Lennon (HQ-24 page 5). Although he had one of the most famous faces in the Western world at this point, the FBI apparently was not confident that local police would be able to recognize the ex-Beatle. The photo, however, is not of Lennon but rather of David Peel, an East Village street singer who had become friends with Lennon and who had an album released on Apple records that year.

John Winston Lennon

John Winston Lennon, a former member of the Beatles Rock Music Group is presently the subject of deportation hearing by the Immigration and Naturalization Service.

Lennon is described as follows:

Name: John Winston Lennon
Race: White
Date of Birth: October 9, 1940
Place of Birth: Liverpool, England
Hair: Brown to Blond
Weight: 160 pounds
Height: Approximately six feet
Build: Slender
Nationality: English
United States   105 Bank Street
Residence: New York City
Arrest Record: 1968 Narcotics Arrest, in
                         England for Possession of
                         Dangerous Drugs (Cannabis)
                         Pled Guilty

Figure 99. HQ-24 page 5.

COMING OUT FOR MCGOVERN The Lennon file contains a page from *Grass Roots*, a publication of the People's Party, reporting that Lennon has "come out in support of McGovern" (HQ-38). The article from *Grass Roots* was sent to Acting Director Gray on August 1, 1972, by the special agent in charge of the San Francisco FBI office.

The ACLU cited this passage in court arguments as evidence that the FBI lacked a legitimate law enforcement purpose in investigating Lennon, pointing out that it was not a crime to support McGovern and that the FBI's real purpose here was to monitor constitutionally protected political activity.

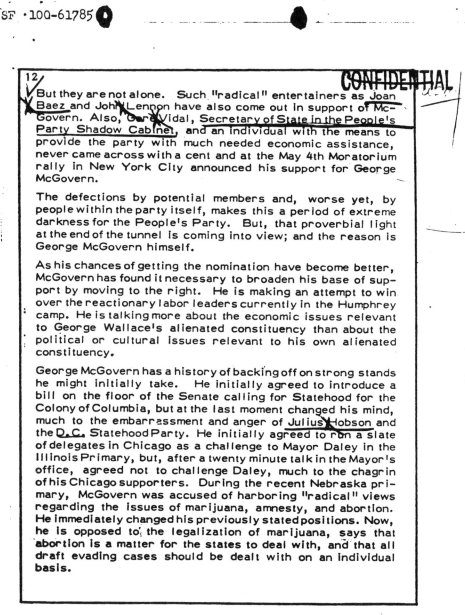

12

But they are not alone. Such "radical" entertainers as Joan Baez and John Lennon have also come out in support of Mc-Govern. Also, Gore Vidal, Secretary of State in the People's Party Shadow Cabinet, and an individual with the means to provide the party with much needed economic assistance, never came across with a cent and at the May 4th Moratorium rally in New York City announced his support for George McGovern.

The defections by potential members and, worse yet, by people within the party itself, makes this a period of extreme darkness for the People's Party. But, that proverbial light at the end of the tunnel is coming into view; and the reason is George McGovern himself.

As his chances of getting the nomination have become better, McGovern has found it necessary to broaden his base of support by moving to the right. He is making an attempt to win over the reactionary labor leaders currently in the Humphrey camp. He is talking more about the economic issues relevant to George Wallace's alienated constituency than about the political or cultural issues relevant to his own alienated constituency.

George McGovern has a history of backing off on strong stands he might initially take. He initially agreed to introduce a bill on the floor of the Senate calling for Statehood for the Colony of Columbia, but at the last moment changed his mind, much to the embarrassment and anger of Julius Hobson and the D.C. Statehood Party. He initially agreed to run a slate of delegates in Chicago as a challenge to Mayor Daley in the Illinois Primary, but, after a twenty minute talk in the Mayor's office, agreed not to challenge Daley, much to the chagrin of his Chicago supporters. During the recent Nebraska primary, McGovern was accused of harboring "radical" views regarding the issues of marijuana, amnesty, and abortion. He immediately changed his previously stated positions. Now, he is opposed to the legalization of marijuana, says that abortion is a matter for the states to deal with, and that all draft evading cases should be dealt with on an individual basis.

- 4 -

Figure 100. HQ-38 page 4.

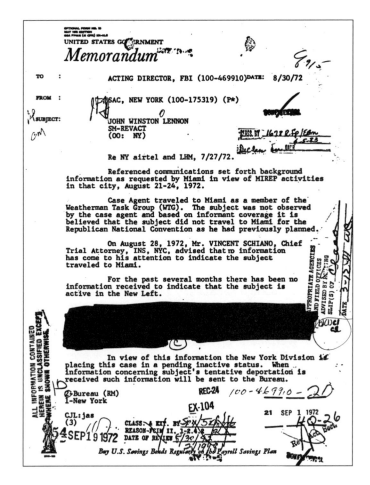

Figure 101a. HQ-26, initial release.

AFTER THE CONVENTION: "PENDING INACTIVE STATUS"   August 30, six days after the end of the Republican convention, Acting Director Gray received a letter (HQ-26) from the special agent in charge of the New York FBI office, reporting that "subject did not travel to Miami for the Republican National Convention," which was true. It adds, "For the past several months there has been no information received to indicate that the subject is active in the New Left." It goes on to report that according to sources, "the subject has fallen out of favor of activists JERRY RUBIN, STEWART ALBERT, and RENNIE DAVIS, due to subject's lack of interest in committing himself to involvement in antiwar and New Left activities." As a result, "the New York Division is placing this case in a pending inactive status."

UNITED STATES GOVERNMENT

Memorandum

TO : ACTING DIRECTOR, FBI (100-469910) DATE: 8/30/72

FROM : SAC, NEW YORK (100-175319) (P*)

SUBJECT: JOHN WINSTON LENNON
SM-REVACT
(OO: NY)

DECLASSIFIED ON 4-27-84
BY 1678 RFp|E8m

CLASS. BY 1678 RFp|E8m
4-5-83

Re NY airtel and LHM, 7/27/72.

Referenced communications set forth background information as requested by Miami in view of MIREP activities in that city, August 21-24, 1972.

Case Agent traveled to Miami as a member of the Weatherman Task Group (WTG). The subject was not observed by the case agent and based on informant coverage it is believed that the subject did not travel to Miami for the Republican National Convention as he had previously planned.

On August 28, 1972, Mr. VINCENT SCHIANO, Chief Trial Attorney, INS, NYC, advised that no information has come to his attention to indicate the subject traveled to Miami.

For the past several months there has been no information received to indicate that the subject is active in the New Left.

Sources; ████████████████ all advised during the month of July, 1972, that the subject has fallen out of the favor of activist JERRY RUBIN, STEWART ALBERT, and RENNIE DAVIS, due to subject's lack of interest in committing himself to involvement in anti-war and New Left activities.

In view of this information the New York Division is placing this case in a pending inactive status. When information concerning subject's tentative deportation is received such information will be sent to the Bureau.

2-Bureau (RM)
1-New York

REC-24   100-469910-20

CJL:jas
(3)

EX-104

CLASS. & EXT. BY SPX/52
REASON-FCIM II. 1-2.4.2
DATE OF REVIEW 6/30/83

21 SEP 1 1972

54 SEP 19 1972

HQ-26

ALL INFORMATION CONTAINED HEREIN IS UNCLASSIFIED EXCEPT WHERE SHOWN OTHERWISE.

62
67D

Figure 101b. HQ-26 after settlement.

NO INFORMATION TO INDICATE LENNON'S PRESENCE IN MIAMI   The special agent in charge of the Miami FBI office wrote a letter (HQ-27) to Acting Director Gray, dated September 28, reporting that "the dissemination program" that sought to have Lennon arrested on drug charges failed. Local police have "no information to indicate the presence of the subject in Miami Beach . . . at any time during the summer of 1972," including the Republican convention. The local FBI promises to "review" the records to determine if Lennon was among the 1,200 people arrested in demonstrations against the Republicans. The FBI seems to think John Lennon could have been arrested demonstrating at the Republican National Convention and no one would have known about it.

UNITED STATES GOVERNMENT

Memorandum

TO : ACTING DIRECTOR, FBI (100-469910) DATE: 9/28/72

FROM : SAC, MIAMI (100-16733) (P)

SUBJECT: JOHN WINSTON LENNON
SM - REVOLUTIONARY ACTIVITIES
(OO: NEW YORK)

Re New York airtel and LHM to Miami, 7/27/72.

Copies of referenced LHM were disseminated to
the Miami Beach Police Department in connection with
the dissemination program in the MIDEM case. The Miami
Beach Police Department and other local authorities
have furnished no information to indicate the presence
of the subject in Miami Beach, Florida, at any time
during the summer of 1972.

The following informants were alerted concerning the subject but were unable to furnish information which would indicate his presence in Miami
Beach: (X)(u)

CLASS. BY 1678 RFP/EBm
4-5-83

CLASS. & EXT. BY
REASON FCIM II
DATE OF REVIEW

APPROPRIATE AGENCIES
AND FIELD OFFICES
ADVISED BY ROUTING
SLIP(S) OF Class

DATE 3-12-91 W

ALL INFORMATION CONTAINED
HEREIN IS UNCLASSIFIED EXCEPT
WHERE SHOWN OTHERWISE

On 8/22/72 and 8/23/72 approximately 1,200
individuals were arrested in Miami Beach by local authorities
during protest demonstrations against the Republican
National Convention. The records relating to these arrests
were photographed by the Miami Office and the film is
currently being processed by the FBI Laboratory. When
the arrest records become available, they will be reviewed

② - Bureau (RM)
2 - New York (100-175319) (RM)
1 - Miami
WED/jah
(5)

REC 64

100-469910

EX-117

OCT 2 1972

57 OCT B3 1972 *Buy U.S. Savings Bonds Regularly on the Payroll Savings Plan*

HQ-27

Figure 102. HQ-27.

"PENDING INACTIVE STATUS" An FBI agent sent this handwritten memo to the special agent in charge of the FBI office in New York, dated October 3, 1972 (NY-54). It reports a phone call from a supervisor stating that Lennon's case should "remain in a pending inactive status until such time as the subject is either deported from the US or until such time his activities warrant case being reopened."

New York had put Lennon's case on "pending inactive status" on August 30, a week after the Republican National Convention (see HQ-26, p. 294). However, Lennon's file was not officially closed until December 8 (see HQ-32, p. 304).

UNITED STATES GOVERNMENT

Memorandum

TO : SAc New York (100-175319) DATE: 10-3-72

FROM : SA ████████████████████ 42(b7c)(1)

SUBJECT: John Winston Lennon
SM - Revact
OO NY

67c)(1) ████████ On 10-3-72 Bureau Supervisor ██████ advised telephonically that captioned case should remain in a pending inactive status until such time as the subject is either deported from the US or until such time ~~warrants~~ his activities warrant case being reopened.

100-175319-

SEARCHED_____ INDEXED _____
SERIALIZED _____ FILED _____
OCT 8 1972
FBI — NEW YORK

ALL INFORMATION CONTAINED
HEREIN IS UNCLASSIFIED
DATE 6-9-92 BY ████████

NY-54

Figure 103. NY-54.

BLACK PAGE: "FOREIGN GOVERNMENT INFORMATION" HQ-28 page 3 has been withheld in its entirety under the national security exemption. This page is described in the FBI's court papers only as a "letter." Even the date is classified. The FBI continues to withhold this page under (b)(1)b2: "information provided by a foreign government with the expectation, expressed or implied, that the information is to be kept in confidence." The FBI stated in court documents that "unauthorized disclosure of foreign government information . . . is presumed to cause damage to the national security. . . . This is because most governments, unlike that of the United States, do not officially acknowledge the existence of certain of their intelligence and security services, much less the scope of their activities and also because the info itself may be sensitive in nature." Release of the information on this page "could reasonably be expected . . . to lead to diplomatic, political, or economic retaliation."

This page follows a letter classified "Secret" from the London legal attaché to Acting Director Gray, dated September 12, 1972, inquiring about the "International Committee for John and Yoko." The ACLU cited this passage in court arguments as evidence that the FBI lacked a legitimate law enforcement purpose in investigating Lennon. The International Committee for John and Yoko was not a criminal organization but rather a group of artists and performers opposing the deportation hearings—a constitutionally protected form of speech that should not have been the target of FBI investigation. This page is still in litigation.

b1

100 — 469910 — 22
HQ-2

Figure 104. HQ-28 page 3.

TWELVE HUNDRED ARREST RECORDS, BUT NONE FOR LENNON   The special agent in charge of the Miami FBI office wrote Acting Director Gray on October 24, 1972, with the final disappointing news that a review of the records of every one of the 1,200 people arrested in demonstrations there "failed to reflect that the subject was one of those arrested" (HQ-29).

Miami points out the unavoidable conclusion: "there is no indication that the subject ever appeared in Miami Beach during either of the national political conventions."

OPTIONAL FORM NO. 10
MAY 1962 EDITION
GSA FPMR (41 CFR) 101-11.6
UNITED STATES GOVERNMENT

Memorandum

TO : ACTING DIRECTOR, FBI (100-469910) DATE: 10-24-72

FROM : SAC, MIAMI (100-16733) (RUC)

SUBJECT: JOHN WINSTON LENNON
SM - RA

(OO: New York)

Re Miami letter to Bureau, 9-28-72.

A review of records relating to the individuals arrested in Miami Beach, Florida, on 8/22 and 23/72, in connection with protest demonstrations against the Republican National Convention, failed to reflect that the subject was one of those arrested.

Inasmuch as there is no indication that the subject ever appeared in Miami Beach during either of the national political conventions in July and August, 1972, no further investigation is being conducted by Miami.

2-Bureau (RM)
2-New York (100-175319) (RM)
1-Miami
WED/al
(5)

ST-114

REC-63 100-469910-23

ALL INFORMATION CONTAINED HEREIN IS UNCLASSIFIED DATE 2/19/81 BY SP4/SEM/MC

3 OCT 27 1972

F Y 73

NOV 3 1972

Rev Act Sect.

Buy U.S. Savings Bonds Regularly on the Payroll Savings Plan

5010-108-02

HQ-29

Figure 105. HQ-29.

"CASE IS BEING CLOSED" The special agent in charge of the FBI in New York City sent an airtel (HQ-32) to Acting Director Gray, dated December 8, 1972, declaring that "in view of subject's inactivity in Revolutionary Activities and his seemingly rejection by NY Radicals, captioned case is being closed in the NY Division." Since New York was the office of origin for the Lennon investigation, this document marks the end of the case. Significantly, the FBI closed its Lennon file one month after Nixon was reelected. On April 21, the FBI had pledged to help "neutralize" Lennon's opposition to Nixon (see HQ-15, p. 238); having succeeded, its job was done.

CONFIDENTIAL   F B I

Date: 12/8/72

Transmit the following in _____
                              (Type in plaintext or code)

Via ___ AIRTEL ___
                              (Priority)

TO: ACTING DIRECTOR, FBI (100-469910)

FROM: SAC, NEW YORK (100-175319)(C)

SUBJECT: JOHN WINSTON LENNON   CLASS. BY 1678 RFP|EBm
           SM - RA   4-6-83
           (OO:NY)   Declass On OADR

ReLegat, London letter, 9/12/72; NYlet, 8/30/72.

Enclosed for the Bureau are ten copies of an LHM captioned "International Committee for John and Yoko,", dated as above. Appropriate copies should be made available to Legat, London, as per their request.

In view of subject's inactivity in Revolutionary Activities and his seemingly rejection by NY Radicals, captioned case is being closed in the NY Division.

In event other information comes to New York's attention indicating subject is active with Revolutionary groups, the case will be re-opened at that time and the Bureau advised accordingly.

The Special Agent of the FBI who contacted INS was SA ███████████

②- Bureau (RM) (Encls. 10)
①- New York

CJL:eps
(4)

ALL INFORMATION CONTAINED HEREIN IS UNCLASSIFIED EXCEPT WHERE SHOWN OTHERWISE.

7 0 DEC 19 1972

Approved: _____   Sent _____ M   Per _____
         Special Agent in Charge
                                    ☆U.S.Government Printing Office: 1972 — 455-574

HQ-32

Figure 107a. HQ-33 page 1, initial release.

BLACK PAGES: "FOREIGN GOVERNMENT INFORMATION," CONTINUED   HQ-
33 is a four-page document completely blacked out and described by the FBI
as "letter with attachment." Even the date is classified. The FBI describes this
document as "information provided by a foreign government with the expectation, expressed or implied, that the information is to be kept in confidence,"
claiming it comes under the national security exemption. The document remains in litigation.

FBI INFO 2/13/96
CLASSIFIED BY: SSA9803RDD/JS
REASON: 1.5 (b)
DECLASSIFY ON: X 5
CA# 83-1720

b1

ST-123

REC-71

V-18

CH 40

DE-1 100- 469910-0

MCT-26 22 AUG 10 1976

UNRECORDED COPY FILED IN

CA# 83-1720
CLASSIFIED DECISIONS FINALIZED
BY DEPARTMENT REVIEW COMMITTEE (DRC)
DATE: 12/10/97   SSA SLD/JS
SLD8 12/10/97

ENCLOSURE

Notice of Classification Action
Cross Ref. File # only
File # 100-469910-25
Classified by: [illegible] RFP/EOM 4-6-83
Declass on: OADR
classified decisions finalized by DRC 2/2/16   [illegible] 2/18/16

28 SEP 1976

b1

HQ-33

Figure 107b. HQ-33 page 1, after court decision.

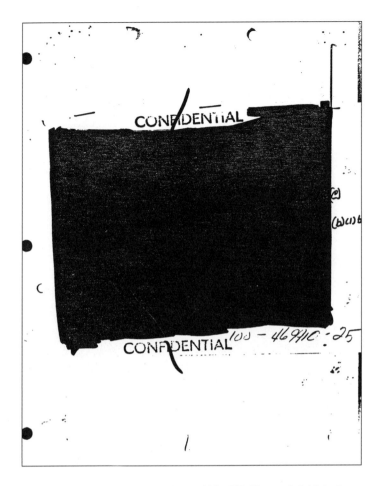

Figure 108a. HQ-33 page 2, initial release.

WHITE AREA RELEASED The second page of HQ-33 remains withheld in its entirety as national security foreign government information. In 1998 "the FBI assured this [foreign] government that it would afford the information and its relationship with the foreign government continued protection requested."

Nevertheless in 1998 the FBI released more of this page, a larger white area, and some new classification markings.

~~CONFIDENTIAL~~

61

ENCLOSURE
~~CONFIDENTIAL~~ 100 - 46990 - 25

HQ-33

Figure 108b. HQ-33 page 2, after court decision.

100 - 469910 -25 HQ

Figure 109. HQ-33 page 3.

61

HQ-3

Figure 110. HQ-33 page 4.

Notes

Introduction

1. The story is told in Jon Wiener, *Come Together: John Lennon in His Time* (New York: Random House, 1984). The John Dean "enemies list" memo was revealed in the *New York Times*, June 29, 1973. For Dean's account of the relationship between the Nixon White House and the FBI, see John Dean, *Blind Ambition: The White House Years* (New York: Simon & Schuster, 1976). For other examples of presidents' political use of the FBI, see Athan Theoharis, *From the Secret Files of J. Edgar Hoover* (Chicago: Ivan R. Dee, 1991), ch. 12.

2. *Access Reports* 17 (October 30, 1991), 5; Marvin Lewis (assistant chief, FBI, FOIA/PA Section), interview with author, April 16, 1992.

3. 5 U.S.C. § 552(b)(1).

4. *EPA v. Mink*, 410 U.S. 73, 95.

5. Quoted in introduction to Athan Theoharis, ed., *A Culture of Secrecy: The Government Versus the People's Right to Know* (Lawrence: University of Kansas Press, 1998), 2–3.

6. Quoted in Daniel Patrick Moynihan, *Secrecy: The American Experience* (New Haven: Yale University Press, 1998), 89, 97.

7. Natalie Robins, *Alien Ink: The FBI's War on Freedom of Expression* (New York: William Morrow, 1992), 32–37; Herbert Mitgang, *Dangerous Dossiers: Exposing the Secret War against America's Greatest Authors* (New York: Ballantine, 1988).

Chapter 1: Getting Started

1. A few documents were withheld under the 5 U.S.C. § 552(b)(3) exemption, "information withheld pursuant to statute." Two statutes were cited: visa records and tax returns. Privacy and confidential sources were both subsections of the same exemption—(b)(7), law enforcement records. The official categories were (b)(7)(C), "unwarranted invasion of personal privacy," and (b)(7)(E), "confidential source material." For subsections of the exemption categories, see glossary.

2. Mark Rosenbaum, interview with author, Los Angeles, February 28, 1998.

3. *Crawford v. Board of Education*, 102 S.Ct. 3211 (1982).

4. *Green v. Anderson*, 115 S.Ct. 1398 (1995).

5. Dan Marmalefsky, interview with author, Los Angeles, February 28, 1998.

6. *Kolender v. Lawson*, 103 S.Ct. 1855 (1983).

7. *Wayte v. U.S.*, 105 S.Ct. 1524 (1985).

8. 5 U.S.C. § 552(a)(4)(B).

9. Executive Order 12356 (April 2, 1982), sec. 1.6(a).

10. Rosenbaum interview.

11. Executive Order 12065 (December 1, 1978).

12. This and all other quotations from plaintiff's and defendant's attorneys are from legal briefs and other court papers, of various titles and dates, in author's possession—unless otherwise cited.

13. The term "Vaughn index" comes from *Vaughn v. Rosen*, 484 F.2d 820 (D.C. Cir. 1973), cert. denied, 415 U.S. 977 (1974).

14. David Margolick, "Japanese-American Judges Reflect on Internment," *New York Times*, May 19, 1995.

15. Ibid.

16. Angus MacKenzie, *Secrets: The CIA's War at Home* (Berkeley: University of California Press, 1997), 9–11.

17. Ibid., 30; see also ibid., 20, 26–29.

18. Ibid., 68–71.

19. Stephen K. Doig, "FBI Ordered to Explain Why Lennon Files Shredded," *Miami Herald*, August 10, 1994.

20. Richard Gid Powers, *Secrecy and Power: The Life of J. Edgar Hoover* (New York: Free Press, 1987), 440, 474.

21. Ibid., 449.

22. William Sullivan testimony, November 1, 1975, quoted in Senate Select Committee to Study Government Operations with Respect to Intelligence Activities, *Final Report*, book 2, 94th Cong., 2d sess., 1976, 14.

23. John Ehrlichman, *Witness to Power* (New York: Simon & Schuster, 1982), 159; *Wilkinson v. FBI*, 633 F.Supp. 336, 349 (C.D. Cal. 1986); Powers, *Secrecy and Power*, 487.

24. Quoted in Jeb Stuart Magruder, *An American Life: One Man's Road to Watergate* (New York: Atheneum, 1974), 89.

25. *Dunaway v. Webster*, 519 F.Supp. 1058, 1065–66, 1070 (N.D. Cal. 1981).

26. *Wilkinson v. FBI*, 99 F.R.D. 148 (C.D. Cal. 1983).

27. *Taylor v. Dept. of the Army*, 684 F.2d 99 (D.C. Cir. 1982).

28. Haldeman described the relationship between the Nixon White House and the FBI in H. R. Haldeman and Joseph DiMona, *The Ends of Power* (New York: Times Books, 1978).

29. Chet Flippo, "Lennon's Lawsuit: Memo from Thurmond," *Rolling Stone*, July 31, 1975, 16. For examples of the 1984 Thurmond story, see *New York Post*, June 30, 1984; *Miami Herald*, June 30, 1984; *Cleveland Plain Dealer*, June 30, 1984; *Detroit Free Press*, June 30, 1984.

30. Ronald Radosh, "John Lennon's Separate Peace," *Washington Post*, July 31, 1984.

31. *Princeton Alumni Weekly*, November 21, 1984, December 19, 1984.

Chapter 2: From District Court to the Supreme Court

1. 132 Cong. Rec. S14039 (September 27, 1986). Penn Kimball figured out who the informers were in his file: Kimball, *The File* (San Diego: Harcourt Brace Jovanovich, 1983).

2. *Clearly v. FBI*, 811 F.2d 421 (8th Cir. 1987).

3. *Kiraly v. FBI*, 728 F.2d 277, 277–79 (6th Cir. 1984).

4. Charles Dickens, *Bleak House* (New York: Penguin ed., 1997), 14–15.

5. Mark Rosenbaum, interview with author, Los Angeles, February 28, 1998.

6. Ibid.

7. Dan Marmalefsky, interview with author, Los Angeles, February 28, 1998.

8. What follows comes from a transcription of the official U.S. government audiotape of the hearing, in author's possession.

9. *Church of Scientology v. U.S. Dept. of the Army*, 611 F.2d 738 (9th Cir. 1979).

10. Marmalefsky interview.

11. *American Jewish Congress v. Department of the Treasury*, 713 F.2d 864; cert. denied, 104 S.Ct. 244 (1983); for a similar ruling, see *Republic of New Afrika v. FBI*, 656 F.Supp. 117 (D.C. Cir. 1986).

12. Jon Pareles, "Caution: Now Entering the War Zone," *New York Times*, February 24, 1991.

13. *Wiener v. FBI*, 943 F.2d 8747, 8748 (9th Cir. 1991).

14. Ibid.

15. Ibid., 8756.

16. Ibid., 8769, 8770.

17. Ibid., 8771, 8772.

18. *Knight v. CIA*, 872 F.2d 660 (5th Cir. 1989).

19. *Wiener v. FBI*, 8765 n19.

20. *Wiener v. FBI*, 8766–67.

21. *Wiener v. FBI*, 8767.

22. The issues range from summary judgment to the adequacy of Vaughn indices to the appropriateness of plaintiff discovery. See, for example, *Schiffer v. FBI*, 78 F.3d 1405, 1409–10 (9th Cir. 1996); *Spurlock v. FBI*, 69 F.3d 1010, 1016 (9th Cir. 1995); *Rosenfeld v. Dept. of Justice*, 51 F.3d 803, 806–7 (9th Cir. 1995); *Church of Scientology Intern v. IRS*, 995 F.2d 916, 920–21 (9th Cir. 1993); *Church of Scientology v. IRS*, 991 F.2d 560, 563 (9th Cir. 1993).

23. Cril Payne, *Deep Cover: An FBI Agent Infiltrates the Radical Underground* (New York: Newsweek Books, 1979).

24. His conviction was overturned on appeal on the grounds that his case should have been severed from the others because of his lawyers' illness. Stanley Kutler, *The Wars of Watergate: The Last Crisis of Richard Nixon* (New York: Knopf, 1990), 465, 576.

25. Rosenbaum interview.

26. Marmalefsky interview.

27. The FBI's first effort to overturn the Ninth Circuit decision was to petition in August 1991 for a "rehearing en banc," an effort to assemble all the judges of the Ninth Circuit Court of Appeals to overrule the three-judge panel. That petition was denied; not a single appellate judge voted in favor of rehearing. 951 F.2d 1073.

28. *Wiener v. FBI*, 943 F.2d 8747 (9th Cir. 1991), cert. denied, 112 S.Ct. 3013 (1992).

29. Rosenbaum interview.

30. *New York Times*, September 28, 1992.

31. Marmalefsky interview.

Chapter 3: Deposing the FBI and CIA

1. *San Francisco Chronicle*, August 20, 1981, quoted in Curt Gentry, *J. Edgar Hoover: The Man and the Secrets* (New York: Norton, 1991), 594. For Felt's side of the story, see W. Mark Felt, *The FBI Pyramid from Inside* (New York: Putnam, 1979).

2. Quoted in Gentry, *Hoover*, 595.

3. The phrase was not original; it came from a district court decision rejecting an FOIA affidavit: *Curran v. Dept. of Justice*, 813 F.2d 477 (1st Cir. 1987).

4. Civil Obedience Act of 1968, 18 U.S.C. 231 (1988); Anti-Riot Act, 18 U.S.C. 2101 (1988).

5. Mark Rosenbaum, interview with author, Los Angeles, February 28, 1998.

6. Dan Marmalefsky, interview with author, Los Angeles, February 28, 1998.

7. *Binion v. Dept. of Justice*, 695 F.2d 1189 (9th Cir. 1983); *Williams v. FBI*, 730 F.2d 885 (2d Cir. 1984).

8. *Williams v. FBI*, 69 F.3d 1155 (D.C. Cir. 1995), 181.

9. Emphasis mine. Here they cited *Pratt v. Webster*, 673 F.2d 408, 422 (D.C. Cir. 1982).

10. *Pratt v. Webster*, 673 F.2d 408 (D.C. Cir. 1982). Rosenbaum and Marmalefsky also cited *Washington Post v. Dept. of State*, 840 F.2d 38 (D.C. Cir. 1988); *Church of Scientology v. IRS*, 991 F.2d 560 (9th Cir. 1993).

11. *Rosenfeld v. Dept. of Justice*, 761 F.Supp. 1440 (N.D. Cal. 1991).

12. Jonah Raskin, *For the Hell of It: The Life and Times of Abbie Hoffman* (Berkeley: University of California Press, 1996), 225.

13. *CIA v. Sims*, 471 U.S. 159 (1985).

14. David Margolick, "Assessing John Lennon," *New York Times*, September 6, 1991.

15. "Bureaucracy Watch: Suspect Beatle," *Los Angeles Times*, June 25, 1992.

16. "Class of '72 Keeps Lennon's Legacy Alive at High School Reunion," *Daytrippin'*, no. 1, December 1997, 24–25.

Chapter 4: The Clinton Administration Takes Action

1. "Statement of the President Regarding Implementation of FOIA," U.S. Newswire, October 4, 1993.

2. Tim Weiner, "Bills Seek to Slash the Number of U.S. Secrets," *New York Times*, March 3, 1994.

3. Ibid.

4. Ibid.

5. Executive Order 12958 (April 17, 1995), 11–12.

6. Ibid.; White House Office of the Press Secretary, Statement by the President, April 17, 1995.

7. "Still Too Many Secrets," *Los Angeles Times* editorial, April 19, 1995.

8. "Clinton Order Declassifies Millions of Records," *Los Angeles Times*, April 18, 1995.

9. The *Times* story, however, failed to report on the fate of the public interest balancing act. Douglas Jehl, "Clinton Revamps Policy on Secrecy of U.S. Documents," *New York Times*, April 18, 1995. See also John Wicklein, "Foiled FOIA," *American Journalism Review*, April 1996, 36–38.

10. Jennifer Weber, "I Am the G-Man," *Sacramento Bee*, December 17, 1995; "Friday Celebrity," *Boston Herald*, December 15, 1995; Michael Fellner Papers, State Historical Society of Wisconsin, Box 19, "Take Over."

11. *Washington Post*, December 12, 1995.

12. *Wiener v. FBI*, Settlement Agreement, September 10, 1997, in author's possession.

13. Mark Rosenbaum, interview with author, Los Angeles, February 28, 1998.

14. R. C. Cobb, *The Police and the People* (Oxford: Clarendon Press, 1970), 5.

15. Ibid.

16. Ibid., 6, 7.

17. "Portrait of a Porker," *Take Over*, January 26, 1976; "The Cow that Came In from the Cold," "Oink," *Take Over*, February 9, 1976.

18. "Sues City for Losing 'Job' as Informant for FBI," *Madison Capital Times*, January 13, 1976.

19. "Maynard Suit Trial Relives Viet War Days," *Madison Capital Times*, August 29, 1979.

20. "Jury Finds Police Negligent; Gives Ex-informant $21,800," *Madison Capital Times*, August 31, 1979.

21. "Whitewash Nets Fink Hefty Sum," *Take Over*, November 9, 1979.

22. "Death Notices," *Madison Capital Times*, July 26, 1997. First-person works by informers tend to be right-wing books of the "I Led Three Lives" variety: Larry Grathwohl, *Bringing Down America: An FBI Informer with the Weathermen* (New Rochelle, N.Y.: Arlington House, 1976), warns that the Weather Underground "has broken our laws many times" and its members "live in dirt and filth" (8, 7). He infiltrated the Weathermen for "many months" before testifying for the Senate Internal Security Subcommittee in 1974. Julia Brown, in *I Testify: My Years as an FBI Undercover Agent* (Boston: Western Islands, 1966), describes herself as "a Negro lady . . . hoodwinked into joining the Community Party," who switched sides and served as an informer for nine years before testifying for HUAC in 1962.

Chapter 5: After the Settlement

1. Dinitia Smith, "F.B.I. Files on Lennon Reveal Little Beyond Some Weird Details," *New York Times*, September 25, 1997.

2. "Keep Politics out of the IRS and FBI," *Tampa Tribune*, October 3, 1997.

3. "Bird-Brained Surveillance," *Denver Post*, September 29, 1997.

4. Dan Rodricks, "That Dangerous Beatle," *Baltimore Sun*, October 3, 1997.

5. Jon Bream, "Yoko Ono's a Proud Mom," *Minneapolis Star-Tribune*, October 14, 1997.

6. Katharine Q. Seelye, "Uptown Manhattan Is Tied Up as Clinton Raises Money," *New York Times*, December 9, 1997.

7. James Fletcher, " 'Bugged' UB40 Sue MI5; Band: They Thought We Were Red Red Swine," *The Mirror*, October 4, 1997. Shayler reported that the rock group UB40 was also the subject of an MI5 file—their reggae cover of "Red, Red Wine" had been an international hit. Lead singer Robin Campbell said, "We have called for the legalization of cannabis, supported Rock against Racism and backed the miners in their strike, but we're just a pop group—we aren't planning to bring down the Government."

8. Nick Fielding, "Turned Over by MI5," *Mail on Sunday*, September 21, 1997.

9. Nick Fielding and Mark Hollingsworth, "Gagged!: Tragic Day for Press Freedom as the Government Halts our MI5 Revelations," *Mail on Sunday*, August 31, 1997.

10. Nick Fielding, "MI5 to Stop Spying on Political Radicals," *Mail on Sunday*, January 11, 1998.

11. Sarah Lyall, "In a Major Policy Change, Britain Moves to Ease Official Secrecy," *New York Times*, December 12, 1997.

12. See Martin Kettle, "MI5 'Helped FBI Spy on Lennon,' " *The Guardian* (London), September 27, 1997.

13. Martin Kettle, interview with author, telephone, September 26, 1997.

14. Mark Rosenbaum, interview with author, Los Angeles, February 28, 1998.

15. Dan Marmalefsky, interview with author, Los Angeles, February 28, 1998.

Conclusion: The Culture of Secrecy

1. Max Weber, "Bureaucracy," in *From Max Weber: Essays in Sociology*, ed. Hans Gerth and C. Wright Mills (New York: Oxford University Press, 1958), 233, 235. Weber found evidence in a characteristically wide range of examples: "The treasury officials of the Persian shah have made a secret doctrine of their budgetary art and even use secret script. The official statistics of Prussia, in general, make public only what cannot do any harm to the intentions of the power-wielding bureaucracy" (233). The only exception he found in the world history of bureaucracy was in imperial China, where "the official Gazette published the personal files and all the reports, petitions and memorials" of the prebendary officials, which meant that the entire work of officials "took place before the broadest public" (437).

2. Tom Blanton, ed., *The White House E-Mail* (New York: New Press, 1995).

3. Scott Armstrong, "The War over Secrecy: Democracy's Most Important Low-Intensity Conflict," in Athan Theoharis, ed., *A Culture of Secrecy* (Lawrence: University of Kansas Press, 1998), 153–54; George Lardner, Jr., "Archivist Was Sounded Out in December on Library Job," *Washington Post*, March 3, 1993.

4. *American Historical Association et al. v. Peterson*, 876 F.Supp. 1300 (D.D.C. 1995).

5. Armstrong, "War over Secrecy," 158, 140; *Armstrong v. Executive Office of the President*, 90 F.3d 553 (D.C. Cir. 1996). The opinion was written by Judge Douglas Ginsburg.

6. Anna Kasten Nelson, "The John F. Kennedy Assassination Records Review Board," in Theoharis, *Culture of Secrecy*, 221, 223.

7. Ibid., 224, 229; Tim Weiner, "A Blast at Secrecy in Kennedy Killing," *New York Times*, September 29, 1998. The review board had five members: John R. Tunheim, a federal district judge in Minnesota, who served as chair; Henry F. Graff, Columbia University historian; Kermit L. Hall, professor of history and law at Ohio State University; William L. Joyce, archivist at Princeton University; and Nelson.

8. The memo was published under the title "Instructions: Lost in Space." *Harper's*, June 1992, 25–26. The document was discovered in 1992 by investigators for the House Subcommittee on Investigations and Oversight; subcommittee chairman Howard Wolpe called it "a very serious and deliberate attempt by [NASA] to subvert not only the Freedom of Information Act but the rights of Congress and the public to review agency decision-making processes."

9. "Gates's Glasnost," *Harper's*, June 1992, 25.

Glossary

108MIG. The 108th Military Intelligence Group.

Airtel. An internal FBI communication urgent enough to be sent the same day it is created but routine enough to be sent by airmail rather than teletype.

(b)(1). National security exemption of the FOIA, which allows agencies to exempt from disclosure any material currently and properly classified in the interests of national security, as defined by the current executive order on classification. Divided into subsections:

(b)(1)b1. "Identity of a foreign government . . . engaged in a cooperative, confidential relationship with the United States."

(b)(1)b2. "Information provided by a foreign government with the expectation, expressed or implied, that the information is to be kept in confidence."

(b)(1)c1. Intelligence source information; "any word, term or phrase which could identify an intelligence source."

(b)(1)c2. Information relating to intelligence source data collection capability.

(b)(1)c3. "Detailed information pertaining to or provided by an intelligence source."

(b)(1)c4. Dates information furnished by an intelligence source.

(b)(1)c5. "Channelization/dissemination instructions"—how "source information is disseminated via proper channels to appropriate collection points."

(b)(1)c6. Date and/or place of specific activity about which an intelligence source reported.

(b)(1)c7. Identity of an intelligence source's contact.

(b)(1)c8. "Intelligence activity information; derivative investigation based upon information obtained during the course of an intelligence activity."

(b)(1)d1. "Intelligence information gathered by the United States about or from a foreign country, group or individual."

(b)(2). Section of the FOIA that permits agencies to withhold information relating solely to internal personnel rules and practices.

(b)(3). Section of FOIA that requires agencies to protect from disclosure information withheld pursuant to statute, including visa and tax records.

(b)(7)(C). FOIA exemption which requires withholding of investigatory records, compiled for law enforcement purposes, that would constitute an unwarranted invasion of the personal privacy of another person. Divided into several subsections:

(b)(7)(C)/(1). Names of FBI agents and clerical personnel.

(b)(7)(C)/(2). Names of nonfederal law enforcement officers.

(b)(7)(C)/(3). Identities of third parties mentioned in an investigative file, including "identifying information of a personal nature."

(b)(7)(C)/(4). Names of government employees.

(b)(7)(C)/(5). Third parties interviewed.

(b)(7)(D). FOIA exemption that requires withholding of investigatory records compiled for law enforcement purposes which would disclose the identity of a confidential source. Divided into several subsections:

(b)(7)(D)/(1). Source symbol numbers or letters.

(b)(7)(D)/(2). Information provided under an express or implied guarantee of confidentiality.

(b)(7)(D)/(3). Nonfederal law enforcement agencies providing information to the FBI on a confidential basis.

(b)(7)(D)/(4). Information from a financial or commercial institution.

(b)(7)(D)/(5). Information provided by individuals interviewed under an express guarantee of confidentiality.

(b)(7)(E). FOIA exemption permitting the withholding of law enforcement records that would reveal secret investigative techniques and procedures.

BU File or Bufile. Bureau files; files located and maintained at FBI headquarters in Washington, D.C.

CALREP. FBI code referring to the 1972 Republican National Convention before it was scheduled to be moved from San Diego to Miami.

DID. Domestic Intelligence Division of the FBI.

Director. FBI Director J. Edgar Hoover.

EO. Executive order on classification, issued by the president, defining "national security" and the restrictions placed on release of information under the FOIA.

EO 12065. Carter executive order on classification, which included a public interest balancing act.

EO 12356. Reagan executive order on classification, which abolished the public interest balancing act.

EO 12958. Clinton executive order on classification, which made the public interest balancing act "a matter of discretion" for government agencies.

EYSIC. Election Year Strategy Information Center, one of the names for the group headed by Rennie Davis planning antiwar demonstrations at the Republican National Convention in 1972.

FOIA. Freedom of Information Act.

Informant. A person who supplies information to the FBI on a regular basis, usually for pay, and often under some kind of contractual agreement; distinguished by the FBI from a "source." The FBI uses this term rather than "informer," which "runs against the American grain" (see Navasky, "Forward," in *Naming Names*).

IS. Internal security; classification code for files and investigations, usually followed by a subcategory, such as "NL" for New Left.

LHM. Letterhead memo; an FBI summary report prepared for dissemination to other agencies that conceals confidential sources.

LNS. Liberation News Service; independent national news network that provided weekly packets of news stories to the underground and alternative press.

MI. The Miami FBI office.

MIDEM. FBI code for 1972 Democratic National Convention, held in Miami.

MIREP. FBI code for 1972 Republican National Convention, held in Miami.

New Left. Subcategory of FBI internal security investigations, referring to student and antiwar activists outside the Communist Party; Lennon was classified for a time as "IS-New Left."

NYO. New York office of the FBI.

OO. Office of origin; the FBI field office with primary responsibility for an investigation. For Lennon, the OO was New York City.

OS. Outside the scope; marginal notation on FOIA-released documents indicating FBI's claim that the withheld material is outside the scope of the FOIA request. "OS" is not one of the exemptions listed in the FOIA.

PCPJ. People's Coalition for Peace and Justice, an antiwar umbrella organization.

REVACT. Revolutionary activities.

RM. Racial matter.

SA. Special agent; an FBI agent.

SAC. Special agent in charge of an FBI field office.

SM. Security matter; classification category for FBI files for investigations of individuals considered potential threats to internal security. Usually followed by a subcategory, such as "NL" for New Left.

Source. A supplier of information to the FBI, usually unpaid, distinguished from "informant." Sources often are people in positions of authority such as employers or landlords.

Teletype. A message sent over the FBI's secure communications network requiring encryption and decryption.

USSS. U.S. Secret Service.

WPP. White Panther Party, John Sinclair's New Left political organization in Michigan.

YES. Youth Election Strategy, the media arm of the group headed by Rennie Davis planning antiwar protests during the 1972 election.

YIP. Youth International Party, a name the FBI took seriously but which was intended as a joke by founder Jerry Rubin. The Yippies nominated a pig for president in Chicago in 1968 and planned demonstrations for the 1972 Republican convention.

Chronology

October 9, 1940 John Winston Lennon born in Liverpool.

December 1962 "Love Me Do," first Beatles hit, tops U.S. charts.

May 1968 Lennon and Yoko Ono spend their first night together, henceforth are inseparable.

October 18, 1968 Lennon and Ono arrested in London on charges of cannabis possession. In November, Lennon pleads guilty to misdemeanor charge, pays a nominal fine, insists that drugs were planted. Conviction will later become pretext for U.S. deportation order.

March 20, 1969 Lennon and Ono marry in Gibraltar.

March 26, 1969 Lennon and Ono's "bed-in for peace" begins in Amsterdam Hilton.

July 7, 1969 "Give Peace a Chance" released in U.S.

April 10, 1970 Paul McCartney announces breakup of the Beatles.

December 11, 1970 *Plastic Ono Band*, first Lennon post-Beatles solo album, released.

August 1971 Lennon and Ono move to New York City, become friends with antiwar activists.

September 9, 1971 *Imagine* album released in U.S.

November 1971 Lennon and Ono move to Bank Street in Greenwich Village.

December 1, 1971 "Happy Xmas/War Is Over" released in U.S.

December 10, 1971 Lennon performs at John Sinclair concert, Ann Arbor, Michigan. FBI informers in audience file reports.

January 21, 1972 FBI officially opens national security investigation of Lennon.

January 23, 1972 J. Edgar Hoover sends coded teletype to President Nixon and the heads of the CIA and military intelligence reporting that Lennon is involved with "movement activities" that "will culminate with demonstrations at the Republican National Convention."

February 4, 1972 Senator Strom Thurmond sends a secret memo to Attorney General John Mitchell outlining Lennon's political plans and suggesting that he be deported.

February 7, 1972 Lennon and Ono demonstrate in New York against British policy in Northern Ireland. Noted in FBI file.

February 14–18, 1972 Lennon and Ono guest host the *Mike Douglas Show.* Noted in FBI file.

March 6, 1972 INS refuses to renew Lennon's visa.

March 16, 1972 Lennon deportation hearing.

April 18, 1972 Lennon deportation hearing.

April 24, 1972 "Woman is the Nigger of the World" released.

April 25, 1972 Hoover sends letter to H. R. Haldeman, assistant to President Nixon, reporting on efforts to deport Lennon.

April 29, 1972 Lennon declares at press conference that deportation action is response to his antiwar stand.

May 2, 1972 J. Edgar Hoover dies; Nixon names Assistant Attorney General L. Patrick Gray Acting Director of FBI.

May 9, 1972 Lennon announces he will not participate in protest activities at Republican National Convention.

May 12, 1972 Lennon deportation hearing.

May 13, 1972 Lennon and Ono participate in antiwar demonstration in NYC. Noted in FBI file.

May 17, 1972 Lennon deportation hearing.

June 12, 1972 *Some Time in New York City* released.

August 21–24, 1972 Republican National Convention in Miami.

August 30, 1972 Lennon's "One to One" concert in Madison Square Garden.

October 24, 1972 FBI's Miami office ends its Lennon investigation.

November 7, 1972 Nixon reelected.

December 8, 1972 FBI officially closes Lennon investigation.

March 2, 1973 Judge Ira Fieldsteen rules that Lennon must leave the U.S. within sixty days. Appeal filed one month later.

August 8, 1974 Nixon resigns.

September 23, 1974 "Whatever Gets You Through the Night" released.

November 2, 1974 Lennon sues INS, arguing he was victim of political vendetta.

June 16, 1975 Lennon sues former Attorneys General John Mitchell and Richard Kleindienst and INS officials, arguing their actions against him were improper.

July 31, 1975 *Rolling Stone* reveals political origins of deportation case, prints copy of 1972 Thurmond memo.

October 7, 1975 U.S. court of appeals overturns INS deportation order.

October 9, 1975 Sean Ono Lennon born.

July 27, 1976 INS grants Lennon permanent residency.

November 12, 1980 "(Just Like) Starting Over" released.

November 15, 1980 *Double Fantasy* released.

December 8, 1980 Lennon killed by Mark David Chapman.

February 12, 1981 FOIA request filed by Jon Wiener for Lennon FBI files.

May 20, 1981 Initial release of FBI files—of 281 pages, 199 withheld in their entirety.

June 17, 1981 Administrative appeal filed.

July 30, 1981 Administrative appeal denied.

March 22, 1983 *Wiener v. FBI* lawsuit filed.

February 29, 1988 Takasugi decision affirms FBI position.

July 24, 1989 ACLU appeal brief filed.

December 5, 1989 Hearing before Ninth Circuit Court of Appeals.

July 12, 1991 Ninth Circuit reverses Takasugi's decision.

April 1992 FBI files petition for Supreme Court review.

June 22, 1992 Supreme Court denies FBI petition. Case remanded to Judge Takasugi's court.

September 11, 1992 FBI files new Vaughn affidavits.

October 16, 1992 Court reopens discovery.

December 16–17, 1992 FBI agents Bolthouse and Davidson, CIA officer Stricker deposed by co-lead counsel Mark Rosenbaum.

January 15, 1993 Subpoenas served on retired FBI agents Shackelford and Miller.

February 19, 1993 D.C. District Court grants FBI motion to quash subpoenas.

October 4, 1993 Judge Takasugi reopens discovery; ACLU team submits interrogatories.

October 4, 1993 Clinton declares "openness initiative"; Attorney General Reno orders internal review of pending FOIA litigation.

November 1, 1993 FBI suggests settlement in exchange for ACLU abandoning discovery. Rejected by ACLU.

December 10 and 27, 1993 FBI makes discretionary release of previously withheld exemption (b)(7) information.

February 1995 ACLU prepares for trial.

April 17, 1995 Clinton issues new executive order on classification, fails to make public interest balancing act mandatory.

December 15, 1995 Takasugi orders FBI to respond to written interrogatories.

February 1996 FBI offers to settle case, opens negotiations.

September 17, 1997 Settlement signed; FBI releases eighty-one pages of previously withheld information; ten "national security" documents remain at issue.

Government Documents

Executive Order 12065, December 1, 1978 (Carter order).

Executive Order 12356, April 2, 1982 (Reagan order).

Executive Order 12958, April 17, 1995 (Clinton order).

Freedom of Information Act. 5 U.S.C. § 552.

"Statement of the Attorney General Regarding Implementation of FOIA." U.S. Newswire, October 4, 1993.

"Statement of the President Regarding Implementation of FOIA." U.S. Newswire, October 4, 1993.

U.S. Department of Justice. Federal Bureau of Investigation. Lennon FBI File, online version. Two hundred forty-eight pages of the Lennon FBI file can be downloaded from the FBI Web site: http://foia.fbi.gov/lennon.htm. (Three hundred ninety pages were released in *Wiener v. FBI.*) This site contains the final released version, without annotation or other explanation or comment except for a brief headnote. The pages are not in chronological order and are not marked with the source or page numbers assigned in the FOIA litigation. Viewing or printing them requires the Adobe Acrobat reader.

U.S. Senate. Select Committee to Study Government Operations with Respect to Intelligence Activities. *Final Report.* 94th Cong., 2d sess., 1976 ("Church Report").

U.S. Senate. Congressional Record. Vol. 132, S14039 (September 27, 1986).

White House Office of the Press Secretary. Statement by the President, April 17, 1995.

Collections

Michael Fellner Papers. State Historical Society of Wisconsin.

Books

Adler, Allan Robert, ed. *Litigation under the Federal Open Government Laws*. Wye Mills, MD: American Civil Liberties Union, 1997.

Blanton, Tom, ed. *The White House E-Mail*. New York: New Press, 1995.

Brown, Julia. *I Testify: My Years as an FBI Undercover Agent*. Boston: Western Islands, 1966.

Buitrago, Ann Mari, and Leon Andrew Immerman. *Are You Now or Have You Ever Been in the FBI Files?* New York: Grove Press, 1981.

Carson, Clayborne. *Malcolm X: The FBI File*. New York: Carrol & Graf, 1991.

Cobb, R. C. *The Police and the People*. Oxford: Clarendon Press, 1970.

Dean, John. *Blind Ambition: The White House Years*. New York: Simon & Schuster, 1976.

Donner, Frank. *The Age of Surveillance: The Aims and Methods of America's Political Intelligence System*. New York: Knopf, 1980.

Ehrlichman, John. *Witness to Power*. New York: Simon & Schuster, 1982.

Felt, W. Mark. *The FBI Pyramid from Inside*. New York: Putnam, 1979.

Garrow, David J. *The FBI and Martin Luther King, Jr*. New York: Penguin, 1981.

Gentry, Curt. *J. Edgar Hoover: The Man and the Secrets*. New York: Norton, 1991.

Grathwohl, Larry. *Bringing Down America: An FBI Informer with the Weathermen*. New Rochelle, N.Y.: Arlington House, 1976.

Haines, Gerald, and David Langart. *Unlocking the Files of the FBI: A Guide to its Records and Classification System*. Wilmington, Del.: Scholarly Resources, 1993.

Haldeman, H. R., and Joseph DiMona. *The Ends of Power*. New York: Times Books, 1978.

Kimball, Penn. *The File: The Chilling True Account of Government Spying on an Innocent Man*. New York: Harcourt Brace, 1983.

Kutler, Stanley. *The Wars of Watergate: The Last Crisis of Richard Nixon*. New York: Knopf, 1990.

MacKenzie, Angus. *Secrets: The CIA's War at Home*. Berkeley: University of California Press, 1997.

Magruder, Jeb Stuart. *An American Life: One Man's Road to Watergate*. New York: Atheneum, 1974.

Mitgang, Herbert. *Dangerous Dossiers: Exposing the Secret War against America's Greatest Authors*. New York: Ballantine, 1988.

Morgan, Richard E. *Domestic Intelligence: Monitoring Dissent in America*. Austin: University of Texas Press, 1980.

Moynihan, Daniel Patrick. *Secrecy: The American Experience*. New Haven: Yale University Press, 1998.

Navasky, Victor. *Naming Names*. New York: Viking, 1980.

Olmsted, Kathryn S. *Challenging the Secret Government: The Post-Watergate Investigations of the CIA and FBI*. Chapel Hill: University of North Carolina, 1996.

O'Reilly, Kenneth. *Racial Matters: The FBI's Secret Files on Black Americans*. New York: Free Press, 1989.

Payne, Cril, *Deep Cover: An FBI Agent Infiltrates the Radical Underground*. New York: Newsweek Books, 1979.

Powers, Richard Gid. *Secrecy and Power: The Life of J. Edgar Hoover.* New York: Free Press, 1987.

Raskin, Jonah. *For the Hell of It: The Life and Times of Abbie Hoffman.* Berkeley: University of California Press, 1996.

Rips, Geoffrey. *Unamerican Activities: The Campaign against the Underground Press.* San Francisco: City Lights, 1981.

Robins, Natalie. *Alien Ink: The FBI's War on Freedom of Expression.* New York: Morrow, 1992.

Solt, Andrew, and Sam Egan. *Imagine: John Lennon.* New York: Macmillan, 1988.

Sullivan, William C., with Bill Brown. *The Bureau: My Thirty Years in Hoover's FBI.* New York: Norton, 1979.

Theoharis, Athan G. *The FBI: An Annotated Bibliography and Research Guide.* New York: Garland, 1994.

——. *Spying on Americans: Political Surveillance from Hoover to the Huston Plan.* Philadelphia: Temple University Press, 1978.

——, ed. *A Culture of Secrecy: The Government Versus the People's Right to Know.* Lawrence: University of Kansas Press, 1998.

——, ed. (with commentary). *From the Secret Files of J. Edgar Hoover.* Chicago: Ivan R. Dee, 1991.

Theoharis, Athan G., Tony G. Poveda, Susan Rosenfield, Richard Gid Powers, eds. *The FBI: A Comprehensive Reference Guide.* Phoenix: Oryx Press, 1999.

Weber, Max. "Bureaucracy." In *From Max Weber: Essays in Sociology.* Edited by Hans Gerth and C. Wright Mills. New York: Oxford University Press, 1958.

Wiener, Jon. *Come Together: John Lennon in His Time.* New York: Random House, 1984.

Zaroulis, Nancy, and Gerald Sullivan. *Who Spoke Up? American Protest against the War in Vietnam, 1963–1975.* Garden City, NJ: Doubleday, 1984.

Articles

Armstrong, Scott. "The War over Secrecy: Democracy's Most Important Low Intensity Conflict." In Athan Theoharis, ed., *The Culture of Secrecy.* Lawrence: University of Kansas Press, 1998.

"Bird-Brained Surveillance." *Denver Post,* September 29, 1997.

Bream, Jon. "Yoko Ono's a Proud Mom." *Minneapolis Star-Tribune,* October 14, 1997.

"Bureaucracy Watch: Suspect Beatle." *Los Angeles Times,* June 25, 1992.

"Clinton Order Declassifies Millions of Records." *Los Angeles Times,* April 18, 1995.

"The Cow that Came In from the Cold." *Take Over,* February 9, 1976.

Doig, Stephen K. "FBI Ordered to Explain Why Lennon Files Shredded." *Miami Herald,* August 10, 1994.

Fielding, Nick. "MI5 to Stop Spying on Political Radicals." *Mail on Sunday,* January 11, 1998.

——. "Turned Over by MI5." *Mail on Sunday,* September 21, 1997.

Fielding, Nick, and Mark Hollingsworth. "Gagged!: Tragic Day for Press Freedom as the Government Halts our MI5 Revelations." *Mail on Sunday,* August 31, 1997.

Fletcher, James. " 'Bugged' UB40 Sue MI5; Band: They Thought We Were Red Red Swine." *The Mirror*, October 4, 1997.

Flippo, Chet. "Lennon's Lawsuit: Memo from Thurmond." *Rolling Stone*, July 31, 1975.

"Friday Celebrity," *Boston Herald*, December 15, 1995.

"Gates's Glasnost." *Harper's*, June 1992.

"Instructions: Lost in Space." *Harper's*, June 1992.

Jehl, Douglas. "Clinton Revamps Policy on Secrecy of U.S. Documents." *New York Times*, April 18, 1995.

"Jury Finds Police Negligent; Gives Ex-informant $21,800." *Madison Capital Times*, August 31, 1979.

"Keep Politics out of the IRS and FBI." *Tampa Tribune*, October 3, 1997.

Kimball, Penn. *The File*. San Diego: Harcourt Brace Jovanovich, 1983.

Kettle, Martin. "MI5 'Helped FBI Spy on Lennon.' " *The Guardian* (London), September 27, 1997.

Lardner, George, Jr. "Archivist Was Sounded Out in December on Library Job," *Washington Post*, March 3, 1993.

Lyall, Sarah. "In a Major Policy Change, Britain Moves to Ease Official Secrecy." *New York Times*, December 12, 1997.

Margolick, David. "Assessing John Lennon." *New York Times*, September 6, 1991.

———. "Japanese-American Judges Reflect on Internment." *New York Times*, May 19, 1995.

"Maynard Suit Trial Relives Viet War Days." *Madison Capital Times*, August 29, 1979.

Nelson, Anna Kasten. "The John F. Kennedy Assassination Records Review Board." In Athan Theoharis, ed., *The Culture of Secrecy*. Lawrence: University of Kansas Press, 1998.

"Oink." *Take Over*, February 9, 1976.

Pareles, Jon. "Caution: Now Entering the War Zone." *New York Times*, February 24, 1991.

"Portrait of a Porker." *Take Over*, January 26, 1976.

Rodricks, Dan. "That Dangerous Beatle." *Baltimore Sun*, October 3, 1997.

Seelye, Katharine Q. "Uptown Manhattan Is Tied Up as Clinton Raises Money." *New York Times*, December 9, 1997.

Smith, Dinitia. "F.B.I. Files on Lennon Reveal Little Beyond Some Weird Details." *New York Times*, September 25, 1997.

"Still Too Many Secrets." *Los Angeles Times*, April 19, 1995.

"Sues City for Losing 'Job' as Informant for FBI." *Madison Capital Times*, January 13, 1976.

Treen, Joe. "Justice for a Beatle." *Rolling Stone*, December 5, 1974.

Weber, Jennifer. "I Am the G-Man," *Sacramento Bee*, December 17, 1995.

Weiner, Tim. "Bills Seek to Slash the Number of U.S. Secrets." *New York Times*, March 3, 1994.

———. "A Blast at Secrecy in Kennedy Killing." *New York Times*, September 29, 1998.

———. "U.S. Plans Secrecy Overhaul to Open Millions of Records." *New York Times*, March 18, 1994.

"Whitewash Nets Fink Hefty Sum." *Take Over*, November 9, 1979.

Wicklein, John. "Foiled FOIA." *American Journalism Review*, April 1996.

Acknowledgments

This project gained immensely from the comments and suggestions of several readers: Eric Foner, Mike Johnson, David Nasaw, and Judy Fiskin. Daniel Holt did all the research in Madison. Scott Armstrong provided valuable help about the CIA "cactus channel." Danilo Bach furnished documentation he found in his own research. David Weiner and Angie Lee worked long and hard on the scanning and page layout of the FBI file pages, the reproduction of which was "powered by Biscuit Technologies."

At the University of California Press, Naomi Schneider's support and enthusiasm for this project was vital. Suzanne Knott solved dozens of problems with admirable calm. Tony Crouch's extra work getting the FBI pages to come out right was crucial.

Attorneys Mark Rosenbaum and Dan Marmalefsky not only wrote the briefs and made the arguments that are the heart of this effort, they also agreed to be interviewed for the book and later each checked the manuscript for errors. This is their story, and the book is dedicated to them.

Index

Abzug, Bella, 26, 156

Affinity Files (Madison, Wisconsin), 89–91

airtels, 108

Albert, Stewart, 4, 122, 294; declaration of, 71–72, 98, 132; in FBI document, 123, 131, 137, 143, 145, 147, 165, 191, 209, 213, 251, 295; Progressive Labor Party, association with, 208

Alien Ink: The FBI's War on Freedom of Expression (Robins), 82

Allamuchy Tribe, in FBI document, 123, 131, 133, 137, 139, 145, 147, 153, 155, 165, 189, 211; FBI file on, 132; FBI memo to INS on, 144–147; Lennon financial contribution to, 132, 138; name change of, 155, 165; New York office of, 130; planning for Republican National Convention by, 136. *See also* Election Year Strategy Information Center (EYSIC)

American Bar Association Committee on Drug Abuse, 37

American Civil Liberties Union (ACLU), 1; goals in taking Wiener case, 16; interrogatories submitted by, 67–68, 82–83; Ninth Circuit Court appeal case of, 39–40, 44; obtaining help of, 15–16; settlement of case, 1, 76–77, 84–86, 92–94, 96–99; Supreme Court appeal brief of, 53–54; trial preparations by, 81–83; *Wiener v. FBI* argument of, 28–32. *See also* Marmalefsky, Dan; Rosenbaum, Mark

American Historical Association, Committee on Access to Documents, 15

American Indian Movement, 174

Angleton, James Jesus, 26

Ann Arbor, Michigan, concert, 77–78, 220, 224; in FBI document, 111–121, 221, 225. *See also* John Sinclair Freedom Rally

Anti-Riot Act, 32, 40, 44, 57, 71, 98

antiwar movement: CIA's surveillance of, 26, 156; in FBI document, 123, 127, 137, 149, 157, 177, 251, 267–269, 271, 295; FBI's monitoring of, 28–29, 88, 134–137; Hoover's opposition to, 28; Lennons' involvement in, 136, 266, 294; trivial information collected on, 87, 122, 176, 250. *See also* Allamuchy Tribe

appeals. *See* Ninth Circuit Court of Appeals appeal; Supreme Court appeal

arena stage, 196, 197

Are You Now or Have You Ever Been in the FBI Files? (Buitrago and Immerman), 174

Armstrong, Scott, 73, 100

Assassination Records Review Board (ARRB), 102–103, 319n7

asterisks, in FBI document, 82–83

Attica Defense Committee, in FBI document, 258–261

Bacall, Lauren, 94

Bacon, Leslie, 4

Baldwin, James, 8

Baltimore Sun, 93

Beatles, 1, 37

Lennon's FBI file opens with a "Confidential
Informant Report" describing his appearance
at the John Sinclair Freedom Rally in Ann
Arbor, Michigan, in 1971 (see pp. 110–19).
© 1971, 1984 John Sinclair

FBI Director J. Edgar Hoover and President Nixon in 1971. Hoover died in May 1972, in the middle of the bureau's attempt to help Nixon deport Lennon. Corbis/Bettman-UPI

Senator Strom Thurmond, whose secret 1972 memo proposed deporting Lennon "as a strategic countermeasure" to his antiwar activities (see pp. 3–4). Courtesy Senator Strom Thurmond

Best wishes to Mr. John Wiener.
Strom Thurmond, U. S. Senator
—S. C.

Jerry Rubin with John and Yoko and Abbie Hoffman. Lennon's friendship with Rubin was noted often in his FBI files (see pp. 174–75, 181). Courtesy Anita Hoffman

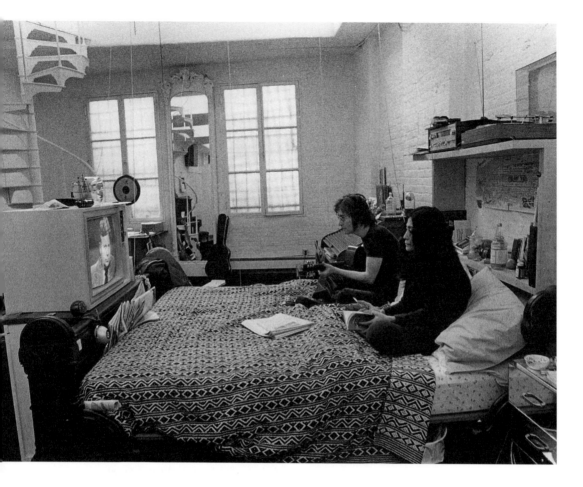

*John and Yoko at their West Village rented
loft, 105 Bank Street, in 1972. The FBI
files said their address at the time was "St.
Regis Hotel, 150 Bank Street"* *(see p. 151).*
Ben Ross

*John and Yoko on the Mike Douglas show,
February 1972. The FBI was watching (see
p. 181).* © *Michael Leshnov*

*John and Yoko meet the press outside
their immigration hearings, May 17, 1972.
J. Edgar Hoover was informed about it in
an urgent coded teletype (see pp. 64–65).*
AP/Wide World Photos

First news of the existence and contents
of the Lennon FBI files made headlines in
the tabloids, among other places. Reprinted
with permission from the New York Post.
©1999, NYP Holdings, Inc.

John and Yoko demonstrating at the South Vietnamese embassy in Washington, D.C., June 1973, seeking freedom for an antiwar Buddhist woman held in prison by the Saigon government. The Washington Post *photo appears in the FBI's Washington field office file on Lennon (see p. 284). Christopher Li, Washington Post*

H. R. Haldeman, assistant to President Nixon, recipient of J. Edgar Hoover's report on the FBI's efforts to help Nixon deport Lennon (see p. 240). Walter McNamee, Newsweek

John and Yoko at an antiwar rally in Manhattan, April 22, 1972, speaking to an audience of 50,000 — and noted by the FBI. Corbis/Bettman-UPI

cartoon by Mike Peters. © *1983 Mike Peters,* Dayton Daily News

cartoon by Signe Wilkinson. © *1983 Signe Wilkinson,* San Jose Mercury News

Press conference, ACLU of Southern
California, announcing progress in Freedom
of Information case. Left to right: attorney
Dan Marmalefsky of Morrison & Foerester,
working pro bono; ACLU Legal Director
Mark Rosenbaum; plaintiff Jon Wiener.
Courtesy Ann Bradley

Text: 10.5/16 Electra   **Display:** Univers Condensed Light and Bold; Grotesque Extra Condensed   **Design:** Nola Burger   **Composition:** Integrated Composition Systems   **Printing and binding:** Edwards Brothers